# The Cultural Life Setting of the Proverbs

# The Cultural Life Setting of the Proverbs

John J. Pilch

Fortress Press
*Minneapolis*

THE CULTURAL LIFE SETTING OF THE PROVERBS

Cover image: © Thinkstock: Stock Photo Traditional Ghee Diya Candles / 78782119

Cover design: Joe Reinke

*Library of Congress Cataloging-in-Publication Data*

Print ISBN: 978-1-5064-0679-4

eBook ISBN: 978-1-5064-0680-0

The paper used in this publication meets the minimum requirements of American National Standard for Information Sciences — Permanence of Paper for Printed Library Materials, ANSI Z329.48-1984.

Manufactured in the U.S.A.

This book was produced using Pressbooks.com, and PDF rendering was done by PrinceXML.

# Contents

# Preface

My colleagues Bruce J. Malina, Richard L. Rohrbaugh, and I wrote a six-volume social-scientific commentary on the New Testament (1992–2013) that proved very helpful for those interested in the circum-Mediterranean cultural context of the Bible. Not only did it open new possibilities for scholars in understanding and interpreting these ancient documents, but it was especially valuable for those involved in a variety of pastoral enterprises in their respective Christian denominations. Preachers, catechists, and the laity in general benefitted from the fresh insights into familiar bible passages. Most commentaries are theologically or religiously oriented, underscoring features of the Bible that might be of use in articulating contemporary denominational Christianity. Others are linguistically or philologically oriented, based on the belief that written documents can be best understood by literary, aesthetic criteria. The distinctive feature of this social-science commentary is that it draws insights from an array of social sciences such as anthropology, social psychology, sociolinguistics, and the like in order to determine the most culturally plausible interpretation of the biblical book of Proverbs. As Patrick Miller points out, "proverbial sayings are inextricably related to culture" (Miller 2006: 170). Problems in translations occur when there is a mismatch between the culture expressed in biblical proverbs and the culture of the target language, English in our case. For example, speaking about marriage and a good wife, Prov. 18:22 is predominantly translated: "He who finds a wife finds a good thing, and obtains favor from the Lord." A contemporary reader would imagine that some ancient version of "match.com" or "eharmony.com" existed to help the aspiring spouse to find himself an ideal match. However, marriages in the circum-Mediterranean world of antiquity (and the present) were arranged by the parents. Ideally, the partner was a patrilateral (or lacking that, a matrilateral) parallel cousin. The marriage was the fusion of the honor of two families for the benefit of each family (Malina 2001: 134–60). Thus the Hebrew word ordinarily translated "find" should more appropriately be rendered "get, acquire," as Hebrew dictionaries indicate. In other words, lucky the fellow whose parents arranged a good and welcome match for him!

The concerns considered here derive from circum-Mediterranean social systems, with the various social structures, cultural values, and understandings of what it meant to be a person who existed at that time and place. Our concern is to discover what the proverbs were expressing within the social setting of their society by examining the typical circum-Mediterranean social behaviors witnessed to in these aphorisms. What social interactions do the proverbs evidence? What sorts of outcomes are expected in this society?

This analysis does not reflect upon each and every proverb in the book of Proverbs. Rather, it focuses on proverbs for which our contemporary understanding can benefit from circum-Mediterranean cultural values and insights. Thus it provides two types of interpretive material. First, by way of clarification, we offer, following the biblical text, short **Textual Notes** relative to select proverbs. These notes draw the reader's attention to dimensions of the social system expressed in the language of each proverb and provide a small-scale social-science commentary that supplements the traditional, more theologically oriented studies available on Proverbs.

Second, at the end of the book I provide a collection of **Reading Scenarios** drawn from anthropological studies of the Mediterranean social system. These scenarios describe elements of the social system that has been encoded in the language of the proverbs in ways that are not always obvious to modern readers. Since most of the reading scenarios apply throughout the proverbs, however, I have duly referenced them in the commentary for the convenience of the reader, using the symbol ▶. Together with the **Textual Notes**, the **Reading Scenarios** offer clues for filling in the unspoken or implicit elements of the writings as a Mediterranean reader would certainly have done. The **Textual Notes** and **Reading Scenarios** help the modern reader develop a considerate posture toward the ancient author and prevent imposing on that author's work interpretations that would be culturally incompatible, as noted above on the topic of "finding an ideal wife" (Prov. 18:22).

The scenarios expressed in the proverbs come from a time and place that for all of us remains foreign territory. It is unlike anything we are likely to imagine from our experience in the modern West. It is a world I invite you to enter as a thoughtful and considerate reader.

Johns Hopkins University
Baltimore, Md.
Feast of John the Baptist, 2015

# Introduction

Like the volumes in the Social Science Commentary on the New Testament, this book seeks to highlight a plausible circum-Mediterranean cultural setting for the aphorisms in the book of Proverbs. Previously, my colleagues and I have used a variety of terms to describe this culture: first-century Eastern Mediterranean, circum-Mediterranean, Middle Eastern, and the like. Each tag had its disadvantages, though anthropologists recognize a large swath of the earth stretching from Turkey to Brazil as a "culture continent" or "culture area" (Foster 1960: 25; Gregg 2005: 4). By this they understand that the entire region shares many cultural elements unchanged over millennia, even as each country and areas within a given country might understand and interpret the element differently. The core value of honor and shame (or dishonor) are two such elements. While I occasionally use these terms in this book, I accept the newly proposed—if still not totally satisfactory—acronym MENA ("Middle East–North Africa"), proposed by Egyptian anthropologists (Gregg 2005: 6; Pilch 2013: 88). The value of the acronym is that it recognizes *diversity* within which culture is not a shared way of life but rather "a constellation of values, meanings, and practices unevenly *distributed* to its members" (Gregg ibid.).

Roland Murphy (1998: 68) correctly observes that "the original setting of a proverb is beyond recovery." However, because they are so inextricably related to their respective cultures, insights from the social sciences can help us to appreciate the import and concern of a proverb even if the original setting is unknown to the reader. In general, the proverbs in 10:1–22:17 and 25–29 were originally independent aphorisms reflecting life in advanced agrarian society. The editorial process of gathering these single sayings into clusters and into a book gave a new interpretation to many of them. As Murphy notes, they became "wisdom literature" (Murphy 1998: 129). My peasant relatives in Poland who till the soil and raise farm animals have a different understanding of Divine Providence, chickens, and eggs as mentioned in Polish proverbs than does their American cousin born and raised in the megalopolis of Brooklyn, New York, who spent most of his adult life in settings of higher learning. Observing a similar difference, this book seeks to understand the cultural life setting of proverbs rather than their literary setting in the book of Proverbs.

The oldest Hebrew fragments of Proverbs we possess were found in Cave Four at Qumran (ca. 30 BCE–50 CE). The Septuagint appears to have used a different Hebrew version, and this and other translations (e.g., Syriac) tried to make sense of puzzling or obscure Hebrew passages by various emendations or reconstructions. This book uses the New Revised Standard Version (NRSV), but adopts the critical assessments and corrections by Richard Clifford (1999), which are, on the whole, reflected in the New American Bible Revised Edition (NABRE, OT 2011).

One difficulty posed by the NRSV is its use of inclusive language. While this may make a pleasing and readable text in English for Western readers, it often misrepresents and distorts the MENA culture in which the proverbs originated. For instance, the literal Hebrew, "son," is replaced with "child." Scholars recognize that proverbs were intended primarily as instructions from a father/teacher to a son/male child. Girls were trained in household tasks by women in the women's quarters. ▶Discipline. Boys were raised by all the women in the women's quarters, together with the girls. Here they were pampered and spoiled. At the age of puberty they were unceremoniously pushed into the harsh men's world, where they had to learn how to be men. One strategy to aid in this task was the application of physical discipline to the boys (Prov. 13:24; 18:19; 22:15;

23:13; 29:15, 17). To change the Hebrew words for "son" or "lad" in these proverbs to "child" unwittingly grants to biblical fundamentalists warrant to physically discipline daughters just as they do sons. This simply didn't happen in MENA cultures. Inclusive language renditions of these proverbs thus distort and misrepresent the culture. To its credit, the NABRE retains the masculine nouns and pronouns in these aphorisms. Moreover, while it inserts inclusive language in other sections of the Bible, it does not do so in Proverbs.

The reader is also invited to pay special attention to a feature of MENA psychology that permeates Proverbs, namely, the tripartite, non-introspective view of the human person. ▶**Three-Zone Personality.** This emic or indigenous view of the human person symbolically understood was given an appropriately derived etic ("outsider") interpretation by Bernard de Géradon (1954, 1958, 1974) a monk of Maredsous abbey who became Abbot of Wavreumont (Belgium) where he died on Nov. 17, 1979. In MENA cultures human beings cannot know others or themselves very well, since they are only able to judge by externals (see 1 Sam. 16:7). Thus they divide the human body into three zones and endow each with symbolic significance. Heart *and* eyes (and all the words that would belong to this semantic field) symbolize a zone of purposeful thinking. The eyes gather information for the heart, the seat of thinking. Mouth *and* ears (and all the words belonging to this semantic field) symbolize a zone of self-expressive speech. The mouth communicates for the ears of others to hear and understand. Hands *and* feet (and all the words belonging to this semantic field) symbolize a zone of purposeful activity. If a zone is not mentioned, the person is malfunctioning in that zone and is not whole, complete, entire, "perfect as your heavenly Father is perfect" (Matt. 5:48). This helps to understand why Murphy insists: "It is important in translating the Bible to render literally the parts of the body that are mentioned, as far as this is possible in the receptor language" (Murphy 1998: 159). Practically all the proverbs reflect this biblical psychological perspective. We have pointed it out in many proverbs, and the reader is invited to tease it out of the proverbs in which we have not mentioned this feature. It will require persistent effort on the part of the reader, but when combined with the information from the other Reading Scenarios, the end result will be a basic grasp of MENA culture and its significance for understanding and interpreting Proverbs.

# 1

---

# Outline of the Book of Proverbs

## I. Proverbs 1–9

### Introduction

*Proverbs 1:1-7*

1 The proverbs of Solomon son of David, king of Israel:
2 For learning about wisdom and instruction,
   for understanding words of insight,
3 for gaining instruction in wise dealing,
   righteousness, justice, and equity;
4 to teach shrewdness to the simple,
   knowledge and prudence to the young—
5 Let the wise also hear and gain in learning,
   and the discerning acquire skill,
6 to understand a proverb and a figure,
   the words of the wise and their riddles.
7 The fear of the Lord is the beginning of knowledge;
   fools despise wisdom and instruction.

These opening verses of Proverbs constitute a unit signaled by an *inclusio*, that is, the repetition of words and ideas as in vv. 2 and 7: "wisdom and instruction." The section is chiastically arranged:

a – 1:2a wisdom and discipline
  b – 1:2b understand
    c – 1:3a instruction/discipline
      d – 1:3b righteousness, justice, equity
    c' – 1:4-5 knowledge/learning
  b' – 1:6 understand
a' – 1:7b wisdom and discipline

Thus the aim of this anthology is to guide a person (mainly youth, but also mature adults as the reference to "the wise" in v. 5 indicates) to proper behavior toward others as expected by God (righteousness and justice) and to making honest and fair decisions, always speaking truth (equity).

*Textual Notes: 1:1-7*

**1:1** Tradition rooted in 1 Kings 5:9-14 ascribed wisdom (especially "proverbs") to Solomon. The biblical book of Proverbs, however, is an anthology, a varied collection of sayings, aphorisms, instructions, and the like, probably compiled by scribes or other functionaries in the royal court. Many reflect folk wisdom gained in the experience of the daily life of ordinary people. The key teachers of this wisdom are the king, the literary tradition recorded by the scribes, and the father (and mother in 1:8 and 6:20).

**1:2** NRSV "instruction" literally means "discipline" in Hebrew (also v. 7). ▶ **Discipline**. It entails both a process (obedience to the teacher and willing acceptance of correction, even physical when necessary; see Pilch 1993) and certain content (the actual instruction, the tradition).

**1:7** Readers of English translations recognize that the word "Lord" presented in such a typeface translates God's name in Hebrew: YHWH. In ordinary typeface, *Lord* is simply a title of respect (or in translations of the Greek scriptures, the proper rendition of *kyrios*). The phrase "fear of the Lord" occurs fourteen times in the book of Proverbs but has nothing to do with emotion. Rather, it is a recognition of and reverence for God demonstrated by obeying God's laws and performing the required rituals (Barré 1981: 41–43).

## Proverbs 1:8–9:18: Instructions of Father and Mother and Lady Wisdom:

*Proverbs 1:8-33*

8 Hear, my child, your father's instruction,
   and do not reject your mother's teaching;
9 for they are a fair garland for your head,
   and pendants for your neck.
10 My child, if sinners entice you,
   do not consent.
11 If they say, "Come with us, let us lie in wait for blood;
   let us wantonly ambush the innocent;
12 like Sheol let us swallow them alive and whole,
   like those who go down to the Pit.
13 We shall find all kinds of costly things;
   we shall fill our houses with booty.
14 Throw in your lot among us;
   we will all have one purse" —
15 my child, do not walk in their way,
   keep your foot from their paths;
16 for their feet run to evil,
   and they hurry to shed blood.
17 For in vain is the net baited
   while the bird is looking on;
18 yet they lie in wait to kill themselves!
   and set an ambush for their own lives!
19 Such is the end of all who are greedy for gain;
   it takes away the life of its possessors.
20 Wisdom cries out in the street;
   in the squares she raises her voice.
21 At the busiest corner she cries out;
   at the entrance of the city gates she speaks:
22 "How long, O simple ones, will you love being simple?
   [How long will scoffers delight in their scoffing
   and fools hate knowledge?]
23 Give heed to my reproof;
   I will pour out my thoughts to you;
   I will make my words known to you.

24 Because I have called and you refused,
    have stretched out my hand and no one heeded,
25 and because you have ignored all my counsel
    and would have none of my reproof,
26 I also will laugh at your calamity;
    I will mock when panic strikes you,
27 when panic strikes you like a storm,
    and your calamity comes like a whirlwind,
    when distress and anguish come upon you.
28 Then they will call upon me,
    but I will not answer;
    they will seek me diligently,
    but will not find me.
29 Because they hated knowledge
    and did not choose the fear of the Lord,
30 would have none of my counsel,
    and despised all my reproof,
31 therefore they shall eat the fruit of their way
    and be sated with their own devices.
32 For waywardness kills the simple,
    and the complacency of fools destroys them;
33 but those who listen to me will be secure
    and will live at ease, without dread of disaster."

Taking a cue from Prov. 9:1 ("Wisdom has built her house, she has set up her seven pillars"), Patrick Skehan—on the basis of meticulous analysis of the entire book—has proposed that the 6th–5th-century BCE author-compiler-designer of Proverbs arranged the text so as to form a structure, a "house," with three distinct parts (Skehan 1971: 27–45). While his proposal has not been widely accepted, the various literary and hermeneutical tools he used in his analysis alert the reader not to neglect such considerations. Though this book seeks to describe a plausible MENA cultural setting for each individual proverb, a similar setting can be recommended for larger collections such as those found in Proverbs 1–9.

Some scholars have identified ten distinct speeches, instructions, or lectures in Prov. 1:1-9 (Whybray 1994: 23–24; Clifford 1999: v–vi), though others are doubtful (Murphy 1998: 8–9). The verses of Proverbs 1 comprise two discrete units: vv. 8-19 are an instruction by father and mother (or teacher) to the son (or pupil, student); vv. 20-33 are a condemnatory speech in prophetic style directed against the people. Some identify vv. 8-19 as Lecture 1 and vv.10-33 as Wisdom poem I (there are three in Proverbs 1–9).

*Textual Notes: 1:8-23*

**1:8-19** The father instructs his (not so) young son to heed his instruction (Hebrew: *mûsār*), which involves (physical) discipline as well as content. The mother is credited with providing "teaching" (Hebrew: *tōrah*), which is an authoritative interpretation of tradition. In MENA cultures, sons give a woman status in the family (1 Sam. 1:1-8). Sons are raised by the women in the women's quarters until the age of puberty, when, without ritual, they are dispatched into the harsh world of the men. The women pamper and spoil their sons, which is why men have to physically discipline them when they join the men's world (Pilch 1993: 101–13). ▶**Discipline.**

Some scholars erroneously claim that these instructions are given to a son as he leaves home on the way to adulthood (Clifford 1999: 38). In MENA cultures sons never leave home (except for wayward or prodigal sons, Luke 15:11-32). They will remain in the patriarch's compound even after they marry. They will, however, be subject to peer pressure from cousins, neighbors, and friends who form a network or group inviting membership. The basic advice is to resist the alluring promises of ill-gotten wealth and success made by these peers. The young man is offered a choice between two ways: a path of righteousness and a path toward wickedness. The theme continues throughout the book. Obeying parental instruction will lead to honorable status (v. 9). ▶**Honor and Shame.**

**1:20-33** This is the first of three Wisdom poems in Proverbs 1–9. While this one rings with threat, the other two (Prov. 8; 9:1-6, 11) proclaim promise. Especially noteworthy in this poem is Wisdom's speaking about herself in the way that the Bible speaks of God. For instance, the sentiment "Then they will call upon me, but I will not answer; they will seek me diligently, but will not find me" (v. 28) is encountered often in the Psalms and the Prophets.

A constant theme of scholarly discussion concerns the attribution to Lady Wisdom of an unexpected level of authority, power, and influence—unexpected, that is, in a presumably misogynistic, patriarchal culture. This is due to a failure to recognize the status of women in this culture. While men behave spontaneously without thought of consequences, women—as in Prov. 31:10-31—demonstrate keen abilities to manage affairs, control events, and be in charge. Men's second and third order (planning and forethought) are first order for women. **According to the Values Orientation Model developed by Kluckhohn and Strodtbeck, all cultures must solve 5 or 6 basic life challenges. Options are limited to three choices in rank order different for men and women. Women's first option is one of the second or third options chosen by men (Pilch amd Malina 2009: xxiv-xl).** In these verses Lady Wisdom finds the people guilty of choosing ignorance and foolishness instead of prudent and wise behavior. She will laugh at them mockingly when terror (NRSV "panic"—the Hebrew word is a variant of šo'ah, a word used in the contemporary world to refer to the Holocaust of World War II) strikes. They are receiving their just deserts for choosing not to heed Wisdom and failing to revere YHWH.

*Proverbs 2:1-22*

1 My child, if you accept my words
  and treasure up my commandments within you,
2 making your ear attentive to wisdom
  and inclining your heart to understanding;
3 if you indeed cry out for insight,
  and raise your voice for understanding;
4 if you seek it like silver,
  and search for it as for hidden treasures—
5 then you will understand the fear of the Lord
  and find the knowledge of God.
6 For the Lord gives wisdom;
  from his mouth come knowledge and understanding;
7 he stores up sound wisdom for the upright;
  he is a shield to those who walk blamelessly,
8 guarding the paths of justice

and preserving the way of his faithful ones.
9  Then you will understand righteousness and justice
   and equity, every good path;
10 for wisdom will come into your heart,
   and knowledge will be pleasant to your soul;
11 prudence will watch over you;
   and understanding will guard you.
12 It will save you from the way of evil,
   from those who speak perversely [falsehoods],
13 who forsake the paths of uprightness
   to walk in the ways of darkness,
14 who rejoice in doing evil
   and delight in the perverseness of evil;
15 those whose paths are crooked,
   and who are devious in their ways.
16 You will be saved from the loose woman,
   from the adulteress with her smooth words,
17 who forsakes the partner of her youth
   and forgets her sacred covenant;
18 for her way leads down to death,
   and her paths to the shades;
19 those who go to her never come back,
   nor do they regain the paths of life.
20 Therefore walk in the way of the good,
   and keep to the paths of the just.
21 For the upright will abide in the land,
   and the innocent will remain in it;
22 but the wicked will be cut off from the land,
   and the treacherous will be rooted out of it.

This is one long acrostic poem. In general, an acrostic poem uses the letters of the Hebrew alphabet, but in many creatively different ways. In Prov. 31:10-31, each of the twenty-two lines begins with a successive letter of the alphabet. This poem (Proverbs 2) uses only two letters: *aleph* (the first letter) is prevalent in vv. 1-11, while *lamed* prevails in vv. 12-22). Verses 1-11 focus on how a son might gain "wisdom," while vv. 12-22 highlight the "way" or the effects of wisdom. The main idea is that education in Israel involves the cooperation of son, father, and God (girls were trained in household duties).

*Textual Notes: 2:1-22*

**2:1-4** The father/teacher exhorts his son to pursue wisdom. The exhortation is phrased in terms of the MENA understanding of the human person based on external observation. ▶ **Three-Zone Personality.** The son/pupil is to listen (mouth–ears), incline his heart (heart–eyes), cry out and raise his voice for insight and understanding (mouth–ears), and seek and search for them like a precious metal (hands–feet). In other words, the pursuit of wisdom should completely engage a person.

**2:5-8** The conditional clauses of vv. 1-4 ("if") find their conclusion in these verses. God grants wisdom, a divine gift. Together, vv. 1-8 demonstrate the complementarity of human initiative and divine benevolence. Fear ("reverence") of the Lord and experiential knowledge of God are the results of one's diligent pursuit of wisdom. They help to keep one on the right path, and God protects the person.

**2:9-11** These verses specify the behavioral results of gaining wisdom: one will understand righteousness, justice, equity, and every good human behavior. These in turn will protect the wise person.

**2:12-15** Here begins the second part of the poem (*lamed*). In general it warns about evil men (vv. 12-15) and women (vv. 16-19) who pose a threat to seekers of righteousness and every good human behavior. Wisdom will protect and save from these dangers.

**2:16-19** For the first time in the book of Proverbs the "deceptive" (loose, forbidden) woman appears (and will reappear again in Prov. 5:1-6; 6:20-35; 7; 9:13-18). In this instance the adulterous woman (v. 17) tempts to sexual activity (v. 19), behavior that leads to death and to Sheol, a place from which there is no return. Reference to her "smooth words" contrasts her "wisdom" with the wisdom offered by God.

**2:20-22** The concluding exhortation in this poem is to continue to behave in accord with God's wisdom. Avoid the allures of wicked men and women. Living to please God will guarantee an enjoyable life ("abide in the land") and preserve from premature death. This is quite unlike the lot of the wicked, who will die prematurely.

## Proverbs 3:1-35

1 My child, do not forget my teaching,
  but let your heart keep my commandments;
2 for length of days and years of life
  and abundant welfare they will give you.
3 Do not let loyalty and faithfulness forsake you;
  bind them around your neck,
4 So you will find favor and good repute
  in the sight of God and of people.
5 Trust in the Lord with all your heart,
  and do not rely on your own insight.
6 In all your ways acknowledge him,
  and he will make straight your paths.
7 Do not be wise in your own eyes;
  fear the Lord, and turn away from evil.
8 It will be a healing for your flesh
  and a refreshment for your body.
9 Honor the Lord with your substance [wealth]
  and with the first fruits of all your produce;
10 then your barns will be filled with plenty,
  and your vats will be bursting with wine.
11 My child, do not despise the Lord's discipline
  or be weary of his reproof,
12 for the Lord reproves the one he loves,
  as a father the son in whom he delights.

Scholars are not agreed on how to structure this poem. The consensus is that vv. 1-12 form a literary unit, but the remaining verses are variously structured. We accept this division: vv. 1-2, 13-18 (20), 21-26, 27-35 (Murphy 1998: 20).

### Textual Notes: 3:1-12

**3:1-2** The Hebrew text literally reports a father addressing his son (NRSV "my child"). The sentiment is repeated in Prov. 4:10; 5:1. The son/ student is exhorted to memorize the teaching (Crenshaw 1998: 93), for it will provide a long life and šālōm, which describes the quality of life: free from anxiety and filled with contentment and happiness (NRSV "welfare").

**3:3-4** The son is urged to cling to two key MENA values: loyalty and faithfulness (*ḥesed w'emet*; Pilch and Malina 2009: 72–75). In a non-introspective culture where it is difficult if not impossible to truly know another person (1 Sam. 16:7), it is critically important to maintain a relationship with those whom one does know well. Hence the significance of loyalty and faithfulness, which also describe relations between God and humans (Exod. 34:6). This text-segment and Prov. 3:21-24 bear striking similarities to Deut. 6:5-9.

NRSV "write them on the tablet of your heart" (compare Jer. 31:33) is lacking in ℵ, B, and other important Greek manuscripts.

**3:5-8** The son/pupil is reminded to be humble (not to rely on personal insight or consider oneself wise in one's own eyes, Prov. 26:5, 12; 28:11) and to behave in a way pleasing to God. The Sage refers to the heart—eyes symbolic body zone (vv. 5, 7). ▶**Three-Zone Personality**. Throughout the book of Proverbs, the eye features in more than forty sayings. Apart from the literal references to human vision, some mentions of the eye represent arrogance (Prov. 6:17; 20:13; 30:13), or an inflated opinion of one's own worth (Prov. 3:7; 12:15; 16:2; 21:2; 26:5, 12, 16; 28:11). In some references the eye represents evil (Prov. 6:13, 17; 10:10, and in 16:30 the "winking of the eye" is one of the metaphors for devising evil. If this is its sense in Prov. 30:17, then the saying speaks of acting with evil intent towards one's parents. The mocking and scorning of one's parents refers to showing them contempt and despising them. To "acknowledge God" (v. 6) is to obey the divine will. The result will be total wellbeing and not just physical health as described in v. 8.

**3:9-10** This is the only time in Proverbs that liturgical sacrifice is prescribed (see Exod. 23:19; 34:26; Deut. 26:1-11; Lev. 23:10-14). The motivation, however, it not simply to express devotion or piety but rather to obtain blessings from God: full barns and new wine (i.e., still-unfermented grape juice). It reflects the MENA value of balanced reciprocity (Malina 2001a: 94-95).

**3:11-12** While true wisdom comes from the Lord, it does not come easily. The previous verses created the impression that good behavior will merit divine blessing. But experience did not bear this out. Hence these verses seek to explain presumably undeserved suffering. Discipline (Hebrew *mûsār*) is physical (Prov. 19:18; 23:13; 29:17) and is part of the educational process rather than simply a form of punishment. Though puzzling to Western readers, the explanation for God's behavior is quite in accord with the MENA understanding of paternal love. The author of Hebrews explains it quite clearly (Heb. 12:5-11). Such a fusion of love and violence is a gross violation of Western cultural values and unfortunately convinces abused persons to remain in and tolerate their circumstances as signs of love.

> 13 Happy are those who find wisdom,
> and those who get understanding,
> 14 for her income is better than silver,
> and her revenue better than gold.
> 15 She is more precious than jewels,
> and nothing you desire can compare with her.
> 16 Long life is in her right hand;
> in her left hand are riches and honor.
> 17 Her ways are ways of pleasantness,
> and all her paths are peace.
> 18 She is a tree of life to those who lay hold of her;
> those who hold her fast are called happy.
> 19 The Lord by wisdom founded the earth;
> by understanding he established the heavens;
> 20 by his knowledge the deeps broke open,
> and the clouds drop down the dew.

Some inclusions signal that these verses form a unit: "happy" (Hebrew *'ašrê*, vv. 13, 18), "understanding" (Hebrew *tbûnâh*, vv. 13, 19), and "wisdom" (Hebrew *hokmâh*, vv. 13, 19).

*Textual Notes: 3:13-20*

**3:13-15** The Hebrew word translated here (v. 13 and in Prov. 3:4; 6:33; 8:17, 35; 18:22; 31:10) as "find" should be preferably translated in these instances as "get, acquire" (*mṣ'*). The corresponding verb in the second half of v. 13 (*pûq*, "obtain") confirms this choice. Moreover, NRSV "happy" translates the Hebrew *'ašrê*, which should more properly be rendered "honorable" or "truly honorable" (See Hanson 1994: 81–111;

Prov. 3:18; 8:32, 34; 14:21; 16:20; 20:7; 28:14; 29:18; 31:28). The one (literally in Hebrew "the man") who acquires wisdom has something more precious than anything else imaginable.

**3:16-18** Wisdom is personified here, as the Sage describes the benefits she bestows: long life (which would include health), wealth, and honorable status (NRSV "called happy"; see Hanson 1994: 81–111), all key MENA values.

**3:19-20** These verses may be a segment of a longer creation report, though here the emphasis is on the role of Wisdom in God's creative activity. While v. 19 reflects the creation report in Genesis, namely, that God sank pillars into the waters as a foundation for the flat earth, v. 20 focuses on that most precious of all elements in the Middle East: water (see Grant 1907: 18–25; Oleson 1992: 883–93). God tamed the primordial waters and set boundaries for them yet provided a necessary supply through rain and rivers or waterways.

> 21 My child, do not let these escape from your sight:
> keep sound wisdom and prudence,
> 22 and they will be life for your soul
> and adornment for your neck.
> 23 Then you will walk on your way securely
> and your foot will not stumble.
> 24 If you sit down, you will not be afraid;
> when you lie down, your sleep will be sweet.
> 25 Do not be afraid of sudden panic,
> or of the storm that strikes the wicked;
> 26 for the Lord will be your confidence
> and will keep your foot from being caught.
> 27 Do not withhold good from those to whom it is due,
> when it is in your power to do it.
> 28 Do not say to your neighbor, "Go, and come again,
> tomorrow I will give it" when you have it with you.
> 29 Do not plan harm against your neighbor
> who lives trustingly beside you.
> 30 Do not quarrel with anyone without cause,
> when no harm has been done to you.
> 31 Do not envy the violent
> and do not choose any of their ways;
> 32 for the perverse are an abomination to the Lord,
> but the upright are in his confidence.

33 The Lord's curse is on the house of the wicked,
    but he blesses the abode of the righteous.
34 Toward the scorners he is scornful,
    but to the humble he shows favor.
35 The wise will inherit honor,
    but stubborn fools, disgrace.

While vv. 1-12 deal with one's relationship with God, vv. 21-35 concern one's relationship with the neighbor (beginning in vv. 27-28 following the introduction in vv. 21-26).

*Textual Notes: 3:21-35*

**3:21-26** Addressing "my son" (NRSV "my child"), the father/teacher promotes the practice of two key wisdom virtues: *tušîyâh* and *mzimmâh*. These words are variously translated. The former (*tušîyâh*) is rendered "sound wisdom" (RSV; NRSV); "deliberation" (NABRE); "proficiency" (Clifford 1999: 56); "discretion" (Murphy 1998: 19); "resourcefulness" (JPS). The main idea is *practical* thinking with a view to deciding efficiently on a proper course of action. The latter (*mzimmâh*) is translated "prudence" (NRSV; Murphy 1998: 19); "discretion" (RSV); "planning" (NABRE); "shrewdness" (Clifford 1999: 56); "foresight" (JPS). Here the reference is to the power or ability to devise. Thus the son/pupil is encouraged to learn how to think clearly in concrete situations.

These virtues will bring actual physical benefits to the son/pupil and protection from violence (vv. 22-25). Such a person should have no fear: God will offer personal protection (v. 26).

**3:27-32** This segment of the poem lists prohibited behaviors against one's neighbor enforced by a motive clause (v. 32). Vv. 27-28 would appear to refer to paying a debt or repaying a loan to a creditor. Justice delayed is justice denied (see Jas. 4:16). Verses 29-30 forbid planning to harm a neighbor and quarreling "without cause." Given the agonistic nature of MENA cultures, quarreling is something of a recreational pastime. ▶**Agonism.** Though this proverb quite likely has in mind unjustified legal disputes, it would also seem to restrain the agonistic tendency, unless there is good reason. Preservation of one's honor and reputation is definitely a good reason to resort to quarreling. To neglect to rescue one's honor is to be shamed, to lose face.

The proverb in vv. 31-32 tries to point out that crime does not pay. The Hebrew word translated "violent" refers especially to physical brutality. The temptation is to imitate that kind of behavior because it seems to pay off. God rejects such behavior. In contrast, the upright, that is, those who do not imitate the reproved behavior, gain an intimate place is God's inner circle (sôd, see Jer. 23:18, 22), a position of trust. Here God reveals divine plans (Amos 3:7) to such as have an intimate and confidential relationship with the deity. It is the opposite of being an abomination in God's sight.

**3:33-35** These concluding verses pronounce God's judgment on the wicked who obtain scorn and disgrace, and divine blessing on the righteous and humble who win divine favor and gain honor.

### Proverbs 4:1-27

1 Listen, children, to a father's instruction,
  and be attentive, that you may gain insight;
2 for I give you good precepts:
  do not forsake my teaching.
3 When I was a son with my father,
  tender, and my mother's favorite,
4 he taught me, and said to me,
  "Let your heart hold fast my words;
  keep my commandments, and live.
5 Get wisdom; get insight:
  do not forget, nor turn away from the words of my mouth.
6 Do not forsake her, and she will keep you;
  love her, and she will guard you.
[7 The beginning of wisdom is this:
  Get wisdom, and whatever else you get, get insight.]
8 Prize her highly, and she will exalt you;
  she will honor you if you embrace her.
9 She will place on your head a fair garland;
  she will bestow on you a beautiful crown."

Scholars agree on the division of this chapter: vv. 1-9, the example of a father; vv. 10-19, the two ways of living one's life; vv. 20-27, life and health that result from following the father's example.

*Textual Notes: 4:1-9*

**4:1-2** A father addresses his sons (plural; NRSV inclusive language "children" is not correct) urging them to listen carefully and hold onto his valuable teaching. This is typical in Proverbs 1–9.

**4:3-5** In vv. 4-9 the father reminisces about his own father's instructions. Mention of his mother reflects the Israelite pattern of rearing sons. ▶**Discipline.** After birth, sons lived in the women's quarters and were raised there by all the women together with the girls. At puberty the son moved into the men's segment of the rigidly gender-divided world, where the father imparted the family wisdom from the grandfather to his own sons. The exhortation was to acquire wisdom and understanding (v. 5) in order to have a long and healthy life.

**4:6, 8-9** Verse 7 has been added to the Hebrew text, drawn most likely from Prov. 1:7; 4:5; 16:16; 17:16. The import of the remaining verses is to personify Wisdom as a woman or wife. She guards (v. 6) and bestows honor (vv. 8-9). The disciple is to "embrace her" (v. 8), traditional love language intended to describe the pursuit of Wisdom as a lifelong endeavor resulting in a wide array of blessings.

10 Hear, my child, and accept my words,
    that the years of your life may be many.
11 I have taught you the way of wisdom;
    I have led you in the paths of uprightness.
12 When you walk, your step will not be hampered;
    and if you run, you will not stumble.
13 Keep hold of instruction; do not let go;
    guard her, for she is your life.
14 Do not enter the path of the wicked,
    and do not walk in the way of evildoers.
15 Avoid it; do not go on it;
    turn away from it and pass on.

16 For they cannot sleep unless they have done wrong;
    they are robbed of sleep unless they have made someone stumble.
17 For they eat the bread of wickedness
    and drink the wine of violence.
18 But the path of the righteous is like the light of dawn,
    which shines brighter and brighter until full day.
19 The way of the wicked is like deep darkness;
    they do not know what they stumble over.

*Textual Notes: 4:10-19*

**4:10-19** These verses exhort the son/pupil to choose good and avoid evil, using the imagery of the Two Ways (vv. 18-19). Obeying the instruction ("words," v. 10) of the father keeps one on the straight path or "way" that God protects. The way or path of the wicked should be avoided at all costs.

20 My child, be attentive to my words;
    incline your ear to my sayings.
21 Do not let them escape from your sight;
    keep them within your heart.
22 For they are life to those who find them,
    and healing to all their flesh.
23 Keep your heart with all vigilance,
    for from it flow the springs of life.
24 Put away from you crooked speech,
    and put devious talk far from you.
25 Let your eyes look directly forward,
    and your gaze be straight before you.
26 Keep straight the path of your feet,
    and all your ways will be sure.
27 Do not swerve to the right or to the left;
    turn your foot away from evil.

*Textual Notes: 4:20-27*

**4:20-27** In these verses a father continues to exhort his son (NRSV "child") to attend to his words, for they are the source of life and health for him. The verses reflect the ancient Israelite understanding of the human person. ▶**Three-Zone Personality**. There are references to heart and eyes, the symbolic body zone of emotion-fused thought (vv.

21, 23, 25), mouth and ears, the symbolic body zone of self-expressive speech (vv. 20, 24), and hands and feet, the symbolic body zone of purposeful activity (vv. 26, 27). This refers to the entire person. Thus the father exhorts his son to obey him wholeheartedly with all his abilities.

## Proverbs 5:1-23

1 My child, be attentive to my wisdom;
   incline your ear to my understanding,
2 so that you may hold on to prudence,
   and your lips may guard knowledge.
3 For the lips of a loose woman drip honey,
   and her speech is smoother than oil;
4 but in the end she is bitter as wormwood,
   sharp as a two-edged sword.
5 Her feet go down to death;
   her steps follow the path to Sheol.
6 She does not keep straight to the path of life;
   her ways wander, and she does not know it.
7 And now, my child, listen to me,
   and do not depart from the words of my mouth.
8 Keep your way far from her,
   and do not go near the door of her house,
9 or you will give your honor to others,
   and your years to the merciless,
10 and strangers will take their fill of your wealth,
   and your labors will go to the house of an alien,
11 and at the end of your life you will groan,
   when your flesh and body are consumed,
12 and you say, "Oh, how I hated discipline,
   and my heart despised reproof!
13 I did not listen to the voice of my teachers
   or incline my ear to my instructors.
14 Now I am at the point of utter ruin
   in the public assembly."
15 Drink water from your own cistern,
   flowing water from your own well.
16 Should your springs be scattered abroad,
   streams of water in the streets?
17 Let them be for yourself alone,
   and not for sharing with strangers.
18 Let your fountain be blessed,

and rejoice in the wife of your youth,
19 a lovely deer, a graceful doe.
   May her breasts satisfy you at all times;
   may you be intoxicated always by her love.
20 Why should you be intoxicated, my son, by another woman
   and embrace the bosom of an adulteress?
21 For human ways are under the eyes of the Lord,
   and he examines all their paths.
22 The iniquities of the wicked ensnare them,
   and they are caught in the toils of their sin.
23 They die for lack of discipline,
   and because of their great folly they are lost.

This poem is the first in the book of Proverbs to develop the danger posed by the "foreign" (NRSV "loose") woman previously mentioned in Prov. 2:16-19 (and again in 5:3; 6:24; 7:5). The context indicates that this is the wife of another man (7:19-20), a woman from another family. Adultery carried grave risks, notably death at the hand of an aggrieved husband or another "next of kin." One would think that that consideration would keep a young man on the "straight and narrow," encouraging him to remain faithful to his wife. However, human beings often take risks without fully appreciating their potential deadly consequences.

*Textual Notes: 5:1-23*

**5:1-14** These verses urge the son (NRSV "child") to heed his father's cautions and teaching about the danger posed by the loose woman. Two symbolic body zones are highlighted: mouth and ears ("lips," "ears," "speech," etc.) and hands and feet ("feet," "path," etc.). ▶ **Three-Zone Personality.** Conspicuously absent is reference to heart and eyes with reference to the loose woman, though that is the zone highlighted for the young married man ("wisdom," "understanding," "prudence," "knowledge," etc.). That symbolic body zone will guide and protect the other two.

The consequences of yielding to the allures of the loose woman in this reflection do not seem to include death! Rather, the reference is to loss of wealth and honor (vv. 9-10), which the young man seems to realize in time to resist the temptation.

**5:15-23** (plus 6:22 following v. 19; see Skehan 1971: 6). In these verses the father/instructor exhorts his son to be faithful to his wife, who will prove to be his delight. She will provide complete satisfaction and be faithful to her husband alone. Like so many women of the Bible, she will prove to be a trustworthy and reliable guide. Verses 21-23 conclude the reflection, reminding the young man that ultimately God sees everything and reacts accordingly. It is lack of discipline that brings the careless young man to ruin.

### Proverbs 6:1-35

1 My child, if you have given your pledge to your neighbor,
   if you have bound yourself to another,
2 you are snared by the utterance of your lips,
   caught by the words of your mouth.
3 So do this, my child, and save yourself,
   for you have come into your neighbor's power:
   go, hurry, and plead with your neighbor.
4 Give your eyes no sleep
   and your eyelids no slumber;
5 save yourself like a gazelle from the hunter,
   like a bird from the hand of the fowler.
6 Go to the ant, you lazybones;
   consider its ways, and be wise.
7 Without having any chief or officer or ruler,
8 it prepares its food in summer,
   and gathers its sustenance in harvest.
9 How long will you lie there, O lazybones?
   When will you rise from your sleep?
10 A little sleep, a little slumber,
   a little folding of the hands to rest,
11 and poverty will come upon you like a robber,
   and want, like an armed warrior.
12 A scoundrel and a villain
   goes around with crooked speech,
13 winking the eyes, shuffling the feet,
   pointing the fingers,
14 with perverted mind devising evil,
   continually sowing discord;

15 on such a one calamity will descend suddenly;
in a moment, damage beyond repair.
16 There are six things that the Lord hates,
seven that are an abomination to him:
17 haughty eyes, a lying tongue,
and hands that shed innocent blood,
18 a heart that devises wicked plans,
feet that hurry to run to evil,
19 a lying witness who testifies falsely,
and one who sows discord in a family.

Scholars agree that vv. 1-19 are an insertion into the series of ten instructions comprising Proverbs 1–9. This text segment consists of four independent pieces: vv. 1-5, the folly of providing backing for a person in debt; vv. 6-11, the damage wreaked by indolence; vv. 12-15, a description of the "man of Belial" (a scoundrel; see also the comment on Prov. 16:27); vv. 16-19, a numerical proverb (see Proverbs 30; also 25–26).

*Textual Notes: 6:1-19*

**6:1-5** *The folly of providing backing for a person in debt.* Biblical law does not make any reference to "giving one's pledge" or "standing surety" for a person in debt. In Prov. 22:26-27 the pledge is financial. However, given the nature of peasant existence (they live at subsistence level with little to no surplus—of anything!—to spare), the pledge may most often have involved something other than money (de Vaux 1961: 170–73). Most often a garment was the pledge, a stand-in for the person of the debtor, but it had to be returned to a poor man at dusk (Exod. 22:25-26; Deut. 24:12-13). Means of livelihood were not to be taken as a pledge (e.g., Deut. 24:6).

Here the father/teacher pleads with his "son" (NRSV "child") to avoid standing surety (Proverbs in general rejects the practice: Prov. 11:15; 17:18; 20:16; 22:26; 27:13). The son is to humble ("shame") himself and do all in his power to convince the "neighbor" to release him from his foolish pledge.

**6:6-11** *The damage wreaked by indolence.* NRSV "lazybones" ("sluggard") is a type in the book of Proverbs (see Prov. 10:4, 26; 15:19; 19:24; 20:4; 21:25; 22:13). Additional reflections on indolence are Prov. 24:30-34 and 26:13-16. Ancient peoples looked to animals as models for human behavior (Job 12:7; Prov. 30:24-30). In this case the ant is contrasted with the lazybones. Entomologists point out that ants are born with an instinct or drive to gather food. Indeed, the ant colony does not have a chief, officer, or ruler. Queens lay eggs but give no orders. Females are the workers fulfilling a variety of necessary tasks by instinct. In contrast, during the harvest period the lazybones shirks his share of the labor, putting the community at risk of running out of provisions. His instinct is sleep rather than work.

**6:12-15** *The Scoundrel.* Using the tripartite symbolic understanding of the human body, the Sage describes the totally wicked person, a scoundrel (literally in Hebrew "man of Belial"; see Prov. 16:27). ▶**Three-Zone Personality.** His speech is deceptive (mouth–ears), his mind devises evil (heart–eyes ), and he intentionally stirs up strife (hands–feet). ▶**Agonism.** While MENA culture is agonistic by its nature, individuals understand full well its potentially damaging consequences and resort to a variety of measures to keep it in check lest it become uncontrollable. Such a person will experience sudden calamity, damage beyond repair.

**6:16-19** *A Numerical Proverb.* The element common to this enumeration is that each of the things listed is an abomination to the Lord (see Prov. 11:20; 12:22; 16:26; 16:25). Once again this text segment resorts to the symbolic understanding of the human body to describe the totality of things the Lord hates. ▶**Three-Zone Personality.** The verses cover each zone (heart–eyes; mouth–ears; hands–feet) twice and conclude with strife, as does the previous segment (v. 14): this time, one who sows discord in the family (v. 19).

20 My child, keep your father's commandment,
   and do not forsake your mother's teaching.
21 Bind them upon your heart always;
   tie them around your neck.
22 When you walk, they will lead you;
   when you lie down, they will watch over you;

and when you awake, they will talk with you.

23 For the commandment is a lamp and the teaching a light,
and the reproofs of discipline are the way of life,

24 to preserve you from the wife of another,
from the smooth tongue of the adulteress.

25 Do not desire her beauty in your heart,
and do not let her capture you with her eyelashes;

26 for a prostitute's fee is only a loaf of bread,
but the wife of another stalks a man's very life.

27 Can fire be carried in the bosom
without burning one's clothes?

28 Or can one walk on hot coals
without scorching the feet?

29 So is he who sleeps with his neighbor's wife;
no one who touches her will go unpunished.

30 Thieves are not despised
who steal only to satisfy their appetite when they are hungry.

31 Yet if they are caught, they will pay sevenfold;
they will forfeit all the goods of their house.

32 But he who commits adultery has no sense;
he who does it destroys himself.

33 He will get wounds and dishonor,
and his disgrace will not be wiped away.

34 For jealousy arouses a husband's fury,
and he shows no restraint when he takes revenge.

35 He will accept no compensation,
and refuses a bribe no matter how great.

This text segment is the second of three instructions concerning adultery in Proverbs 1–9 (5:1-23; 6:20-35; 7). The poem can be divided into three parts.

I. Verses 20-24 exhort the son to take his father and mother's instruction to heart, for they will guide him and prevent him from yielding to the temptation of adultery.

II. Verses 25-29 compare the cost of prostitution (only a loaf of bread) with the cost of adultery (threat to one's life and damage to one's very self).

III. Verses 30-35 compare theft with adultery. Reparation for the former can easily be made monetarily, but adultery risks retaliation and loss of honor, the core MENA cultural value without which it is difficult to live. The exhortation to avoid adultery is not about developing a strong appreciation of one's wife, as in Proverbs 5, but rather the fear of irremediable loss of honor and possibly even one's life. ▶ Adultery.

*Textual Notes: 6:20-35*

**6:20-35** Medical and social scientists, especially those who use the ethnographic data in the Human Relations Area Files (HRAF) at Yale University, prefer to speak of "extramarital sex" or an "extramarital relationship" instead of "adultery," which carries with it the notion of condemnation or sin in the Judaeo-Christian and Islamic world (Levinson 1995: 242–47). It has to be understood instead within the notion of marriage as "a culturally specific set of behaviors rather than as some abstract universal human institution" (Pilch 2012: 123). The meanings ascribed to marriage are culturally quite specific; hence the meaning of adultery is similarly culturally specific. ▶ Adultery. While in the United States adultery is usually interpreted as deviant marital (sexual) behavior, in ancient Israel it was one set of specific male actions that dishonored or shamed other males and was an abomination to God. Malina has traced its evolving meaning through the historical development of ancient Israel (Malina 2001: 134–60).

Given the social reality in which the ancient MENA peasant lived, a reader wonders how effective the parents' instruction would be. Village population was small, and privacy did not exist. Everyone's business consisted in minding the business of everyone else. Surely in the smallest village some foolish adulterer was known to all and despised. It would seem that the very existence of such a guilty person would pose a stark warning to young married men tempted to commit adultery. If the perpetrator was already dead, that fact would pose an even stronger warning. Hence the necessity of understanding marriage and extramarital sex in its cultural context in order to fully understand the significance of and expected potential for these parental instructions.

## Proverbs 7:1-27

1 My child, keep my words and
   store up my commandments with you;
2 keep my commandments and live,
   keep my teachings as the apple of your eye;
3 bind them on your fingers,
   write them on the tablet of your heart.
4 Say to wisdom, "You are my sister,"
   and call insight your intimate friend,
5 that they may keep you from the loose woman,
   from the adulteress with her smooth words.
6 For at the window of my house
   I looked out through my lattice,
7 and I saw among the simple ones,
   I observed among the youths,
   a young man without sense,
8 passing along the street near her corner,
   taking the road to her house
9 in the twilight, in the evening,
   at the time of night and darkness.
10 Then a woman comes toward him,
   decked out like a prostitute, wily of heart.
11 She is loud and wayward;
   her feet do not stay at home;
12 now in the street, now in the squares,
   and at every corner she lies in wait.
13 She seizes him and kisses him,
   and with impudent face she says to him:
14 "I had to offer sacrifices,
   and today I have paid my vows;
15 so now I have come out to meet you,
   to seek you eagerly, and I have found you!
16 I have decked my couch with coverings,
   colored spreads of Egyptian linen;
17 I have perfumed my bed with myrrh,
   aloes, and cinnamon.
18 Come, let us take our fill of love until morning;
   let us delight ourselves with love.
19 For my husband is not at home;
   he has gone on a long journey.
20 He took a bag of money with him;
   he will not come home until full moon."
21 With much seductive speech she persuades him;

with her smooth talk she compels him.
22 Right away he follows her,
and goes like an ox to the slaughter,
or bounds like a stag toward the trap
23 until an arrow pierces its entrails.
He is like a bird rushing into a snare,
not knowing that it will cost him his life.
24 And now, my children, listen to me,
and be attentive to the words of my mouth.
25 Do not let your hearts turn aside to her ways;
do not stray into her paths.
26 for many are those she has laid low,
and numerous are her victims.
27 Her house is the way to Sheol,
going down to the chambers of death.

This final warning about adultery completes the sequence. Prov. 2:16-19 introduces the wayward woman as one hindrance to acquiring wisdom. The warning is further elaborated in Prov. 5:1-23 and 6:20-35. Proverbs 7 graphically describes the threat of death posed by this woman.

*Textual Notes: 7:1-27*

**7:1-5** A father addresses this warning to his son (NRSV "child") with the imperative "live!" (See Gen. 20:7; 42:18; Jer. 27:12, 17; Ezek. 18:32, in which this same word occurs in a context of avoiding death). He uses love language ("sister," "friend") to refer to Wisdom, suggesting the son should direct his attention and affection to Lady Wisdom. Sadly, the son says nothing as the story continues, and is led like an animal to his death.

**7:6-13** The father relates in vivid terms a scene he witnessed: the behavior of a young man with no sense (literally in Hebrew "lacking heart," the part of the body symbolically representing the zone of emotion-fused thinking: ▶**Three-Zone Personality**). From what follows it is clear that this lad is stupid, perhaps naïve and gullible as young people sometimes can be. He deliberately places himself in a situation of high-risk temptation. In short order the married temptress dressed like a harlot meets and seduces him.

The youth interprets her statement about "paying her vow" as an invitation to a meal at which the meat from the (thanksgiving) "sacrifice of well-being" to God will be served (see Lev. 7:15-17). There will be plenty of food that must be consumed. Yet as the woman continues she makes it quite clear that she has much more in mind. As noted, he says nothing, but accepts her invitation and goes to his death (vv. 21-23). The father then addresses his warning to all sons (NRSV "my children"). The story should serve as an example for them.

From a cultural perspective the concern of the father is quite understandable even if the scenario he paints has little plausibility. Villages were small and not very populous. Inhabitants were mostly related. Everyone knew everyone else, and surely a woman of this nature would be known to all. While the temptation of a ready and willing consort would be strong, the mortal threat she posed would be known to all. The father would thus be repeating the obvious. Would it be more persuasive than the reality (e.g., previous victims of her treachery)? Moreover, if this scenario occurred previously, the aggrieved husband may well have killed the lover and perhaps even the wife. If he failed to do anything and she continued her adulterous behavior the husband would be shamed in the village as a cuckold. Taking long trips would not absolve him from his cultural obligation. Thus this scenario is definitely an example story (e.g., Prov. 24:30-34), a teaching story with little cultural plausibility. However, it could be adequate for a simple youth, a young man with no sense (stupid).

## Proverbs 8:1-36

1 Does not wisdom call,
  and does not understanding raise her voice?
2 On the heights, beside the way,
  at the crossroads she takes her stand;
3 beside the gates in front of the town,
  at the entrance of the portals she cries out:
4 "To you, O people, I call,
  and my cry is to all that live.

5 O simple ones, learn prudence;
  acquire intelligence, you who lack it.
6 Hear, for I will speak noble things,
  and from my lips will come what is right;
7 for my mouth will utter truth;
  wickedness is an abomination to my lips.
8 All the words of my mouth are righteous;
  there is nothing twisted or crooked in them.
9 They are all straight to one who understands
  and right to those who find knowledge.
10 Take my instruction instead of silver,
  and knowledge rather than choice gold;
11 for wisdom is better than jewels,
  and all that you may desire cannot compare with her.
12 I, wisdom, live with prudence,
  and I attain knowledge and discretion.
[13 The fear of the Lord is hatred of evil.] [gloss from 3:7]
  Pride and arrogance and the way of evil
  and perverted speech I hate.
14 I have good advice and sound wisdom;
  I have insight, I have strength.
15 By me kings reign,
  and rulers decree what is just;
16 by me rulers rule,
  and nobles, all who govern rightly.
17 I love those who love me,
  and those who seek me diligently find me.
18 Riches and honor are with me,
  enduring wealth and prosperity.
19 My fruit is better than gold, even fine gold,
  and my yield than choice silver.
20 I walk in the way of righteousness,
  along the paths of justice,
21 endowing with wealth those who love me,
  and filling their treasuries.
22 The Lord created me at the beginning of his work,
  the first of his acts of long ago.
23 Ages ago I was set up,
  at the first, before the beginning of the earth.
24 When there were no depths I was brought forth,
  when there were no springs abounding with water.
25 Before the mountains had been shaped,
  before the hills, I was brought forth—
26 when he had not yet made earth and fields,
  or the world's first bits of soil.

27 When he established the heavens, I was there,
  when he drew a circle on the face of the deep,
28 when he made firm the skies above,
  when he established the fountains of the deep,
29 when he assigned to the sea its limit,
  so that the waters might not transgress his command,
  when he marked out the foundations of the earth,
30 then I was beside him, like a master worker;
  and I was daily his delight, rejoicing before him always,
31 rejoicing in his inhabited world
  and delighting in the human race.
32 And now, my children, listen to me:
  happy are those who keep my ways.
33 Hear instruction and be wise,
  and do not neglect it.
34 Happy is the one who listens to me,
  watching daily at my gates,
  waiting beside my doors.
35 For whoever finds me finds life
  and obtains favor from the Lord;
36 but those who miss me injure themselves;
  all who hate me love death."

Within Proverbs 1–9, chapter 8 is a follow-up to Prov. 1:2-33, Lady Wisdom's first speech. In that address she threatens to depart from anyone who rejects her. Proverbs 8, in contrast, presents a catalogue of Wisdom's virtues and the potential gifts she can bestow on those who pay attention and accept her invitation to become her disciples. It is structured in four sections (vv. 1-10; 12-21; 22-31; 32-36).

*Textual Notes: 8:1-36*

**8:1-10** Standing at the highest and centermost part of the city, Wisdom boldly invites all to become her disciples. She assures passersby that her instruction is entirely trustworthy and reliable, deserving to be accepted. (v. 11 may be borrowed from Prov. 3:14-15; see Skehan 1979: 368).

**8:12-21** Lady Wisdom recounts what she loves and hates. Kings are mentioned because this was the social institution that mediated divine wisdom to human beings (see 1 Kgs. 3:5-14). In this segment the poem draws a contrast with the adulterous woman of Proverbs 5. Lady Wisdom bestows as her everlasting gifts the very things the adulterous woman took away.

**8:22-31** God created Wisdom before everything else, and God was present with Wisdom, which enjoys being with God. This a position of special honor, something very significant in MENA culture. She especially rejoices in seeing God in the act of creation.

**8:32-36** Truly honorable (v. 34, NRSV "happy"; Hanson 1994: 81-111) is the disciple of Wisdom who accepts her invitation. The choice is a matter of life and death.

## Proverbs 9:1-18

1 Wisdom has built her house,
   she has hewn her seven pillars.
2 She has slaughtered her animals, she has mixed her wine,
   she has also set her table.
3 She has sent out her servant girls,
   she calls from the highest places in the town,
4 "You that are simple, turn in here!"
   To those without sense she says,
5 "Come, eat of my bread
   and drink of the wine I have mixed.
6 Lay aside immaturity, and live,
   and walk in the way of insight."
7 Whoever corrects a scoffer wins abuse;
   whoever rebukes the wicked gets hurt.
8 A scoffer who is rebuked will only hate you;
   the wise, when rebuked, will love you.
9 Give instruction to the wise, and they will become wiser still;
   teach the righteous and they will gain in learning.
10 The fear of the Lord is the beginning of wisdom,
   and the knowledge of the Holy One is insight.
11 For by me your days will be multiplied,
   and years will be added to your life.
12 If you are wise, you are wise for yourself;
   if you scoff, you alone will bear it.
13 The foolish woman is loud;
   she is ignorant and knows nothing.
14 She sits at the door of her house,
   on a seat at the high places of the town,

15 calling to those who pass by,
  who are going straight on their way,
16 "You who are simple, turn in here!"
  And to those without sense she says,
17 "Stolen water is sweet,
  and bread eaten in secret is pleasant."
18 But they do not know that the dead are there,
  that her guests are in the depths of Sheol.

This final chapter of the introduction to the book of Proverbs contrasts two women and their respective invitations: Lady Wisdom (Prov. 9:1-6, 11) and Lady Folly (Prov. 9:13-18). Five independent sayings have been inserted at a later time (vv. 7-10, 12).

*Textual Notes: 9:1-18*

**9:1** The theme of Lady Wisdom building her house occurs also in Prov. 14:1; 24:3. The seven columns may be her teachings in Proverbs 1–8, supports for the house. Prov. 10:1–22:16 will expand the teaching in contrasting the wise and the righteous.

**9:2-3** When the house is constructed, invitations to the festal banquet (wine mixed with spices) are issued in the upper city.

**9:4-6, 11** The invitees are the "simple," "those without sense"; the literal Hebrew is "those who lack heart" (see Prov. 12:1, "fools"), the symbolic body zone of emotion-fused thinking. ▶**Three-Zone Personality**.

**9:7-10, 12** These verses echo words and motifs from Proverbs 1 in a way that forms an *inclusio*. They are a later addition to the poem.

**9:7-9** The Sages routinely cautioned that attempting to correct a scoffer may be futile (see also Prov. 22:10). The wise person will be grateful and become even wiser.

**9:10** The true beginning of wisdom is acknowledging YHWH as the one true and only God deserving obedience and respectful ritual.

**9:12** A difficult verse whose meaning—without adequate context—remains too obscure to interpret.

**9:13-18** Lady Folly has nothing worthwhile to offer at her banquet.

She proffers adultery, sexuality stolen from the household of another, which can only lead to death and destruction.

## II. Proverbs 10:1–22:16

### The Proverbs of Solomon

Scholars are agreed that this second section of the Book of Proverbs (10:1–22:16) is indeed a collection with a discernible unity. The numerical value of Solomon's name in Hebrew (300 + 30 + 40 + 5) is 375, the number of proverbs in this collection. This is not only an indication of literary skill but perhaps also a mnemonic aid in this oral culture. The proverbs are linked by "catchwords," e.g., righteous/wicked, wise/fool, and the like. Chapters 10–12 are dominated by righteous/wicked contrasts, 13–15 by wise/fool contrasts. Nevertheless, the proverb retains its own meaning despite its collocation in this collection. As R. N. Whybray notes, the sayings in 10:1–22:17 and chapters 25–29 reflect "self contained proverbs reflecting a largely agricultural society uninfluenced by the interests of a scribal class" (*Composition*, 129). We focus on that meaning from a Middle Eastern cultural perspective.

### Proverbs 10:1-31

1 The proverbs of Solomon.
   A wise child makes a glad father,
   but a foolish child is a mother's grief.
2 Treasures gained by wickedness do not profit,
   but righteousness delivers from death.
3 The Lord does not let the righteous go hungry,
   but he thwarts the craving of the wicked.
4 A slack hand causes poverty,
   but the hand of the diligent makes rich.
5 A child who gathers in summer is prudent,
   but a child who sleeps in harvest brings shame.
6 Blessings are on the head of the righteous,
   but the mouth of the wicked conceals violence.
7 The memory of the righteous is a blessing,
   but the name of the wicked will rot.
8 The wise of heart will heed commandments,

but a babbling fool will come to ruin.
9 Whoever walks in integrity walks securely,
  but whoever follows perverse ways will be found out.
10 Whoever winks the eye causes trouble,
  but the one who rebukes boldly makes peace.
11 The mouth of the righteous is a fountain of life,
  but the mouth of the wicked conceals violence.
12 Hatred stirs up strife,
  but love covers all offenses.
13 On the lips of one who has understanding wisdom is found,
  but a rod is for the back of one who lacks sense.
14 The wise lay up knowledge,
  but the babbling of a fool brings ruin near.
15 The wealth of the rich is their fortress;
  the poverty of the poor is their ruin.
16 The wage of the righteous leads to life,
  the gain of the wicked to sin.
17 Whoever heeds instruction is on the path to life,
  but one who rejects a rebuke goes astray.
18 Lying lips conceal hatred,
  and whoever utters slander is a fool.
19 When words are many, transgression is not lacking,
  but the prudent are restrained in speech.
20 The tongue of the righteous is choice silver;
  the mind of the wicked is of little worth.
21 The lips of the righteous feed many,
  but fools die for lack of sense.
22 The blessing of the Lord makes rich,
  and he adds no sorrow with it.
23 Doing wrong is like sport to a fool,
  but wise conduct is pleasure to a person of understanding.
24 What the wicked dread will come upon them,
  but the desire of the righteous will be granted.
25 When the tempest passes, the wicked are no more,
  but the righteous are established forever.
26 Like vinegar to the teeth,
  and smoke to the eyes,
  so are the lazy to their employers.
27 The fear of the Lord prolongs life,
  but the years of the wicked will be short.
28 The hope of the righteous ends in gladness,
  but the expectation of the wicked comes to nothing.
29 The way of the Lord is a stronghold for the upright,
  but destruction for evildoers.
30 The righteous will never be removed,

but the wicked will not remain in the land.
31 The mouth of the righteous brings forth wisdom,
but the perverse tongue will be cut off.
32 The lips of the righteous know what is acceptable,
but the mouth of the wicked what is perverse.

Antithetic parallelism prevails in this section, frequently contrasting the righteous and the wicked (10:2, 3, 6, 7, 11, 16, 20, 21, 24, 25, 28, 29, 30, 31, 32). But who are the righteous (most often ṣaddiq) and the wicked (most often reša')? This is never clearly spelled out. Instead, representative behaviors are described. However, later rabbinic reflection identified two kinds of righteous people: the ḥasid and the ṣaddiq (Pilch 2002: 38–40). Both aimed to please God. The ḥasid was satisfied with fulfilling the basic requirements of righteousness, while the ṣaddiq went over and beyond the "basic" to reduce or eliminate the risk of failing to please God.

From the cultural perspective of an agricultural society, surely Prov. 10:4 and 10:5 refer to a person (literally, 10:5 says "shameful son") who does not pull his weight in the common family enterprise. Subsistence depended on a successful harvest. High taxation left the family precious little to live on, all the less if the crop was deficient. Commitment to the family was an essential element of building a "house," a community, a central theme of Proverbs. Laziness or shirking one's duty was not what a righteous person should do. It was not pleasing to God.

*Textual Notes: 10:1-31*

**10:1** Establishing and maintaining a house is a major theme not only in Proverbs 1–9; the theme is further developed throughout the rest of the book. The relationships between son, father, and mother occur repeatedly: see Prov. 15:20; 17:21, 25; 19:13, 26; 23:22-26. There are also repeated references to spousal relationships: 12:4; 14:1; 18:22; 19:14; 21:9, 19). This is completely understandable since kinship is one of the two major social institutions of circum-Mediterranean culture. All of life hinges around kinship and politics. ►**Kinship.** ►**Politics.**

Everything else is subsumed under them. Here the focus is on the son and the effect his wise or foolish behavior has on his father and mother.

**10:4** Though poverty and wealth in the Bible are not necessarily or primarily economic concepts, that is precisely the context in this aphorism (see also Prov. 6:6-11; 12:24, 27; 13:4). The reference is to human labor and its fruits. ▶**Rich and Poor.**

**10:5** The Hebrew contrasts two kinds of sons: an honorable one who is responsible and diligent, participating in the harvest for the benefit of the entire family, and a shameful one who is lazy ("sleeps in harvest"). ▶**Honor and Shame.** Compare Prov. 17:2.

**10:8** "Wise of heart" contrasts with "lacking heart" (6:32; 7:7; 9:4, 16). ▶**Three-Zone Personality.** The heart–eyes symbolic body zone is linked with hands–feet (purposeful activity) in the wise person, in contrast with the mouth–ears of the fool ("babbling fool").

**10:10** "Winking [literally: pinching] the eye" (see Ps. 35:19; Prov. 16:30) continues to elude precise definition. Most interpreters relate this gesture to the circum-Mediterranean cultural belief in the "evil eye," that is, the belief that some people can cause real harm by their gaze, by staring (Kotze 2010). Since eyes are connected to the heart in biblical psychology, and evil springs from the heart, it makes sense that the eyes project what is in the heart. ▶**Three-Zone Personality.** Winking the eye is thus identified as an insidiously malicious gesture, a non-verbal manner of communicating hostility. However, the context of each occurrence suggests the need for nuanced interpretation. In this instance the ambiguous non-verbal communication ("winking the eye") is contrasted with clear verbal communication ("rebukes boldly"), producing bad and good results respectively ("trouble," "peace").

**10:12** MENA culture is agonistic. ▶**Agonism.** Hatred is anger expressed, which automatically stirs up strife. The key to peace and harmony is to forgive offenses or disregard them so as not to stir up strife.

**10:18** Scholars prefer to translate this proverb thus: "Whoever conceals hatred has lying lips; whoever reveals slander is a fool." This gives the aphorism an antithetical form otherwise lacking: "conceals," "reveals." While the reflection sounds very commonsensical, it has special significance in circum-Mediterranean culture where secrecy, deception, and lying are acceptable strategies for maintaining and safeguarding honor. This helps us understand the preoccupation with speech in this section: "mouth" (vv. 6, 11, 14, 31, 41), "lips" (vv. 8, 13, 18, 19, 21, 32), "tongue" (vv. 20, 31), "words" (v. 19), and "rebuke" (vv. 10, 17).

This proverb is something of a cultural truism. The one who conceals hatred must lie in order to avoid initiating a feud. Feuds can escalate to violence, which in turn can result in bloodshed. The cost of shedding blood is too much to risk, hence lying in this part of the verse is what everyone expects. Only one's family deserves the truth. It is permissible and expected that one should lie to outsiders. ▶Lying. The one who reveals the true deficiencies and failures of others—especially outsiders—is indeed a fool who risks serious, perhaps even mortal consequences. A contemporary Western reader must beware of imposing on lies in Middle Eastern culture the moral evaluation they carry in Western culture.

**10:21** NRSV "lack of sense" is literally in Hebrew "lacking heart." ▶Three-Zone Personality. The four verses (vv. 18-21) focus on the mouth–ears symbolic body zone as deficient in one or another sense. The end result is undesirable and thus should be avoided.

**10:23** NRSV "doing wrong" is actually lewdness, or committing a forbidden sexual act (Judg. 20:6; Ezek. 16:43; 23:48). It described a truly heinous crime like incest, adultery, or idolatry. The point is that a fool has no idea of the seriousness of his crime. Ignorance, however, will not excuse him.

**10:26** The lazy person or sluggard is a type in Proverbs (e.g., Prov. 26:13-16). The word (aṣēl) appears some fourteen times in Proverbs (and only once elsewhere). Even when the word is not used, the idea may be present (Prov. 10:4, 5). For the most part the context is advanced agrarian society and its requirements. Laziness is of no help.

Thus a lazy person is as irritating as vinegar to the teeth or smoke to the eyes.

**10:27** "Fear of the Lord" occurs fourteen times in the book of Proverbs (e.g., 1:7; 10:27; 14:26-27; 15:16, 33; 16:6; 20:23; 22:4; etc.) and is not an emotion. (See the comment on Prov. 1:7.)

### Proverbs 11:1-31

1 A false balance is an abomination to the Lord,
   but an accurate weight is his delight.
2 When pride comes, then comes disgrace;
   but wisdom is with the humble.
3 The integrity of the upright guides them,
   but the crookedness of the treacherous destroys them.
4 Riches do not profit in the day of wrath,
   but righteousness delivers from death.
5 The righteousness of the blameless keeps their ways straight,
   but the wicked fall by their own wickedness.
6 The righteousness of the upright saves them,
   but the treacherous are taken captive by their schemes.
7 When the wicked die, their hope perishes,
   and the expectation of the godless comes to nothing.
8 The righteous are delivered from trouble,
   and the wicked get into it instead.
9 With their mouths the godless would destroy their neighbors,
   but by knowledge the righteous are delivered.
10 When it goes well with the righteous, the city rejoices;
   and when the wicked perish, there is jubilation.
11 By the blessing of the upright a city is exalted,
   but it is overthrown by the mouth of the wicked.
12 Whoever belittles another lacks sense,
   but an intelligent person remains silent.
13 A gossip goes about telling secrets,
   but one who is trustworthy in spirit keeps a confidence.
14 Where there is no guidance, a nation falls,
   but in an abundance of counselors there is safety.
15 To guarantee loans for a stranger brings trouble,
   but there is safety in refusing to do so.
16 A gracious woman gets honor,
   but she who hates virtue is covered with shame.
   The timid become destitute,
   but the aggressive gain riches.
17 Those who are kind reward themselves,

but the cruel do themselves harm.
18 The wicked earn no real gain,
but those who sow righteousness get a true reward
19 Whoever is steadfast in righteousness will live,
but whoever pursues evil will die.
20 Crooked minds are an abomination to the Lord,
but those of blameless ways are his delight.
21 Be assured, the wicked will not go unpunished,
but those who are righteous will escape.
22 Like a gold ring in a pig's snout
is a beautiful woman without good sense.
23 The desire of the righteous ends only in good;
the expectation of the wicked in wrath.
24 Some give freely, yet grow all the richer;
others withhold what is due, and only suffer want.
25 A generous person will be enriched,
and one who gives water will get water.
26 The people curse those who hold back grain,
but a blessing is on the head of those who sell it.
27 Whoever diligently seeks good seeks favor,
but evil comes to the one who searches for it.
28 Those who trust in their riches will wither,
but the righteous will flourish like green leaves.
29 Those who trouble their households will inherit wind,
and the fool will be servant to the wise.
30 The fruit of the righteous is a tree of life,
but violence takes lives away.
31 If the righteous are repaid on earth,
how much more the wicked and the sinner!

This chapter continues the contrast between the righteous and the wicked, with the vast majority of its aphorisms cast in antithetical form.

*Textual Notes: 11:1-31*

**11:1** Weights and measures pertain especially to the market place. In the contemporary Western mind this relates to economy, especially a market economy. ▶**Economy.** In the ancient world, economy was not a free-standing social institution but was embedded in kinship and politics. ▶**Kinship.** ▶**Politics.** The Greek word *oikonomia* refers to managing one's household: providing for the needs of one's family.

This would be domestic economy (kinship). Political economy described the relationship of citizens to their country. In modern terminology this would be the nation or state, entities that did not exist before the eighteenth century (Pilch 2012: 64). Political economy involved "land tenure, with control of labor and resources through debts, taxation, and other forms of redistribution" (Oakman 2012: 27). In particular, this involved commerce between countries, carried out by merchants, that necessitated weights and measures, since money was not widely used as a medium of exchange (Oakman 2002: 342).

Proverbs indicates the cultural belief that human beings are incapable of creating consistently accurate weights. Only God could determine these (Prov. 16:11). God's surrogate, the king, was to promulgate and enforce them (see 2 Sam. 14:26, "king's weight" or "royal standard"). Deuteronomy cautioned against using two different weights in weighing out payments (Deut. 25:13-16). A seller would use a heavier weight in order to obtain more money. A buyer would choose a light one to calculate payments (see Amos 8:5-6). According to Deuteronomy, the mere possession of two weights is dishonest. Their use is repugnant (an "abomination") to God (Prov. 16:11; 20:10, 23).

**11:2** Though the Hebrew word translated "humble" appears only here in the Hebrew Bible, the concept occurs often (e.g., Prov. 15:33; 18:12). As a Middle Eastern value, humility, or being humble, has a different meaning than in the West (Malina 2009: 118–20). It belongs to the realm of honor, the MENA core value, and it means staying within one's inherited social status. Humble persons do not claim more than life has bestowed upon them. The key strategy for assuring this is to stay a step below or behind one's rightful status. Pride is the opposite, and hence merits shame. The wise assure their rightful situation as such by not claiming more than they deserve.

**11:3-6** These verses are to be read in the context of commerce introduced in v. 1. NRSV integrity versus crookedness (v. 3) is better rendered honesty versus duplicity, precisely the problem when choosing to use false weights. Riches (v. 4), no matter how gained, are useless in any kind of misfortune ("day of wrath"). Only righteousness guarantees vindication. In v. 6b a preferable translation would be "deceivers are trapped by their greed [Hebrew *hawwat*]," much more suited to the world of ancient commerce.

**11:7** As is the case again and again in the book of Proverbs, v. 7 in Hebrew is very difficult and challenging to translate. Given the context established by v. 1 and developed in vv. 3-6, a preferable translation would be: "expectation pinned on wealth is destroyed." Thus these proverbs comfort the peasant in agrarian society who had no money and quite probably envied those who did. In the final analysis wealth does no one any good in times of crisis.

**11:9-12** This cluster of proverbs deals with speech and the well-being of a city. The cultural context is secrecy, deception, and lying. ▶**Lying.** Cultural wisdom advises restraint in communication. Since honor depends on a claim to value and public acknowledgment of that claim, the less people know, the less likely they are to challenge a claim. Honor is protected. But outsiders are never satisfied and probe deeper, hence the strategy of deception. One leaks misleading or even false information to derail the investigations of others. As a last resort one lies to protect honor and to cover many other circumstances. It was quite common in antiquity for people to tell lies (or even the truth) about others—even neighbors!—in order to impugn their reputation, their honor. Only a fool, or a wicked or godless person, would do that, because the retaliation would be in kind (Prov. 25:7c-10). A wise person knows that self-restraint and silence are always the best course (Prov. 11:9).

The next two verses (vv. 10-11) center on the city. Modern readers must be careful not to imagine that any ancient cities were anything at all like contemporary cities (Rohrbaugh 2007a; 1996). Biblical references to "cities" are in reality to villages or hamlets for the most part, with very small populations. In this context the behavior and achievements of one person (upright or wicked) have a huge impact on the community. The populace rejoices at the success of the upright as it does at the destruction of the wicked (v. 10). The good words or "blessing" of the upright build up the community just as the words of the wicked tear it down (v. 11).

Finally, v. 12 returns to the theme of v. 9, that is, refraining from doing damage to one's neighbor. "To belittle" is to express contempt (see Prov. 30:17; 2 Kgs. 19:21). In Prov. 14:21 such contempt is considered a sin. In contrast, keeping silent is a sign of wisdom, whether by virtue of prudence or out of concern for the community's well-being.

**11:13** NRSV translates "slander" as "gossip." The Hebrew word for slander (*rākal*) literally means "to traffic, trade, sell." Because merchants spread gossip, the Hebrew word for "trade" took on the meaning of gossip, too. (See the comment on Prov. 16:28 below.) The antithesis or contrast in this proverb is between "going about" and "standing still" (literal Hebrew; NRSV "trustworthy"). Against this background the NRSV "gossip" makes sense, but "trustworthy in spirit" blurs the contrast. It would be better to translate "stable in spirit."

**11:15** Proverbs discourages the practice of giving surety for another, that is, guaranteeing that a debtor will repay the creditor (6:1; 17:18; 20:16; 22:26; 27:13). If the debtor defaults, the one giving surety will be burdened with the debt. This is all the more important when the debtor is a neighbor, friend, or stranger, and not a family member. Given the cultural conviction that all goods are limited and already distributed, giving surety is too great a risk and has potentially calamitous consequences. ▶ **Limited Good.**

**11:16** NRSV renders the Greek expansion that attempted to explain the Hebrew text: "a gracious woman gets honor, but the aggressive gain riches." In this culture, of course, honor is preferable to riches, yet in each case the means (charm; aggression) have limits. The same is true of the honor and riches they gain. Everything is fleeting. On the other hand, as Proverbs notes, Wisdom bestows lasting honor and wealth (Prov. 3:16; 8:18).

**11:20** NRSV "crooked minds" renders the literal Hebrew "crooked hearts," the symbolic body zone of emotion-fused thinking. ▶ **Three-Zone Personality.** The heart/mind motivates and initiates human activity in the symbolic body zone of hands–feet. In this proverb crooked hearts are an abomination to the Lord because they do not produce proper behavior. In contrast, God's delight is in those who behave properly, whose "way is blameless." (See Prov. 17:20.)

**11:22** The humor of this proverb is rooted in the imagery, and its appeal is buttressed by onomatopoeia in Hebrew. The first line is dominated by the melodic repetition of the letter "z": *nezem zāhāb bᵉap azīr* ("a gold ring in the snout of a pig").

**11:24-25** These proverbs extol the virtue of giving to others, of being open-handed and open-hearted (see Deut. 15:1-11, cautioning against casting the evil-eye on a needy person; Sir. 19:1-13). The New Testament echo of this idea (Mark 4:25; Matt. 13:12; Luke 19:26) puts the concept in the passive voice, indicating that God will repay the generosity. ▶ **Evil Eye.**

**11:29** This reflection on running one's household returns to the major theme of Proverbs. The Hebrew word translated "trouble" means to create trouble or danger without reason. Obviously, such behavior can cost a troublemaker his or her inheritance. Such a person is a fool who will end up serving the one who has safeguarded family and household, a truly wise person.

**11:30** This proverb poses a challenge. NRSV opts to translate: "violence takes lives away," but perhaps a preferable rendition would be "one who takes lives [in a positive sense] is a sage" (Clifford 1999: 126–27).

### Proverbs 12:1-28

1 Whoever loves discipline loves knowledge,
  but those who hate to be rebuked are stupid.
2 The good obtain favor from the Lord,
  but those who devise evil he condemns.
3 No one finds security by wickedness,
  but the root of the righteous will never be moved.
4 A good wife is the crown of her husband,
  but she who brings shame is like rottenness in his bones.
5 The thoughts of the righteous are just;
  the advice of the wicked is treacherous.

6 The words of the wicked are a deadly ambush,
   but the speech of the upright delivers them.
7 The wicked are overthrown and are no more,
   but the house of the righteous will stand.
8 One is commended for good sense,
   but a perverse mind is despised.
9 Better to be despised and have a servant
   than to be self important and lack food.
10 The righteous know the needs of their animals,
    but the mercy of the wicked is cruel.
11 Those who till their land will have plenty of food,
    but those who follow worthless pursuits have no sense.
12 The wicked covet the proceeds of wickedness,
    but the root of the righteous bears fruit.
13 The evil are ensnared by the transgression of their lips,
    but the righteous escape from trouble.
14 From the fruit of the mouth one is filled with good things,
    and manual labor has its reward.
15 Fools think their own way is right,
    but the wise listen to advice.
16 Fools show their anger at once,
    but the prudent ignore an insult.
17 Whoever speaks the truth gives honest evidence,
    but a false witness speaks deceitfully.
18 Rash words are like sword thrusts,
    but the tongue of the wise brings healing.
19 Truthful lips endure forever,
    but a lying tongue lasts only a moment.
20 Deceit is in the mind of those who plan evil,
    but those who counsel peace have joy.
21 No harm happens to the righteous,
    but the wicked are filled with trouble.
22 Lying lips are an abomination to the Lord,
    but those who act faithfully are his delight.
23 One who is clever conceals knowledge,
    but the mind of a fool broadcasts folly.
24 The hand of the diligent will rule,
    while the lazy will be put to forced labor.
25 Anxiety weighs down the human heart,
    but a good word cheers it up.
26 The righteous gives good advice to friends,
    but the way of the wicked leads astray.
27 The lazy do not roast their game,
    but the diligent obtain precious wealth.

28 In the path of righteousness there is life,
   in walking its path there is no death.

**12:4** The Hebrew phrase here translated as "good wife" is later rendered "capable wife" (Prov. 31:10). Many commentators interpret these instances as examples of good judgment on the part of the husband. Nothing could be further from the truth, since marriage in the ancient (and contemporary) circum-Mediterranean world is the fusion of the honor of two families represented by these individuals. Moreover, marriages are arranged. They represent the choices of the parents who do the arranging. The respective spouses have no option but to accept the decision made for them. Since God assigns one's parents, and the parents select the marriage partners for their children, Jesus' interpretation of Gen. 2:24 is perfectly intelligible: "What God has joined together, let no one separate" (Matt. 19:24-26).

Reference to bones in proverbs ("rottenness in the bones") still remains something of a mystery. It is obviously a condition of ill health, a lack of complete well-being. Medico-centric interpretations consider it to be something akin to caries, which affects teeth and bones (Toverud 1923). However, scholars recognize that the ancient Israelites ascribed psychological and even spiritual experiences to certain bodily organs. Thus "rot in the bones" in this verse is intended to contrast with "crown": a wife who brings shame besmirches her husband's honor, but worse yet, the honor of his entire family, since, as noted, marriage fuses the honor of two families. Compare Prov. 14:30.

### Textual Notes: 12:1-28

**12:5** NRSV "thoughts" and "advice" actually refer to plans, intentions. The contrast with "just" is "deceit," that is, the plans of the wicked will come to naught.

**12:9** There are twenty-three instances of "better ... than ..." sayings in Proverbs (e.g., 15:16, 17; 16:8, 19; 17:1; 19:1). The meaning here (and in all of them) is that one ought to be satisfied with one's honest lot (one servant), rather than put on airs while in reality having nothing to boast about.

**12:10** The reference here is to domestic animals. While scholars caution against any attempt to identify with precision the animals mentioned in the Bible, domestic animals include the camel and horse family (horses, asses, and mules), large cattle, and small ruminants (mainly sheep and goats). These latter animals provided meat, milk, cheese, skin, and wool or goats' hair (see Prov. 27:23-27). Dogs were principally feral scavengers and provided a safeguard against disease by eating refuse in the city. If they were domesticated at all, it was only as young dogs who were later returned to the wild. They were not pets. Thus it makes sense to care for the domestic animals rather than mistreat them with cruelty as did the wicked.

**12:11** This is one of many aphorisms in the book criticizing laziness and promoting diligence (see Prov. 10:4, 5; 12:11, 24, 27; 13:4; 17:2; 18:9; 19:24; 24:30-34; 26:15; etc.). In advanced agrarian, pre-industrial society, labor was hard and intensive, and the rewards were sometimes incommensurate. This, in addition to high taxation (more like exploitation), made it imperative for every family member to bear the burden of contributing to family welfare. Diligent industriousness was a matter of life and death, literally.

**12:13-23** This cluster of proverbs deals with speech. In the ancient world only the family had a "right to know." One should never lie to one's family, though lying is acceptable toward everyone outside the family, who have no "right to know." ▶**Lying**. Honor, the core cultural value, is the basis for this cultural practice. The more others know, the less opportunity for making honor claims that will be acknowledged and approved by outsiders.

**12:16** By ignoring an insult the wise person escapes potential physical harm. In contrast, the fool responds to an insult immediately and without thinking of the consequences. Acknowledging an insult leads to feud, which can escalate to violence and ultimately result in bloodshed. Once that happens it is almost impossible to bring closure to this tragedy, which could have been avoided by ignoring the insult.

It is part and parcel of agonistic MENA culture. ▶ **Agonism**. Recall that normative inconsistency is also a MENA cultural value. Hence one can resort to a violent response on some occasions but avoid it in others.

**12:17** This proverb concerns legal testimony. The law court is the context for the meaning of the Hebrew word translated "speaks" (see also Prov. 6:19; 14:5, 25; 19:5, 9). One should pay attention to the way in which a witness speaks outside of court to determine whether he is speaking truthfully in court. However, the circum-Mediterranean world knows that, in general, justice is not likely to be served in courts. The common advice is to settle out of court (Prov. 25:7c-10; Matt. 5:25-26). This proverb presents obvious advice, even if it is rare in actual circum-Mediterranean experience. It is an instance of the customary circum-Mediterranean contrast between the ideal (e.g., truthful witness and honest evidence) and reality (deceit).

**12:19** Even though lying is common and accepted in MENA culture as a strategy in service of honor, it will easily be discovered. The truth, in contrast, will endure. It is also possible to understand the proverb as saying that those who speak the truth are protected by God and hence live long lives, while liars can expect punishment from God; they will not prosper.

**12:22** While there is no explicit contrast between the wicked and righteous in this aphorism, the behaviors describe precisely those kinds of persons. Noteworthy is the phrase "an abomination to the Lord." It occurs eleven times in Proverbs (3:32; 6:16; 11:1, 20; 12:22; 15:8, 9, 26; 16:5; 17:15; 20:23) to describe improper deeds, though not necessarily violations of the Mosaic law as in Deuteronomy. Here the contrast is between lying and telling the truth ("acting faithfully"). Though it is an "abomination to the Lord," lying remained a core strategy for safeguarding one's honor in this culture and was a very common practice. ▶ **Lying**.

**12:24** See the comment on Prov. 12:11. This proverb is cast in hyperbolic terms in order to motivate everyone, but especially sons, to diligent industriousness for the good of the family. If one does not do it freely and willingly, one will be forced to do it in oppressive circumstances (see Exod. 1:11; 1 Kgs. 5:13).

**12:27** Though the Hebrew of this aphorism is uncertain, the contrast between sloth and diligence is patent. The lazy person will not even obtain the food of the poor (birds) while the industrious will have plenty (See the comment on Prov. 12:11).

**12:28** This general conclusion to Proverbs 12 repeats a reference to the traditional "two ways" (see Prov. 2:12; Habel 1972). The text is quite corrupt and difficult. NRSV accepts the Masoretic text, but other scholars prefer a different interpretation and translation:

> "On the path of righteousness is life,
> But the way of malice leads to death."

The problem with the NRSV and other such renditions is the suggestion of "resurrection" ("no death"), something syntactically and ideologically unlikely in Proverbs, which pre-dates the first biblical reference to resurrection, Dan. 12:1-3, ca. 164 BCE.

### Proverbs 13:1-25

1 A wise child loves discipline,
   but a scoffer does not listen to rebuke.
2 From the fruit of their words good persons eat good things,
   but the desire of the treacherous is for wrongdoing.
3 Those who guard their mouths preserve their lives;
   those who open wide their lips come to ruin.
4 The appetite of the lazy craves, and gets nothing,
   while the appetite of the diligent is richly supplied.
5 The righteous hate falsehood,
   but the wicked act shamefully and disgracefully.
6 Righteousness guards one whose way is upright,
   but sin overthrows the wicked.
7 Some pretend to be rich, yet have nothing;
   others pretend to be poor, yet have great wealth.
8 Wealth is a ransom for a person's life,
   but the poor get no threats.
9 The light of the righteous rejoices,
   but the lamp of the wicked goes out.
10 By insolence the heedless make strife,

but wisdom is with those who take advice.
11 Wealth hastily gotten will dwindle,
   but those who gather little by little will increase it.
12 Hope deferred makes the heart sick,
   but a desire fulfilled is a tree of life.
13 Those who despise the word bring destruction on themselves,
   but those who respect the commandment will be rewarded.
14 The teaching of the wise is a fountain of life,
   so that one may avoid the snares of death.
15 Good sense wins favor,
   but the way of the faithless is their ruin.
16 The clever do all things intelligently,
   but the fool displays folly.
17 A bad messenger brings trouble,
   but a faithful envoy, healing.
18 Poverty and disgrace are for the one who ignores instruction,
   but one who heeds reproof is honored.
19 A desire realized is sweet to the soul,
   but to turn away from evil is an abomination to fools.
20 Whoever walks with the wise becomes wise,
   but the companion of fools suffers harm.
21 Misfortune pursues sinners,
   but prosperity rewards the righteous.
22 The good leave an inheritance to their children's children,
   but the sinner's wealth is laid up for the righteous.
23 The field of the poor may yield much food,
   but it is swept away through injustice.
24 Those who spare the rod hate their children [lit: sons],
   but those who love them are diligent to discipline them.
25 The righteous have enough to satisfy their appetite,
   but the belly of the wicked is empty.

*Textual Notes: 13:1-25*

**13:1** NRSV inclusive language changes the meaning of this proverb in a way that runs contrary to the context and the culture. There is no reference to women in chapter 13, and the literal translation of this verse should be "a wise son" rather than "a wise child." ▶**Inclusive language.** This proverb continues the reflection on adult children and their mother and father that began in 10:1.

**13:7-8** These aphorisms concern wealth and poverty. Verse 7 once again reflects circum-Mediterranean cultural values. Pretending, or "making oneself out to be [something]," is a common practice. The person who has nothing "makes oneself out to be" rich (the ideal) but in actuality has nothing (reality). The second part of the verse could be understood as an example of cultural humility. ▶ **Humility.** A wealthy man dare not risk presenting himself as something more than he is. Hence he acts poor not just to conceal his real wealth but to give others the opportunity to publicly acknowledge his true worth. It is also important to remember that wealth and poverty are not primarily or principally economic designations in the Bible. They rather point to status, reputation, honor-rating (Malina 1986a; 2001a; 2001b). ▶ **Rich and Poor.**

The first part of v. 8 is clear: people of wealth can ransom their own lives. The second line is simply a guess (e.g., the poor cannot even hear the threats of kidnappers) because the text is unrecoverable.

**13:10** This is one of many aphorisms in the book of Proverbs commenting on strife (Prov. 15:18; 18:6; 20:3; 22:10). ▶ **Agonism.** The word translated "heedless" is literally "empty," that is, a person with no sense or awareness of the consequences of his actions.

**13:11** As already noted, wealth need not be understood primarily in economic terms. However, in this proverb such a meaning is plausible. In the ancient circum-Mediterranean world a sudden increase in wealth was suspect (see Prov. 20:21; 28:20). The reason for this is the peasant cultural belief that all things of value were finite in quantity and already distributed. ▶ **Limited Good.** There was no more to be had. A sudden increase in wealth raises the question: "where did this come from?" A common suspicion is theft. Wealth as such is never considered evil in Proverbs, nor in general in the Hebrew Bible. It is thought to be a divine blessing, the result of time-consuming and laborious effort (Prov. 10:4b).

**13:12** "Tree of life" in Proverbs is simply a metaphor describing the good life one achieves by heeding the advice of Wisdom (see Prov. 3:18; 11:30; 15:4; compare Prov. 13:14). It does not share in the mythological background of Gen. 2:9 ("tree of life") or the references in Akkadian and Egyptian literature. Such an association occurs in the New

Testament references: Rev. 2:7; 22:2, 14, 19 (Malina and Pilch 2000: 247–49). However, the image should not be associated with the "tree of life" or "tree of the world" discussed by cultural anthropologists (Goodman 1990: 200–4).

**13:17** Messengers played an important role in oral culture. They could simply make a report (Job 1:14) or act as representatives on behalf of the one who sent them. In the latter case they might carry on negotiations such as buying or selling a piece of land, or livestock, or produce. They would be trusted to agree on a good price. Thus the point of this proverb is not about the message but the character of the messenger: bad! He acts for his own benefit and not that of the one who sent him. As such, his character contrasts with that of the faithful envoy, who brings healing, that is, peace of mind (see Prov. 14:30).

**13:18** NRSV "ignores" translates a Hebrew word that carries the sense of stubborn self-willed, totally irresponsible behavior. Hence the Hebrew word, *mûsār*, is correctly translated as "instruction," as here, though it often means physical discipline and is translated in this way elsewhere (Deut. 11:2; Prov. 3:11). ▶**Discipline.** Honor that comes to the one who heeds reproof, that is, who takes instruction to heart and lives by it, is granted by the community. The social context of this proverb is central to its meaning, because the economic well-being of the individual and the family depends on approval and acceptance by the community.

**13:21-22** Lineage and inheritance were keenly important in ancient Israel. It was considered a disaster if one had no heirs (Eccl. 2:18-21; 4:7-8; 6:1-2) to inherit one's wealth. Recall that wealth included status and honor rating as well as possessions. This calamity was wished upon the wicked (Ps. 109:6-20; Job 27:13-19). The proverb claims that (but does not explain how) the righteous will obtain the ill-gotten goods of the sinners.

**13:23** This aphorism reflects the common experience of the poor in early Israel. The harvest of the poor was good, but it was stolen through exorbitant levies (e.g., Amos 5:11). Israel recognize that the poor, indeed every person, has rights (Heb. *mišpaṭîm*; see Isa. 10:2; Job 36:6) that must be respected and honored, even by God (Job 34:5).

**13:24** Inclusive language translations of this verse not only misrepresent ancient circum-Mediterranean culture but give warrant to biblical fundamentalists to physically chastise their daughters as well as their sons (Dobson 1996). This proverb concerns only sons: "who spares the rod hates his son." Reference to "rod" confirms that the Hebrew word translated "discipline" (*mûsār*) is to be understood as physical, corporal punishment (see also Prov. 16:22; 22:15). ▶ **Discipline.** Encouraging physical discipline of children is a common theme in wisdom literature (see Prov. 3:12; 19:18; 22:15; 23:13-14; 29:15, 17; Sir. 7:23; 30:1-13).

## Proverbs 14:1-35

1  The wise woman builds her house,
    but the foolish tears it down with her own hands.
2  Those who walk uprightly fear the Lord,
    but one who is devious in conduct despises him.
3  The talk of fools is a rod for their backs,
    but the lips of the wise preserve them.
4  Where there are no oxen, there is no grain;
    abundant crops come by the strength of the ox.
5  A faithful witness does not lie,
    but a false witness breathes out lies.
6  A scoffer seeks wisdom in vain,
    but knowledge is easy for one who understands.
7  Leave the presence of a fool,
    for there you do not find words of knowledge.
8  It is the wisdom of the clever to understand where they go,
    but the folly of fools misleads.
9  Fools mock at the guilt offering,
    but the upright enjoy God's favor.
10 The heart knows its own bitterness,
    and no stranger shares its joy.
11 The house of the wicked is destroyed,
    but the tent of the upright flourishes.
12 There is a way that seems right to a person,
    but its end is the way to death.
13 Even in laughter the heart is sad,
    and the end of joy is grief.

14 The perverse get what their ways deserve,
   and the good, what their deeds deserve.
15 The simple believe everything,
   but the clever consider their steps.
16 The wise are cautious and turn away from evil,
   but the fool throws off restraint and is careless.
17 One who is quick-tempered acts foolishly,
   and the schemer is hated.
18 The simple are adorned with folly,
   but the clever are crowned with knowledge.
19 The evil bow down before the good,
   the wicked at the gates of the righteous.
20 The poor are disliked even by their neighbors,
   but the rich have many friends.
21 Those who despise their neighbors are sinners,
   but happy are those who are kind to the poor.
22 Do they not err that plan evil?
   Those who plan good find loyalty and faithfulness.
23 In all toil there is profit,
   but mere talk leads only to poverty.
24 The crown of the wise is their wisdom,
   but folly is the garland of fools.
25 A truthful witness saves lives,
   but one who utters lies is a betrayer.
26 In the fear of the Lord one has strong confidence,
   and one's children will have a refuge.
27 The fear of the Lord is a fountain of life,
   so that one may avoid the snares of death.
28 The glory of a king is a multitude of people;
   without people a prince is ruined.
29 Whoever is slow to anger has great understanding,
   but one who has a hasty temper exalts folly.
30 A tranquil mind gives life to the flesh,
   but passion makes the bones rot.
31 Those who oppress the poor insult their Maker,
   but those who are kind to the needy honor him.
32 The wicked are overthrown by their evil doing,
   but the righteous find a refuge in their integrity.
33 Wisdom is at home in the mind of one who has understanding,
   but it is not known in the heart of fools.
34 Righteousness exalts a nation,
   but sin is a reproach to any people.
35 A servant who deals wisely has the king's favor,
   but his wrath falls on one who acts shamefully.

*Textual Notes: 14:1-35*

**14:2** This proverb contains one of the fourteen occurrences of the phrase "fear of the Lord." Readers of English-language Bible translations recognize that Lord translates "YHWH," God's proper name. Fear is not an emotion but rather recognizing who YHWH is, who the human being is, and behaving accordingly. Thus fear of the Lord entails obedience and reverence. As a result, fear of the Lord results in wisdom, which according to v. 1 strives to build a household rather than destroy it. In v. 2, good conduct ("walking uprightly") demonstrates fear of the Lord, while one who is devious despises the Lord.

**14:3** This aphorism is yet another example of obscure meaning in the Hebrew text that unfortunately invites creative translations. The Hebrew word in this verse, *hoter*, means "rod," and literally the text says "rod of pride." The word occurs only once again in the Bible: Isa. 10:5, where it means "twig" or "sprout." In Aramaic, however, the word can mean "rod" (for punishment), and this very likely influenced the NRSV translators to render this phrase "rod for the back." However, "rod of pride" is a Semitism meaning a "rod performing prideful activities." Thus the speech of fools is produced by "a rod of prideful activities," namely, the tongue, whereas the lips (mouth, words) of wise persons protects them. ▶**Three-Zone Personality**. The focus here is on the mouth–ears symbolic body zone, the zone of self-expressive speech.

**14:4** NRSV favors an emendation of this verse that most scholars deem unnecessary. Moreover, the English translation is somewhat confusing. "There is no grain" means that if one has no oxen one obviously doesn't need to feed them. One apparently saves money. The English translation, however, could lead one to think that without oxen one will not be able to produce and harvest grain. This would seem to be confirmed by the second half of the verse. However, no one interprets the verse in this way. Farm animals such as oxen were critically important in pre-industrial advanced agrarian societies like that of ancient Israel.

**14:5** Another proverb treating of a lying witness (Prov. 6:19; 12:17; 14:25; 19:5, 9, 28; 25:18). ▶**Lying.** That this observation is repeated so frequently in spite of the Decalogue (Exod. 20:16) strongly suggests that it was a very common occurrence. As already noted, the ancient world was accustomed to lying witnesses in law courts; hence no one expected to find justice in that venue.

**14:10** References to the heart occur a few times in Proverbs (12:25; 13:12, 19; 14:13; 17:3) and reflect the non-, indeed anti-introspective understanding of the human person in the Bible. ▶**Three-Zone Personality.** Only God can know the human heart (1 Sam. 16:7; Ps. 44:21; Prov. 17:3; 21:2; 24:12). This anti-introspective understanding of the human person helps appreciate the fact that many physical health problems in the Bible are somatizations of unresolved psychological problems. Medical anthropologists call this a conversion disorder, that is, the internal state is "converted" into a physical symptom (Howard 2001: 59–60). The proverb thus states the culturally obvious experience. The person does indeed feel bitterness in the heart (but does not know why or what to do about it), while no outsider is at all able to appreciate or empathize with another's joy.

**14:13** Like v. 10 above, so too this proverb reflects the anti-introspective understanding of the human person in circum-Mediterranean culture. One cannot judge by appearances, which can be deceptive. Moreover, joy sometimes ends in grief.

**14:17** "Quick-tempered" translates a Hebrew phrase that literally means "short of nose." Non-introspective ancient Israelites somatized their emotions and expressed them accordingly (Pilch 1999: 8–13). The Middle Eastern temperament is primarily oriented toward spontaneity, that is, acting without careful planning or consideration of the consequences (Pilch and Malina 2009: 56–57). Everyone in this culture is quick-tempered. The expectation is that a relative or friend would intervene and prevent the person from acting foolishly. The contrast with the quick-tempered person is the "schemer." The Hebrew word can have a positive or negative meaning. In a positive sense it would be translated "cleverness, shrewdness," and the like. NRSV prefers "prudence" or "discretion," neutral terms with no moral connotations (see Prov. 1:4; 2:11; 3:21; 5:2; 8:12). Here the word is part of a Hebrew phrase, "a person of schemes," with a definite negative connotation (see also Prov. 12:2; 24:8).

**14:19** The synonymous parallelism in this verse is unusual in this collection dominated by antithetic parallelism. The idea is that the wicked are vanquished ("bow down") by the good and pay homage to it. Further, they are eventually reduced to begging at the good man's door, a symbol of extreme humiliation.

**14:20-21** Once again it is important to keep in mind that rich and poor are not primarily economic markers. In v. 20, neighbors understandably despise the poor "next door" because these poor seek help from them. The peasant population was not well off and had little to share with the poor next door. Indeed, in these circumstances peasants are notoriously selfish and reluctant to share. In v. 21, NRSV translates "sinners" for those who "miss the mark." However, given the contrast with "happy are those . . ." in the next line, perhaps it is preferable to replace "sinners" with "those who miss or fail to obtain happiness." However, "sinners" could be acceptable by comparison with Prov. 14:31; 17:5; 19:17. Moreover, NRSV "happy" translates the Hebrew ʔašrê, which should more properly be translated "honorable" or "truly honorable" (See Hanson 1994: 81–111; Prov. 3:18; 8:32, 34; 14:21; 16:20; 20:7; 28:14; 29:18; 31:28).

**14:25** See 14:5 above. One who utters lies is literally in Hebrew "spouter of lies" (see Prov. 6:19; 14:5; 19:5, 9). One example of "spouters of lies" can be found in the tragic story of Naboth (1 Kings 21).

**14:26-27** Both proverbs promote and extol the value of "the fear of the Lord," a theme in Proverbs (Prov. 1:7; 10:27; 14:26-27; 15:16, 33; 16:6; 20:23; 22:4). It is not an emotion but rather describes proper respect for the deity and keeping the divine commandments. Verse 26 highlights the value of such behavior for one's children. Verse 27 affirms that fear of the Lord can prevent one from committing evil deeds that would cause premature death.

**14:29-30** In v. 29, NRSV "slow to anger" translates Hebrew "long of nose" (see v. 17 above), while NRSV "hasty temper" translates Hebrew "shortness of spirit/breath." This is another example of the tendency of anti-introspective peasants to somatize internal states (see Pilch 1999: 8–13). Being "slow to anger" leads to great wisdom or understanding, while "hasty temper" increases folly. Verse 30 presents yet another somatization of emotions. The Hebrew word translated by NRSV as "passion" (or jealousy) derives from the color (red) produced in the face by deep emotion. The reference is thus not to an internal state but rather to its external manifestation. This urges reconsideration of the phrase "rot in the bones." Medico-centric interpretations consider it to be something akin to caries, which affects teeth and bones (Toverud 1923). However, scholars recognize that the ancient Israelites ascribed psychological and even spiritual experiences to certain bodily organs. Thus "rot in the bones" in this verse is intended to contrast with "tranquil mind," so that "disturbed mind" might be a preferable rendition. Compare Prov. 12:4.

**14:31** Once again the descriptor "poor" is not primarily an economic designation but rather an indication of temporary loss of inherited status (Malina 2001: 99–100). "You always have the poor with you" (Matt. 26:11; Mark 14:7; John 12:8) describes a revolving class of people who lose their status temporarily. Their cultural obligation is to regain their rightful status as expeditiously as possible. God empathizes with the poor, and one's relationship with God depends on how one treats the poor.

### Proverbs 15:1-33

1  A soft answer turns away wrath,
   but a harsh word stirs up anger.
2  The tongue of the wise dispenses knowledge,
   but the mouths of fools pour out folly.
3  The eyes of the Lord are in every place,
   keeping watch on the evil and the good.

4 A gentle tongue is a tree of life,
   but perverseness in it breaks the spirit.
5 A fool despises a parent's instruction,
   but the one who heeds admonition is prudent.
6 In the house of the righteous there is much treasure,
   but trouble befalls the income of the wicked.
7 The lips of the wise spread knowledge;
   not so the minds of fools.
8 The sacrifice of the wicked is an abomination to the Lord,
   but the prayer of the upright is his delight.
9 The way of the wicked is an abomination to the Lord,
   but he loves the one who pursues righteousness.
10 There is severe discipline for one who forsakes the way,
   but one who hates a rebuke will die.
11 Sheol and Abaddon lie open before the Lord,
   how much more human hearts!
12 Scoffers do not like to be rebuked;
   they will not go to the wise.
13 A glad heart makes a cheerful countenance,
   but by sorrow of heart the spirit is broken.
14 The mind of one who has understanding seeks knowledge,
   but the mouths of fools feed on folly.
15 All the days of the poor are hard,
   but a cheerful heart has a continual feast.
16 Better is a little with the fear of the Lord
   than great treasure and trouble with it.
17 Better is a dinner of vegetables where love is
   than a fatted ox and hatred with it.
18 Those who are hot-tempered stir up strife,
   but those who are slow to anger calm contention.
19 The way of the lazy is overgrown with thorns,
   but the path of the upright is a level highway.
20 A wise child makes a glad father,
   but the foolish despise their mothers.
21 Folly is a joy to one who has no sense,
   but a person of understanding walks straight ahead.
22 Without counsel, plans go wrong,
   but with many advisers they succeed.
23 To make an apt answer is a joy to anyone,
   and a word in season, how good it is!
24 For the wise the path of life leads upward,
   in order to avoid Sheol below.
25 The Lord tears down the house of the proud,
   but maintains the widow's boundaries.
26 Evil plans are an abomination to the Lord,

but gracious words are pure.
27 Those who are greedy for unjust gain make trouble for their
households,
but those who hate bribes will live.
28 The mind of the righteous ponders how to answer,
but the mouth of the wicked pours out evil.
29 The Lord is far from the wicked,
but he hears the prayer of the righteous.
30 The light of the eyes rejoices the heart,
and good news refreshes the body.
31 The ear that heeds wholesome admonition
will lodge among the wise.
32 Those who ignore instruction despise themselves,
but those who heed admonition gain understanding.
33 The fear of the Lord is instruction in wisdom,
and humility goes before honor.

In terms of literary form, the antithetical parallelism diminishes in this chapter. The power of the spoken word, the symbolic body zone of mouth–ears, is a frequent topic (vv. 1, 2, 5, 7, 23, 26, 28). ▶ **Three-Zone Personality**.

*Textual Notes: 15:1-33*

**15:1** Once again in this proverb we find somatization of emotions. The Hebrew word translated "wrath" means "heat," which often accompanies the feeling of wrath. In addition, the Hebrew word translated "anger" ("stirs up anger") is literally "nose," whose nostrils usually flare when anger is aroused. The proverb relates the obvious, namely, that restraint in speech can mollify angry outbursts from others, while a harsh word (literally in Hebrew "a word of pain") can have the opposite effect.

**15:3** The context of this proverb could well be the cultural value placed on secrecy, deception, and lying. ▶ **Lying**. Life is challenging under such circumstances. Will the wicked get their just deserts? Will the righteous be recognized and rewarded? The comforting thought is that the omniscient God sees all and notes it well. There is no place on earth that is inaccessible to God (Sir. 23:19).

**15:4** Gentle speech in contrast to lying gives life to others (see Ezek.

47:12), while a lying tongue deceives and demoralizes others. The reference is to the mouth–ears symbolic body zone. ▶**Three-Zone Personality**. Again, the proverb can be appreciated in the context of secrecy, deception, and lying as acceptable strategies for defending honor (even baseless honor) in a culture where this is a core value. ▶**Lying**.

**15:5** The Hebrew vocabulary of this verse reflects that of Proverbs 1–9, the instructions of a father to his son (or teacher to pupil). While NRSV translates the Hebrew (*mûsâr*) as "instruction," the word "admonition" in the second half of the verse suggests "discipline" as preferable. The discipline, of course, is physical and painful (See the comment on Prov. 13:18). ▶**Discipline**.

**15:8** This is the vocabulary of ritual, as in Deut. 7:25 (see also Prov. 11:1). Offerings made by people who displease God are abominations (see Isa. 1:10-17; 29:10). A (rather crass) Moroccan Arabic proverb presents a similar sentiment: "The anus of the one who prays is cleaner than the mouth of one who has given up praying" (Westermarck 1931: 238, #1314).

**15:9** This proverb moves the thought of v. 8 from sanctuary to daily life. The phrase "pursues righteousness" connotes a serious and determined intention to live a life pleasing to God.

**15:10** The Hebrew word translated "discipline" never means punishment in Proverbs (NRSV's interpretation); in this book, discipline is always something good even if it is physical. The preferable rendition of this verse would be: "Discipline is bad [or distasteful] for one who forsakes the way." The consequence of hating correction (second part of the verse) is premature death.

**15:11** Nothing is hidden from God, including the human heart. Non-introspective circum-Mediterranean cultures recognized that human beings could not read hearts. Only God has that ability (1 Sam. 16:7). The heart in ancient Mediterranean psychology was the seat of thinking and willing. Heart and eyes are often paired in biblical psychology; they are the source of emotion-fused thinking (see Prov.

21:2, 4; 23:26). The heart receives its input from the eyes (Prov. 15:30).
▶**Three-Zone Personality**.

**15:13-17** This cluster of proverbs is linked by the Hebrew words for "heart" (vv. 13, 14, 15) and "better" (vv. 15-17; in v. 15 NRSV translates the Hebrew "good heart" as "cheerful").

**15:13** Internal emotions find outward expression most often on the human countenance. A happy heart is reflected in a smiling face. But a broken heart, or despondency, can break one's spirit ("a crushed spirit": see Prov. 17:22; 18:14). If the Hebrew "spirit" is rendered as "breath," then a physical manifestation of this state is portrayed (cp. Prov. 17:22; 18:14; Sir. 13:25-26).

**15:14** NRSV correctly translates the literal Hebrew "the *heart* of one who has understanding" as "the *mind* of one who has understanding." The activities of the heart in biblical psychology are to see, know, understand, think, remember, choose, feel, consider, look at, and the like. ▶**Three-Zone Personality**. Thus the contrast is between one who seeks knowledge to serve the common good and the fool who traffics in folly.

**15:15** Scholars consider this a contradictory proverb, but perhaps it is just an observation about the real life of poor people. All of life for the indigent is evil (literal Hebrew). Recall that "poor" is not primarily an economic designation. ▶**Rich and Poor**. It rather describes the inability of a person or group to maintain their inherited status, thus a certain kind of powerlessness—the common lot of peasants. In contrast, one who is cheerful of heart, who is not powerless, enjoys life like a banquet. It almost sounds like Auntie Mame's observation to her orphaned nephew, Patrick: "Life is a banquet, and most poor suckers are starving to death."

**15:16-17** Now follow two proverbs in the familiar "better" format. They do not relate to the "poor" of v. 15. Verse 16 contrasts great treasure, accompanied by unspecified turmoil or trouble, with little, accompanied by reverence and respect for the Lord. The context of v. 17 might plausibly be hospitality, which in the Middle East is extended chiefly by males exclusively to strangers. To one's family and relatives one extends steadfast lovingkindness (Pilch 2015: 498–501). ▶Hospitality. In this context the sense of the proverb is that a guest seated at a feast featuring a fatted ox may well be the guest of a greedy person who is not inclined to share. That greedy person casts an evil eye on the guest and the meal, causing great havoc, perhaps even nausea (see Prov. 23:6-8). ▶Evil Eye. It is far better to be the guest of a host whose invitation to a simple meal is made out of a desire for fellowship and with love.

**15:18** This proverb is well suited to circum-Mediterranean culture, which by nature is agonistic, that is, conflict-prone. ▶Agonism. Being hot-tempered can be considered an element of the typical or modal MENA personality (see Prov. 29:22; Sir. 28:8-11). Agonism permeates all of life. A Syro-Lebanese proverb observes: "At each meal a quarrel, with each bite a worry." Self-control is not considered a possibility, and loss of self-control is normal and expected. The contrast here is between a "man of heat" and one "slow to anger" (literally: "long of nose"). The person slow to anger behaves much like God (Exod. 34:6; Num. 14:18; Neh. 9:17; etc.), thus one who strives to be holy as God is holy (Lev. 11:44-45).

**15:20-23** The Hebrew word translated "joy" serves as a catchword linking these verses (20, 21, 23) together. The point is that adult children reflect the good and/or inappropriate parenting skills of their mother and father. Proverbs—the wise advice of elders passed on to youngsters—is quite harsh toward disobedient children (Prov. 19:16; 20:20; 28:34; 30:11). That it is at all necessary to keep repeating these cautions in addition to God's word in the Decalogue (Exod. 20:12; Deut. 5:16) suggests that such miscreant behavior was common in ancient Israel. **Disobeying Parents is miscreant behavior. The repeated emphasis on obedience suggests that God's own command did not prevent it.**

**15:20** The Hebrew literally contrasts a wise "son" with a "fool of a man," misrepresented by NRSV's inclusive rendition "child."

**15:22** Western individualistic wisdom believes that "too many cooks spoil the broth." In contrast, collectivistic MENA societies believe that the input of many (an entire family, for instance) guarantees the success of a plan (Hebrew singular in the second part of the proverb). ▶ **Collectivistic Society.**

**15:23** This proverb's advice is illustrated in Sir. 32:3-9, which lists occasions when it is appropriate to speak or to be silent.

**15:25-33** Scholars call this cluster of aphorisms the YHWH proverbs, since God's name appears in four of them (vv. 25, 26, 29, 33), including the first and last. Thematically, Proverbs 25–29 deals with righteousness and wickedness, while Proverbs 31–33 concerns instruction and admonition.

**15:25** The contrast here is between the proud or haughty and the (quite probably childless) widow. The proud or haughty are powerful, and the widow by definition is powerless. ▶ **Widow.** Ancestral land was critical in ancient Israel, and loss of this land was catastrophic. If a widow had no grown sons she was entrusted with her husband's property. If she had a young son, when he became of age he took over the property and was responsible for caring for his mother. The biblical warnings against defrauding a childless widow who did not remarry indicate that widows did in fact possess property (see Deut. 10:18; 27:19; Isa. 1:17, 23; Jer. 7:6; 22:3). This proverb reveals a distinctive Israelite belief that God personally would support the right of a widow to keep possession of her property (Prov. 23:10-11). Property boundaries were marked by stones, which could be easily moved (Deut. 19:14; Isa. 5:8; Hos. 5:10; Prov. 22:28).

**15:27** In a limited-good culture such as ancient Israel and all peasant societies, the guiding belief is that there is no more where this came from. Everything of value is finite in quantity and already distributed. ▶ **Limited Good.** Increase of any kind other than by luck or fortune is viewed suspiciously. It is unjust gain, and those who actively seek such gain are greedy, that is, they manifest that they are not content with their lot but want more, which means someone else will have less. Peasant life is a zero-sum game. Thus such greedy persons will bring down major calamity (NRSV "trouble") upon their households. It is the wrong way to build a house (Prov. 1:11-14).

The second line makes it clear that bribery of some sort is going on (Hebrew *mattānâh*, "gifts": Langston 1991: 19). Bribery appears to have been a common practice, for it is severely condemned in the Bible (Exod. 23:8; Deut. 16:19; 27:25; Prov. 17:23). However, sometimes a bribe is expedient (Prov. 17:23), illustrating another feature of this culture: normative inconsistency. ▶**Normative Inconsistency**. In this proverb, however, the advice is that refusing to engage in bribes will lead to a long life, thanks to God's protection.

**15:28** NRSV "mind" translates the Hebrew word for "heart," the seat of thinking. ▶**Three-Zone Personality**. Two symbolic body zones are highlighted: heart–eyes, the zone of emotion-fused thought, and mouth–ears, the zone of self-expressive speech.

**15:29** Both the wicked and the righteous pray, but God only attends to the prayer of the righteous. Prayer is a socially meaningful symbolic act of communication, directed to the person or persons perceived as somehow supporting, maintaining, and controlling the order of existence of the one praying (Malina 1980: 214–20). ▶**Prayer**. This social science definition helps us understand why God would not attend to the prayer of the wicked. However, the psalms of lament frequently complain that God has neglected to hear and respond to the prayers of the suppliant (e.g., Psalm 22).

**15:30** This aphorism reflects a key concept of ancient biology, namely, that the eyes shoot out light that enables a person to see (extramission theories; Gross 1999: 58–64). Matthew's Jesus observes that the eye is the lamp of the body. A lamp gives off light; hence the eye emanates the light that is within the body, light the ancient Greeks believed was caused by fire inside the body/eye. A blind person has only darkness in the body, which shoots darkness out of the eyes and prevents sight (Matt. 6:22-23).

In ancient biblical psychology, eyes–heart were one of three zones of the body interpreted symbolically. ▶**Three-Zone Personality**. The eyes collected information to feed to the heart, the organ of thinking. The result is emotion-fused thinking. Further, as already noted, the eyes could see because light emanated from them. Thus in this proverb the light emanating from the eyes of another person brings joy to the person looked at.

The next line points to a second zone of the body symbolically interpreted: mouth–ears. This is the zone of self-expressive speech delivered by one and heard by another. NRSV "refreshes the body" translates the literal Hebrew: "puts fat on the bones." The phrase describes the total well-being of the human person. "Puts fat on the bones" (well-being) contrasts with "rot in the bones" (Prov. 12:4; 14:30), the opposite of well-being.

**15:31** The compiler of the book of Proverbs may have been guided by the views of biblical psychology, which identifies three zones of the body interpreted symbolically: eyes–heart, mouth–ears, and hands–feet. ▶**Three-Zone Personality.** Mention of ears in the preceding proverb suggests linking it with another proverb about the ears. NRSV "wholesome admonition" renders the literal Hebrew "admonition of life," that is, admonition that leads to life. Such a one merits a place among the wise.

**15:32** NRSV "gain understanding" translates the literal Hebrew "gain heart," the seat of understanding in biblical psychology. It is parallel to "selves" in the first line, which in Hebrew is *nepeš*, usually translated "soul" but designating the entire self. ▶**Nepeš/soul.** Those two elements of the biblical understanding of the human person are intimately connected. Thus to ignore instruction (Hebrew *mûsār*, which should preferably be translated "discipline") is to reject or loathe one's very self. To heed admonition or reproof leads to wisdom.

**15:33** Humility in biblical culture is a socially acknowledged claim to neutrality in the competition of life. ▶**Humility.** It prompts a person to deliberately stay a step behind or below her or his rightful status so as not to create the impression of yearning for more credit (honor) than one is due. From this perspective it is easy to understand that humility precedes honor. Fear of the Lord, that is, acknowledging and respecting God's superiority to humanity, is wise behavior, a clear expression of humility that will gain honor from God, the only honor that counts.

## Proverbs 16:1-33

1  The plans of the mind belong to mortals,
   but the answer of the tongue is from the Lord.
2  All one's ways may be pure in one's own eyes,
   but the Lord weighs the spirit.
3  Commit your work to the Lord,
   and your plans will be established.
4  The Lord has made everything for its purpose,
   even the wicked for the day of trouble.
5  All those who are arrogant are an abomination to the Lord;
   be assured, they will not go unpunished.
6  By loyalty and faithfulness iniquity is atoned for,
   and by the fear of the Lord one avoids evil.
7  When the ways of people please the Lord,
   he causes even their enemies to be at peace with them.
8  Better is a little with righteousness
   than large income with injustice.
9  The human mind plans the way,
   but the Lord directs the steps.
10 Inspired decisions are on the lips of a king;
   his mouth does not sin in judgment.
11 Honest balances and scales are the Lord's;
   all the weights in the bag are his work.
12 It is an abomination to kings to do evil,
   for the throne is established by righteousness.
13 Righteous lips are the delight of a king,
   and he loves those who speak what is right.
14 A king's wrath is a messenger of death,
   and whoever is wise will appease it.
15 In the light of a king's face there is life,
   and his favor is like the clouds that bring the spring rain.
16 How much better to get wisdom than gold!
   To get understanding is to be chosen rather than silver.
17 The highway of the upright avoids evil;
   those who guard their way preserve their lives.
18 Pride goes before destruction,
   and a haughty spirit before a fall.
19 It is better to be of a lowly spirit among the poor
   than to divide the spoil with the proud.
20 Those who are attentive to a matter will prosper,
   and happy are those who trust in the Lord.
21 The wise of heart is called perceptive,
   and pleasant speech increases persuasiveness.

22 Wisdom is a fountain of life to one who has it,
  but folly is the punishment of fools.
23 The mind of the wise makes their speech judicious,
  and adds persuasiveness to their lips.
24 Pleasant words are like a honeycomb,
  sweetness to the soul and health to the body.
25 Sometimes there is a way that seems to be right,
  but in the end it is the way to death.
26 The appetite of workers works for them;
  their hunger urges them on.
27 Scoundrels concoct evil,
  and their speech is like a scorching fire.
28 A perverse person spreads strife,
  and a whisperer separates close friends.
29 The violent entice their neighbors,
  and lead them in a way that is not good.
30 One who winks the eyes plans perverse things;
  one who compresses the lips brings evil to pass.
31 Gray hair is a crown of glory;
  it is gained in a righteous life.
32 One who is slow to anger is better than the mighty,
  and one whose temper is controlled than one who captures a city.
33 The lot is cast into the lap,
  but the decision is the Lord's alone.

The Masoretes (8th to 10th centuries CE) identified Prov. 16:17 as the very center of the book of Proverbs. This, of course, refers to the written text. Scholars note that Prov. 16:1–22:16 differs from Proverbs 10–15 in that antithetical parallelism prevails in the latter; it slowly disappears and is replaced by synonymous parallelism in the former. Prov. 16:1–9 may have preexisted as a unit even before its collection in this book. The unit is called the YHWH proverbs since this name appears in every proverb except v. 8. Verse 1 also forms an *inclusio* with v. 33. In our book, however, while acknowledging the literary context of the proverb, we focus on the cultural life-setting of each proverb standing on its own. What cultural values help to understand the proverb as its creators and tradents understood it?

## Textual Notes: 16:1-33

**16:1** NRSV "Plans of the mind" is in Hebrew literally "arrangements of the heart." The word "heart" is associated with "tongue" in the second line, reflecting the tripartite view of the human person in biblical psychology. ▶**Three-Zone Personality**. Eyes–heart and mouth (tongue)–ears are mentioned; hands–feet—the zone of purposeful activity—is not explicitly mentioned, but perhaps implied. Thus human beings imagine projects to be accomplished, but God is the one who brings them to fruition.

**16:2** NRSV "weighs the spirit" is literally in Hebrew "weighs the spirits." The meaning is the same as Prov. 21:2, "weighs the heart," a common reference to God's evaluation of human motives (Prov. 17:3; 24:12) 7:10; 17:3; Jer. 11:20 [heart and mind, literally "kidneys and heart"]; 17:10; 20:12). ▶**Three-Zone Personality**. A popular contemporary translation of "weighs the spirits" is "measurer of motives" (NABRE), an etic (that is," outsider") interpretation of the emic (or indigenous) biblical text. It is an appropriate rendition, but it conceals the insight of ancient biblical psychology.

**16:4** This proverb raises the issue of predestination in the modern mind. However, that was not the understanding of the ancients. The Bible does not speak explicitly of free will but implies it, for example, in Deut. 30:19: "I have set before you life and death . . . Choose life!" Sirach makes the first explicit mention of free will (Sir. 15:11-14), but notes that God left the human creature "in the power of his own free choice" (NRSV). Literally in Hebrew, God left the human creature in the power of "his own inclination (yeṣer)." According to the rabbinic interpretation of Gen. 2:7 ("formed," yaṣar), God implanted two drives or inclinations (yeṣerim) in the human heart: one toward good and one toward evil. Sadly, the one toward evil seemed to dominate (Gen. 6:5; 8:21). While this indicates an element of freedom, it also includes an element of apparent determinism. The Bible does not seem to be bothered by the tension (Amos 3:6). God decides everything, including the appropriate fate for evil people (Sir. 33:7-15; 39:12-31).

**16:5** "Arrogant" in Hebrew is literally "proud of heart," yet another reference to biblical psychology's understanding of the human person. ▶**Three-Zone Personality.** The proud of heart are an abomination to the Lord, that is, unacceptable to God. The same judgment applies to those with "haughty eyes" (Prov. 6:16-17, in which the three zones are explicitly identified: eyes–heart; mouth–ears; hands–feet).

**16:6** NRSV "loyalty and faithfulness" translate the Hebrew ḥesed w'emet, "steadfast lovingkindness and faithfulness." This describes God in Exod. 34:6 and should be the pattern for relating to other human beings (Prov. 3:3). These virtues are synonymous with fear of the Lord, that is, respectful acknowledgment of God's status.

**16:7** To understand how an enemy can become at peace with those he opposes, it helps to appreciate that MENA culture recognizes shifting loyalties. An Arab proverb states: "I against my brother; my brother and I against our cousins; my brother, I, and our cousins against our neighbors," and so on. Circumstances change shifting loyalties. Thus when one's behavior pleases God, the deity can inspire or activate shifting loyalties so that enemies can live at peace with one another (Gen. 26:26-31; Gen. 44–45).

**16:8** NRSV "income" is anachronistic and misleading. The Hebrew literally means "increase." In the zero-sum economy of antiquity any increase was believed to have come at a loss to someone else. The word "income" restricts the sense of increase to money, which was not available to the vast majority of peasants.

**16:9** NRSV "the human mind" is an etic or "outsider" translation of the emic or indigenous phrase "the heart of man" (literal Hebrew). This is in synonymous parallelism with "steps" in the next line, once again reflecting the understanding of human beings in biblical psychology: heart–eyes and hands–feet. The Lord brings human plans to fruition.

**16:10-15** As the preceding aphorisms were considered YHWH proverbs because of the mention of God's name, these five are known as "royal proverbs" because of their treatment of the king and his duties. YHWH proverbs and royal proverbs were associated because the king was representative of God, ruling in the deity's stead. Hence many of the duties and attributes of YHWH are also ascribed to the king, who is supposed to reflect them.

**16:10** NRSV "inspired decisions" translates the Hebrew *qesem*, usually rendered "oracle" and connoting divination (see Deut. 18:10), something strictly forbidden. Here, however, the word is used in a positive sense, hence translated "inspired decisions." All kings who rule in God's name are presumed to have special abilities for performing their duties, especially their judicial obligations (1 Kgs. 3:28; Ps. 72:2). David is alleged to have "wisdom like the wisdom of the angel of God to know all things that are on the earth" (2 Sam. 14:20). It is plausible that the king—like holy people in the Israelite tradition—had ready access to the realm of God and God's advice in alternate states of consciousness. ▶**Alternate States of Consciousness.** This could be a dream, trance, vision, or the like. Thus his judgments can indeed be considered to be inspired.

**16:11** See the comment on 11:1.

**16:12** NRSV translation of the first line is misleading. The more appropriate translation would be: "Doing evil is an abomination [i.e., abhorrent] to kings." The reference is not to kings who do evil, as the NRSV would have it, but rather malefactors in royal service. A king's throne or rule will endure only if justice rules, hence he must rid his staff of evildoers (see Ps. 101; Prov. 20:8; 25:5; 29:14). This is another example of the cultural practice of shifting loyalties. The person in royal service probably was selected under one set of circumstances, but when these changed he would have to be dismissed.

**16:13** This proverb describes the kind of courtier who would please the king, namely, a truthful one. Focus on "lips" and "speaking" is a reference to the mouth-ears symbolic zone of the human body, the zone of self-expressive speech. ▶**Three-Zone Personality.**

**16:14-15** These aphorisms tell of the king's power over life and death. Verse 14 advises a person how to avoid the consequence of royal wrath (or anger), which is death. While in the West wrath or anger is an emotion one should control, in MENA culture it is a response to a manifest slight. It is an act of revenge for the slight or the challenge posed to the honor of a person, in this instance the king (Malina and Pilch 2007). The king's revenge is death for the one who stirred his anger. He sends someone to carry out the revenge (2 Kgs. 6:32-33). A wise person will, however, know how to defuse the wrath and escape the deserved revenge (Prov. 15:1, 4; see 1 Sam. 25; Dan. 2).

Verse 15 presents the contrast to wrath and death, namely a favorable disposition toward another person. The phrase "light of the face" is used in Job 29:26, but the Bible mainly uses it to describe God's favor (Ps. 4:6; 44:3; 89:15). It is prominent in the blessing of Aaron: "the Lord make his face to shine upon you" (Num. 6:25). Thus the king is to imitate God in showing favor to his subjects.

**16:17** As noted above, this verse marks the exact middle of the book of Proverbs. Scholars believe that the compiler intentionally placed it here as a reminder of the theme of the two ways in Proverbs 1–9 (see Prov. 4:10-19). The way of the righteous keeps one from harm but, as the second part of the verse points out, one must make a constant effort to stay on this path. Doing so will save one's life (compare Prov. 19:16; 21:23; 22:5).

**16:18** This aphorism springs from the MENA cultural value of humility, which entails respecting others and not even giving a hint of trying to be superior. ▶**Humility**. To accomplish this, an honorable person puts oneself one step behind the rightful status. This allows others to invite that person to acknowledge and take up that rightful status. This proverb spells out the disastrous consequences of pride and a haughty spirit. They lead to one's downfall.

**16:20** NRSV "happy" translates the Hebrew ʾašrê, which should more properly be given as "honorable" or "truly honorable " (See Hanson 1994: 81–111; Prov. 3:18; 8:32, 34; 14:21; 16:20; 20:7; 28:14; 29:18; 31:28). The one who trusts in the Lord is a truly honorable person.

**16:21** This proverb once again draws on biblical psychology. ▶**Three-Zone Personality**. The emic phrase "wise of heart" reflects the symbolic body zone of eyes–heart, the zone of emotion-fused thinking, and "sweetness of lips" (literal Hebrew rendered appropriately by NRSV in etic terms as "pleasant speech") reflects the symbolic body zone of mouth–ears, the zone of self- expressive speech. The mouth speaks out of the fullness of the heart, and wisdom presented in appealing terms can be convincing.

**16:22** On "fountain of life" see Prov. 10:11; 13:14; 14:27. The second part of this proverb is challenging to translate. NRSV interprets it as folly being the discipline of fools (in the sense of punishment—see Prov. 13:24; 22:15). ▶ **Discipline.** Other interpretations are that it is useless to discipline fools, for they still learn nothing—or the opposite, that they are disciplined only in folly.

**16:23** Literally in Hebrew "mind of the wise" is "heart of the wise." This is yet another reflection of biblical psychology, that is, the biblical understanding that the heart is the source of knowledge and understanding (heart–eyes). In this proverb the heart is the source of persuasion (mouth–ears). ▶ **Three-Zone Personality.**

**16:24** "Pleasant words" present a reflection on the mouth–ears symbolic body zone. ▶ **Three-Zone Personality**. Pleasant words are like honey dripping from a honeycomb. The image of words dripping upon hearers is frequent in the Bible (Prov. 5:3; Job 29:22). NRSV "soul" translates the Hebrew word *nepeš,* which literally means "throat" or "palate." ▶ **Nepeš/soul.** Here palate would be more appropriate. NRSV "health to the body" translates the Hebrew "healing" or "strengthening the bones." "Bones" refers to the total well-being of a person (see Prov. 15:30). In an agonistic culture where insult is a normal part of social communication, pleasant words as this proverb describes them offer welcome respite. The proverb also suggests tempering harsh speech.

**16:26** NRSV "appetite" translates the Hebrew word *nepeš* (palate, throat; hunger; often, soul). ▶ **Nepeš/soul.** It is paired in this proverb (as often in the Bible) with the Hebrew word *peh* ("mouth"; NRSV: "hunger") in the second line (see Prov. 13:2; 21:23; Job 7:11; Eccl. 6:7). The proverb states a truism: one works in order to gain the basic necessities of life, namely, food and drink. However, Qoheleth's observation (Eccl. 6:7) suggests that filling the stomach alone does not satisfy the whole person. There is more to life than nourishment.

Once again the non-introspective observation in this proverb focusing on parts of the body illustrates how the ancients could reach toward deeper meanings from that perspective.

**16:27-30** These three proverbs deal with the symbolic body zone of mouth–ears, specifically the effects of the speech of wicked people (compare Prov. 6:12-15, 16-19). ▶ **Three-Zone Personality.** Verses 27-29 each begin with the Hebrew word 'îš (man, a person; inclusive language translation NRSV renders each use of 'îš in the plural, allowing women to be included in this rogues' gallery).

**16:27** NRSV "scoundrels" translates the Hebrew "man of Belial." The origins of the word *Belial* are uncertain, but it is not a name. It is rather a descriptor most likely signifying depravity or wickedness, much worse than simply worthlessness. Such a person literally "digs evil," an unusual phrase perhaps derived from "dig a pit" (into which others might fall; Ps. 7:16; 57:7; 119:85; Prov. 26:27; Jer. 18:20, 22). His words (mouth–ears symbolic body zone) are like a destructive fire (see Jas. 3:6). ▶ **Three-Zone Personality.** His speech disturbs social harmony and destroys the community.

**16:28** NRSV "perverse person" translates the Hebrew "man who speaks *tahpukôt*," related to the word meaning "overturn, overthrow." We are still in the mouth–ears symbolic body zone (see Prov. 2:12; 6:19). ▶ **Three-Zone Personality.** Such a person "turns things upside down" by stirring up strife or quarrels. The meaning of the Hebrew word translated "whisperer" is uncertain, but the word is particular to and frequent in the book of Proverbs (Prov. 18:8; 26:20, 22). A plausible translation could be "backbiter" or "talebearer" (Clifford 1999: 162) or better yet, "gossiper" (Murphy 1998: 118). As Richard Rohrbaugh notes (Rohrbaugh 2007b: 126), while gossip is a nearly universal phenomenon and not distinctive to Mediterranean culture, it is more significant in non-literate as compared with literate societies. Moreover, ethnographers note that Mediterranean culture has had a profound impact on gossip in that context. Because of core MENA values of honor and shame, gossip can create either shame or honor even if there is no foundation in reality. This proverb highlights its deleterious effects on friendship. Rohrbaugh helpfully lists the Hebrew words pertaining to the semantic field of gossip, many of which appear in Proverbs (Rohrbaugh 2007b: 134–35).

**16:29** A violent person in this context is one who hurts a neighbor by enticing or seducing the neighbor to walk a path that is not good (see Prov. 1:8-19). Enticing, seducing, inviting are activities of the mouth–ears symbolic body zone. ▶**Three-Zone Personality**. Violence need not be physical (Pilch 1997: 310–13). It can be verbal.

**16:30** Two symbolic body zones are represented in this proverb: eyes–heart (zone of emotion-fused thinking) and mouth–ears (zone of self-expressive speech). ▶**Three-Zone Personality**. Both activities ("winks the eyes" [Prov. 6:13; 10:10] and "compresses the lips") are recognized as forms of non-verbal communication (Pilch 1996: 172–76). (See the comment on Prov. 10:10.) This proverb instructs on how to "read" and interpret the gestures of another person, particularly one who is up to no good. Judging by externals is the only way non-introspective MENA persons can assess others (1 Sam. 16:7).

**16:31** NRSV "righteous life" translates the Hebrew "way of righteousness," reiterating the theme of two ways so frequent in the book of Proverbs.

**16:32** NRSV "slow to anger" translates the Hebrew "long of nose" (see comments on Prov. 14:29; 15:18), reflecting the non-introspective tendency to somatize emotions. In view of the agonistic nature of MENA culture, it is not surprising that exhortations to patience are frequent in Proverbs. ▶**Agonism**. In this "better than" proverb a patient person is exalted over a warrior, a mighty person. The second line explains the first: one who controls his spirit (literal Hebrew; synonymous with "long of nose") is better than one who can capture a city.

**16:33** Casting lots was a means for determining God's will concerning the proper course of action one should take. Scholars are not agreed concerning what the lots were (dice?) and the way in which they were used. This proverb says they were cast into the folds of a garment. Saul was chosen first king of Israel by lot (1 Sam. 10:17-27).

After its conquest, the land was divided by casting lots (Num. 26:55; Josh. 14:2). Matthias, the successor to Judas, was chosen by lot (Acts 1:26). The point of the proverb is that ultimately God decides how the lots turn out, indicating the divine will in a particular matter.

## Proverbs 17:1-28

1 Better is a dry morsel with quiet
   than a house full of feasting with strife.
2 A slave who deals wisely will rule over a child who acts shamefully,
   and will share the inheritance as one of the family.
3 The crucible is for silver, and the furnace is for gold,
   but the Lord tests the heart.
4 An evildoer listens to wicked lips,
   and a liar gives heed to a mischievous tongue.
5 Those who mock the poor insult their Maker;
   those who are glad at calamity will not go unpunished.
6 Grandchildren are the crown of the aged,
   and the glory of children is their parents.
7 Fine speech is not becoming to a fool;
   still less is false speech to a ruler.
8 A bribe is like a magic stone in the eyes of those who give it;
   wherever they turn they prosper.
9 One who forgives an affront fosters friendship,
   but one who dwells on disputes will alienate a friend.
10 A rebuke strikes deeper into a discerning person
   than a hundred blows into a fool.
11 Evil people seek only rebellion,
   but a cruel messenger will be sent against them.
12 Better to meet a she bear robbed of its cubs
   than to confront a fool immersed in folly.
13 Evil will not depart from the house of one
   who returns evil for good.
14 The beginning of strife is like letting out water;
   so stop before the quarrel breaks out.
15 One who justifies the wicked and one who condemns the righteous
   are both alike an abomination to the Lord.
16 Why should fools have a price in hand to buy wisdom,
   when they have no mind to learn?
17 A friend loves at all times,
   and kinsfolk are born to share adversity.
18 It is senseless to give a pledge,
   to become surety for a neighbor.

19 One who loves transgression loves strife;
   one who builds a high threshold invites broken bones.
20 The crooked of mind do not prosper,
   and the perverse of tongue fall into calamity.
21 The one who begets a fool gets trouble;
   the parent of a fool has no joy.
22 A cheerful heart is a good medicine,
   but a downcast spirit dries up the bones.
23 The wicked accept a concealed bribe
   to pervert the ways of justice.
24 The discerning person looks to wisdom,
   but the eyes of a fool to the ends of the earth.
25 Foolish children are a grief to their father
   and bitterness to her who bore them.
26 To impose a fine on the innocent is not right,
   or to flog the noble for their integrity.
27 One who spares words is knowledgeable;
   one who is cool in spirit has understanding.
28 Even fools who keep silent are considered wise;
   when they close their lips, they are deemed intelligent.

*Textual Note: 17:1-28*

**17:1** See the comments on Prov. 15:16-17 and 16:8. NRSV "feasting with strife" is literally in Hebrew "sacrifices" [*zbāḥîm*] of strife." Some scholars see here an implied contrast between *zbāḥîm* (a slaughter victim, partly burnt; or sacrifices in general) celebrated in peace (e.g., 1 Sam. 20:6, 9, the family feast of David at Bethlehem) and the family feast mentioned in this proverb that is shared after such a sacrifice, but with quarrels. Such family quarrels were common in this agonistic culture, even on sacred occasions. ▶**Agonism.**

**17:2** The Hebrew literally contrasts a clever or shrewd family servant with a son who acts shamefully. ▶**Honor and Shame.** NRSV's inclusive term "child" muddles the picture. In the next line, the Hebrew literally says, "will share inheritance with the brothers." The inclusive word "family" replacing "brothers" (and "child" replacing "son") may misrepresent the original cultural context of the proverb. If taken literally, this proverb may be very old, predating the (pre-monarchical?) period when daughters were able to inherit in the absence of sons (Num. 27:1-11; 36:1-12; Josh. 17:3-6; see Ben-Barak 1980). The basic idea here echoes that of Prov. 12:24.

**17:3** We have already noted that this non-introspective MENA society believed that only God could read the human heart: its thoughts, motivations, and the like (see Prov. 14:10). Thus God alone tests human hearts (Ps. 26:2; 66:10; Jer. 9:7-8; 17:9-10; 20:12). The insight this proverb contributes is that God can also purify hearts as the crucible and furnace do for precious metals.

**17:4** Lips and tongue belong to the mouth–ears symbolic body-zone. ►**Three-Zone Personality**. The self-expressive speech of this zone reflected in this proverb is a lie, or more precisely, gossip. (See the comment on Prov. 16:28.) ►**Lying**. Keep in mind that secrecy, deception, and lying are culturally legitimate strategies for preserving one's honor in this culture. It makes life difficult, all the more so when, as this proverb points out, such a gossip or liar is an evildoer. In other words, the evildoer knows that his speech is malicious and destructive but does it anyway, perhaps not so much in service of his own reputation or honor, but simply to destroy the reputation of another.

**17:5** Wealth and poverty are not primarily or principally economic designations in the Bible. They rather point to status, reputation, honor-rating (Malina 1986a; 2001a; 2001b). ►**Rich and Poor**. Everyone is expected to maintain the born, or inherited, status. Sometimes a person temporarily falls below that status. The cultural obligation is to regain one's status as soon as possible. In the Bible, God has special concern for the poor, and whoever would mock the poor insults God (Prov. 14:31; 22:22; 29:13). Insulting God is considered sin in the Bible, that is, shaming God. Following the cultural rules of honor and shame, God must redress that shame. Hence the passive voice ("will not go unpunished") in the second line is a theological or divine passive and refers to God's response to the guilty party.

**17:6** Literally, this proverb is about males: grandsons, fathers, sons. "Grandsons are the crown of old men, the glory of sons is their fathers." The NRSV inclusive translation reflects the contemporary

Western view rather than MENA culture, which prizes sons as a special mark of honor.

**17:7** NRSV "speech" is literally "lips" in the Hebrew text. In either case the proverb refers to the mouth–ears symbolic body zone. ▶**Three-Zone Personality**. The contrast is between a fool (in this case someone who contributes nothing to society) and a prince or noble person. One would be stunned to hear a fool saying something of significance but shocked and disappointed to learn that a person of power and influence lies or engages in deceitful speech. ▶**Lying**.

**17:8** Anthropologists distinguish two kinds of bribes: transactional and variance. Transactional bribes are "fees" or "gifts" that anyone can use to facilitate or expedite a transaction. A variance bribe adversely affects the administration of justice (Langston 1991). Bribes in the Bible are mostly of the variance kind and are usually condemned because God shows no partiality (Deut. 10:17; 2 Chr. 19:7), which of course the briber seeks. This proverb, however, views the bribe from a neutral perspective, that is, as a type of gift, a normal part of everyday life. The giver of a bribe has a sense of power, for he always gets what he wants.

**17:9** MENA societies are known for shifting allegiances and loyalties. However, it is important to have some basic support in life notably from family and friends. Thus, while some relatives or friends may come and go in one's intimate circle it is important to have some stable relationships. Forgiveness guarantees a lasting friendship. The Hebrew word translated "affront" (pešaʻ) connotes rebellion (see 1 Kgs. 12:19) and is used in the Hebrew Bible to convey affront both toward humans and, especially, toward God. Thus the proverb implies forgoing revenge for a serious affront. Rather, the one insulted should cover or forgive it for the sake of maintaining a friendship. Harping on the affront will rupture the friendship (see Lev. 19:18).

**17:14** This proverb addresses the effects of agonism, a key value in MENA cultures. ▶**Agonism**. Conflict-prone individuals should consider the consequences. Conflict may lead to violence, which in turn may produce bloodshed. Blood-feud is long-lasting and almost impossible to settle in MENA cultures. Thus starting an argument is like opening a sluice. There is no telling or predicting where the water will go. Therefore, stop the argument before it even begins. If it has begun, a mediator should be summoned at the earliest to halt the process.

**17:15** The language of this proverb is juridical, concerning law courts (Deut. 25:1-3) and, in this instance, the perversion of justice. NRSV "justifies" and "condemns" mutes the judicial tone and would be better translated "acquits" and "convicts." Specifically, this concerns corrupt judges (Exod. 23:6-8; Deut. 16:18-20; Isa. 5:23). MENA societies of antiquity doubted that justice could be obtained in the courts. Better to settle before going to court than to risk unpredictable outcomes (Prov. 25:8-10; Matt. 25:25-26). This perversion of justice is such an abomination to God that the perpetrators will have to answer to divine justice.

**17:16** NRSV "mind" is literally "heart," reflecting the eyes–heart symbolic body zone. ►**Three-Zone Personality**. Though the fool has the means for acquiring wisdom, he will not use them.

**17:17** Scholars are not agreed whether this is proverb is in antithetical or synonymous parallelism. Either way, it speaks well of friends and brothers (literal Hebrew). A friend's love is for all time, but a brother—as go'ēl or next of kin (see Lev. 25:25; Num. 35:9-15; Sir. 30:6)—fulfills a special duty to family members in time of adversity.

**17:18** The topic of giving surety is frequent in Proverbs (Prov. 6:1; 11:15; 17:18; 20:16; 22:26-27; 27:13). It is uniformly strongly discouraged as foolish, or as in this proverb literally "lacking heart," the symbolic body zone of emotion-fused thinking. ►**Three-Zone Personality**. The cultural reason for this is the value of limited good. ►**Limited Good**. Once it is lost, there simply is no more where this came from. Ben Sira gives the opposite advice, so long as the benefactor is certain he will have the means to cover the debt in case of default (Sir. 29:14-20).

**17:19** The first line of this proverb fits agonistic MENA culture. ►**Agonism**. In place of NRSV "loves," substitute "holds onto" or "clings to." Instead of "forgiving and forgetting" affronts, conflict-prone individuals cling to them simply to stir up trouble for the fun of it. The second line defies interpretation. Architecturally it remains a puzzle, unless it means that something poorly constructed will come tumbling down. Others interpret "high door" as mouth, hence "proud speech," a self-destructive activity of the mouth–ears symbolic body zone. ▶Three-Zone Personality.

**17:20** NRSV "crooked of mind" translates the Hebrew "crooked of heart," referring to the heart–eyes symbolic body zone. ▶Three-Zone Personality. Such will not find good (NRSV "prosper"). The perverse tongue refers to the mouth–ears symbolic body zone, and such will fall into evil, implying the hands–feet symbolic body zone. The proverb describes a totally corrupt person, lacking in all the symbolic body zones.

**17:21** A number of proverbs speak about a shameful and stupid son (Prov. 10:1; 15:20; 17:25; 19:13), sometimes contrasting him with a wise son (Prov. 10:1; 13:1; 15:20). The son's character reflects on the honor status of a family and most especially his father. NRSV "parent" blunts the cultural significance of the son. While the birth of a son gives his mother status and is her social security for life, the wise or foolish behavior of the son reflects more on the father. His tasks are to insure filial loyalty to him and the family and to be able to impose his will on the son. If the son is stupid and foolish, this suggests that the father failed in his duty to raise a wise and honorable son (Pilch 1993). Such a son is no joy and brings his father only sorrow.

**17:22** This proverb refers to the symbolic body zone of heart–eyes, the zone of emotion-fused thinking. ▶Three-Zone Personality. The first line has an uncertain Hebrew word difficult to translate. Some suggest "face," so "a cheerful heart makes a happy face." Others (NRSV) opt for "health, heal," so "a cheerful heart is good medicine." However one translates it, the cheerful heart is contrasted with a downcast spirit (ruah), which robs the body of its vitality ("dries up the bones"—see Prov. 12:4; 14:30). Compare Prov. 15:13; 18:14.

**17:23** See the comment on Prov. 17:8 above.

**17:25** See the comment on Prov. 17:21 above. NRSV's inclusive translation ("children," "them") once again misrepresents MENA culture's high expectations of sons (Hebrew). A wise (adult) son brings honor to both father and mother, but a fool is a grief to his father, who is judged by outsiders as a failure in this regard, and bitterness to his mother, who can expect no assistance from him. Rebecca understandably favored her wise son, Jacob, over her first-born son, Esau, who behaved foolishly in the story (Gen. 25:29-34; 27).

**17:26** See the comment on Prov. 17:15. This proverb pertains to the judicial system behaving at its worst.

**17:27** The first line of this proverb refers to the mouth–ears symbolic body zone. ▶**Three-Zone Personality**. A wise person (heart–eyes) thinks clearly and is succinct in speech (mouth–ears). Such a "cool in spirit" person clearly has understanding. The phrase "cool in spirit" is a *hapax legomenon* in the Hebrew Bible (that is, it occurs only once). In the Egyptian wisdom tradition it contrasts with "heated man" and describes a person who has self-restraint and is moderate in speech. It probably carries the same meaning here.

**17:28** This proverb offers sound advice to the fool concerning the mouth–ears symbolic body zone (keeping silent; having closed lips). ▶**Three-Zone Personality**. Rather than "pouring out folly" (Prov. 15:2), which is a fool's proclivity, keeping one's mouth shut projects an image of a wise and intelligent person. In MENA cultures, appearances count more than reality. Thus one is always "making oneself out to be someone other than he is." If a fool has any sense at all he would heed this advice and gain honor, which would otherwise elude him.

### Proverbs 18:1-24

1 The one who lives alone is self-indulgent,
  showing contempt for all who have sound judgment.
2 A fool takes no pleasure in understanding,
  but only in expressing personal opinion.
3 When wickedness comes, contempt comes also;
  and with dishonor comes disgrace.
4 The words of the mouth are deep waters;
  the fountain of wisdom is a gushing stream.
5 It is not right to be partial to the guilty,
  or to subvert the innocent in judgment.
6 A fool's lips bring strife,

and a fool's mouth invites a flogging.

7 The mouths of fools are their ruin,
and their lips a snare to themselves.

8 The words of a whisperer are like delicious morsels;
they go down into the inner parts of the body.

9 One who is slack in work
is close kin to a vandal.

10 The name of the Lord is a strong tower;
the righteous run into it and are safe.

11 The wealth of the rich is their strong city;
in their imagination it is like a high wall.

12 Before destruction one's heart is haughty,
but humility goes before honor.

13 If one gives answer before hearing,
it is folly and shame.

14 The human spirit will endure sickness;
but a broken spirit who can bear?

15 An intelligent mind acquires knowledge,
and the ear of the wise seeks knowledge.

16 A gift opens doors;
it gives access to the great.

17 The one who first states a case seems right,
until the other comes and cross-examines.

18 Casting the lot puts an end to disputes
and decides between powerful contenders.

19 An ally offended is stronger than a city;
such quarreling is like the bars of a castle.

20 From the fruit of the mouth one's stomach is satisfied;
the yield of the lips brings satisfaction.

21 Death and life are in the power of the tongue,
and those who love it will eat its fruits.

22 He who finds a wife finds a good thing,
and obtains favor from the Lord.

23 The poor use entreaties,
but the rich answer roughly.

24 Some friends play at friendship
but a true friend sticks closer than one's kin.

There is no specific organizing theme for this chapter, but Luis Alonso Schökel notes that the mouth–ears symbolic body zone (speaking and listening) is represented in many of the proverbs: 18:2, 4, 6, 7, 8, 13, 15, 20, 21, 23 (Alonso Schökel and Vilchez 1984).

*Textual Notes: 18:1-24*

**18:1** MENA societies, like eighty percent of the population on the face of the planet at the present time, are collectivistic rather than individualistic. ▶**Collectivistic Society.** In brief, this means that members find their identity in the group and submit to the will and judgment of the group, chiefly the family but also friends, village, etc. NRSV "lives alone" may be misleading. To live alone would mean that one has no network of kin or friends, which is an impossibility in collectivistic society. It is equivalent to suicide. The Hebrew word means "separated," "estranged," "alienated." Thus the estranged person is separated (voluntarily or involuntarily) from the primary group, determined to follow his or her own will without regard for the community, indeed, quarreling with opposing opinions.

**18:2** Clearly, anyone in MENA cultures who refuses to consider the wisdom of the group is thought a fool. Such a person is not as interested in the wisdom of others as collectivistic individuals are but prefers rather to share what is (literally in Hebrew) in the heart, the symbolic body zone of emotion-fused thinking. ▶**Three-Zone Personality.** Such a one prefers to promote his or her own opinion, which is foolishness (see Prov. 12:23; 13:16).

**18:3** This proverb implicitly appeals to the MENA society's esteem of an honorable reputation. ▶**Honor and Shame.** It paints the shameful results of wicked behavior: contempt, literally "lightness"—the opposite of "heaviness/honor" in Hebrew (*kābôd*; NRSV translates "dishonor)—and disgrace (or reproach). The person faced with these distasteful consequences of shame should be motivated to strive after honorable behavior.

**18:4** Another proverb focused on symbolic body zones. ▶**Three-Zone Personality.** The image of deep waters is best explained by Prov. 20:5, which refers to the heart of a person (heart–eyes symbolic body zone = deep waters) as the source of that person's deep thoughts eventually expressed in words (mouth–ears symbolic body zone). The second line is best read without "is." Human words are like a gushing stream, a fount of wisdom for others (see Prov. 10:11; 13:14; 15:27; 16:22).

**18:5** This is one of a handful of "not good" proverbs describing activities that violate the good order of society (see Prov. 16:29; 17:26; 20:23; 24:23; 28:21). Some scholars think it might be a euphemism for "criminal" or "disastrous." This proverb describes the behavior of corrupt judges in legal cases who show partiality by pardoning the guilty and condemning the innocent. NRSV "partial to the guilty" is literally in Hebrew "lifting up the face" of the guilty. It describes judicial bias in Lev. 19:15 and Ps. 82:2; see Deut. 10:17. In MENA cultures the human body is the screen on which honor is displayed and claimed. The most important part is the head, face, and eyes, the very front of the human body. Thus "to lift up the face," "to save face," "to lose face," and similar phrases all concern honor (Neyrey 1998: 24). In this proverb, honor is given to a dishonorable person.

**18:6** This proverb deals with the mouth–ears symbolic body zone. ▶**Three-Zone Personality.** Once more in Proverbs (compare Prov. 17:14; 20:3) it describes the consequences of a fool's unguarded and ill-considered speech. Such behavior not only initiates strife but may well provoke retaliatory blows (not necessarily judicial punishment as NRSV's "flogging" suggests).

**18:7** Another proverb dealing with the mouth–ears symbolic body zone. ▶**Three-Zone Personality.** The compiler quite probably arranged these proverbs on the basis of chiastic structure: v. 6: lips, mouth; v. 7: mouth, lips. While proverbs concerning this body zone most often relate the injury fools inflict on others, this one highlights the drastic consequences for the fool personally.

**18:8** This proverb is identical with Prov. 26:22. Its topic is gossip. (See the comment on Prov. 16:28.) The aphorism describes the irresistible appeal of gossip, likening it to tasty bits of food, devoured greedily and transported deep within the human body. The Hebrew translated "inner parts" (NRSV) [of the body] actually means storeroom. Gossip is not only relished but stored for further enjoyment on future retrieval and, of course, quite likely to be repeated.

**18:9** Yet another aphorism criticizing laziness. (See comment on Prov. 12:11.) The word translated "vandal" is literally "destroyer." It occurs again in Prov. 28:24b relative to gross mistreatment of parents, hence a destroyer of the family and, by extension, wider society. Because kinship was one of the two formal social institutions of ancient MENA society (the other being politics), it was imperative that each family member contribute to the well-being of the group. ▶**Kinship**. ▶**Politics**. This proverb condemns as a destroyer the one who shirks this duty.

**18:12** See comments on 16:18a, and 15:33b. Humility in biblical culture is a socially acknowledged claim to neutrality in the competition of life. ▶**Humility**. It prompts persons to deliberately stay a step behind or below their rightful status so as not to create the impression of yearning for more credit (honor) than one is due. From this perspective it is easy to understand that humility precedes honor (or "glory;" see Prov. 15:33; 22:4). The rallying cry of some Christians—"Give God the glory!"—is part of the semantic field of honor. The proverb warns against being proud or haughty (see also Prov. 11:2; 29:23). Since honor and shame are core of MENA societies, proverbs such as this seek to impress upon members the importance of honor and the potential threats to it. Honor once lost is never regained. It is tantamount to death ("destruction").

**18:13** Yet another proverb concerning the mouth–ears symbolic body zone. ▶**Three-Zone Personality**. Self-expressive speech is an important element in communication, but only if it is not premature and waits respectfully for its turn. Sirach makes this quite explicit (Sir. 11:8). Such behavior is disgraceful and personally humiliating, not to mention rude and insulting to the speaker so interrupted.

**18:14** The Hebrew word *ruah* is polysemic. It means wind (air in motion), breath, and spirit simultaneously. In this proverb the reflection concerns the nature and abilities of the human spirit. It has the capability, strength, and determination to deal with sickness, but a crushed spirit is robbed of this potency. It loses its confidence, determination, and ability to overcome adversity.

**18:15** This proverb relates to two symbolic body zones: heart (NRSV "mind")-eyes, and mouth–ears. ▶**Three-Zone Personality.** The "heart" and the "ear" are two parts of the human body by which knowledge is acquired. The Hebrew word translated "knowledge" (dāʿat) is not simply factual information but rather connotes critical assessment that leads to practical decisions for action. Thus it includes the third symbolic body zone, hands–feet. The proverb exhorts a person to be totally involved in the search for practical knowledge and committed to executing what needs to be done.

**18:16** Scholars are divided on the interpretation of this proverb. Is the topic a "gift" or a "bribe?" The cluster of Proverbs 16–19 would seem to favor "bribe" (see also Prov. 15:27; 17:8, 23), but considered on its own this aphorism probably refers to "gift" plain and simple. The distinction is subtle, since a gift in MENA societies always expects reciprocity, that is, something in return. There are no "free" gifts (Stansell 1999: 69). Thus the proverb is simply a reminder of a key cultural strategy for obtaining necessary or desired goods.

**18:17** The context of this proverb is the law court. It is advice intended for the judge: hear all sides of a matter before rendering a decision. As already noted in this book, law courts were not usually considered just (see Mic. 7:3). Litigants were urged to settle out of court (Prov. 25:7c-10; Matt. 5:25-26). In this proverb the first person is the defendant (literally in Hebrew "innocent"), the second (literally "neighbor") is the plaintiff or accuser. Not all judges possessed the sagacity of Solomon (1 Kgs. 3:16-28).

**18:18** God determines the outcome of casting lots. (See comment on Prov. 16:33.) Thus casting lots keeps powerful contenders, perhaps on the verge of violence, apart. MENA cultures ordinarily seek a mediator to settle disputes to forestall feud, violence, and bloodshed. In this instance God is the mediator through the casting of lots.

**18:19** NRSV "ally" is literally "brother." Family quarrels, even after resolution, leave a bitter residue, festering resentment or worse (see Prov. 18:1 above). This proverb presents the "real." The psalmist states the "ideal": "How very good and pleasant it is when kindred [lit.

"brothers"] live together in unity!" (Ps. 133:1). ▶Normative Inconsistency. The enigmatic Hebrew of the second line of this proverb (disputed by scholars) could plausibly mean that such quarrels and their consequences are as difficult to resolve as breaching castle gates, the most protected part of a city.

**18:20** Still another proverb in this chapter referring to the mouth–ears symbolic body zone ("fruit of the mouth"—see Prov. 12:14; 13:2; "lips"). ▶Three-Zone Personality. The odd imagery is intentional: fruit of the mouth (words that emanate from the lips) somehow satisfies the stomach. However, Bernard de Géradon's three-zone anthropological model helps to make sense of it (de Géradon 1974). In Prov. 18:8 and 20:27 the belly (Hebrew *been*) bears more than a physiological meaning. It refers to the inner part of a human person (hence translated "innermost part"). Thus just as food satisfies the appetite (stomach), so good speech is itself satisfying and fulfilling for a person's well-being.

**18:21** Another proverb referring to the mouth–ears symbolic body zone ("tongue"). ▶Three-Zone Personality. The Hebrew word translated "love" is perhaps better rendered "choose," as in Prov. 12:1; 20:13; 29:3. Thus, depending on what one communicates, one literally chooses death or life (see Sir. 37:18). In a culture in which lying and deception are acceptable strategies for defending one's honorable reputation, a speaker must be wary of the consequences of speech. An insult could result in real physical harm, including death.

**18:22** Perhaps more than any other aphorism in the book of Proverbs, this one is most often misunderstood and interpreted ethnocentrically. The Hebrew word translated here as "find" also means "get, acquire" (see Prov. 3:13). In many MENA societies, and certainly in biblical culture, marriage partners do not self-select as in the West. Marriage partners are *betrothed* because the marriage is arranged by the fathers of the partners with input from the mothers. In the West, marriage partners are *engaged* because they select one another, even in the face of parental and family opposition. Marriage in the MENA world is the fusion of the honor of two extended families primarily with a view to political and/or economic advantage for both. The ideal partner for the male is a patrilateral parallel cousin or "father's brother's daughter (FBD)" (e.g., Gen. 24:15). Absent that possibility, it can be mother's brother's daughter (Gen. 28:1-2). Marriages are endogamous. The partners do not "search" and "find" (Malina 2001a: 134–60).

Viewed in this cultural context, the proverb praises the diligent efforts of the mother and father, the ones who arrange the marriage. Since God chooses one's parents, the marriage arranged by parents is assumed to be arranged by God, as the second line affirms and Israelites believed (Matt. 19:6). The literal Hebrew phrase "finding a good" means having a stroke of good fortune, prospering (see Prov. 16:20; 17:20; 19:8). How could it be otherwise, since it is a gift from God through the parents? (Prov. 19:14; 12:2). The lucky groom is aware of Prov. 11:16: "A gracious woman gets honor, but she who hates virtue is covered with shame" and Prov. 12:4: "A good wife is the crown of her husband, but she who brings shame is like rottenness in his bones." He hopes to sing the praises of his wife as in Prov. 31:10-31, thanks to God having worked through the parents.

**18:23** Poverty and wealth in the Bible are not necessarily and primarily economic concepts. ▶**Rich and Poor**. Their primary referent is status. The poor have temporarily lost their inherited status, which is why they, unlike the wealthy, are powerless. Their primary task is to restore themselves to their inherited status. Hence their behavior should necessarily be deferential so as not to jeopardize that move. This reference to the wealthy (like others as well—Prov. 22:7; 28:6, 11) is hostile, though the proverb itself simply describes life as it really is for these two classes of people.

**18:24** NRSV "kin" in the second line is literally "brother" in Hebrew. This helps us understand the aphorism's point. Brothers in MENA societies have fluctuating relationships. An Arab proverb observes: "I against my brother; I and my brother against our cousin; etc." The Bible reports a number of troubled fraternal relationships beginning with Cain and Abel. One cannot always depend on one's brother, even if that brother is expected to play the role of *go'el*, next-of-kin. (See comment on Prov. 17:17.) Hence the value of a "true friend." The literal Hebrew is "one more loving and closer [or more clinging to] than a brother."

### Proverbs 19:1-29

1 Better the poor walking in integrity
   than one perverse of speech who is a fool.
2 Desire without knowledge is not good,
   and one who moves too hurriedly misses the way.
3 One's own folly leads to ruin,
   yet the heart rages against the Lord.
4 Wealth brings many friends,
   but the poor are left friendless.
5 A false witness will not go unpunished,
   and a liar will not escape.
6 Many seek the favor of the generous,
   and everyone is a friend to a giver of gifts.
7 If the poor are hated even by their kin,
   how much more are they shunned by their friends!
   When they call after them, they are not there.
8 To get wisdom is to love oneself;
   to keep understanding is to prosper.
9 A false witness will not go unpunished,
   and the liar will perish.
10 It is not fitting for a fool to live in luxury,
   much less for a slave to rule over princes.
11 Those with good sense are slow to anger,
   and it is their glory to overlook an offense.
12 A king's anger is like the growling of a lion,
   but his favor is like dew on the grass.
13 A stupid child is ruin to a father,
   and a wife's quarreling is a continual dripping of rain.
14 House and wealth are inherited from parents,
   but a prudent wife is from the Lord.
15 Laziness brings on deep sleep;
   an idle person will suffer hunger.
16 Those who keep the commandment will live;
   those who are heedless of their ways will die.
17 Whoever is kind to the poor lends to the Lord,
   and will be repaid in full.
18 Discipline your children while there is hope;
   do not set your heart on their destruction.

19 A violent-tempered person will pay the penalty;
   if you effect a rescue, you will only have to do it again.
20 Listen to advice and accept instruction,
   that you may gain wisdom for the future.
21 The human mind may devise many plans,
   but it is the purpose of the Lord that will be established.
22 What is desirable in a person is loyalty,
   and it is better to be poor than a liar.
23 The fear of the Lord is life indeed;
   filled with it one rests secure and suffers no harm.
24 The lazy person buries a hand in the dish,
   and will not even bring it back to the mouth.
25 Strike a scoffer, and the simple will learn prudence;
   reprove the intelligent, and they will gain knowledge.
26 Those who do violence to their father and chase away their mother
   are children who cause shame and bring reproach.
27 Cease straying, my child, from the words of knowledge,
   in order that you may hear instruction.
28 A worthless witness mocks at justice,
   and the mouth of the wicked devours iniquity.
29 Condemnation is ready for scoffers,
   and flogging for the backs of fools.

In this chapter there is more synonymous parallelism than antithetic. The chapter has no obvious structure.

*Textual Notes: 19:1-29*

**19:1** Because of its similarity to Prov. 28:6, some scholars amend the second line to that aphorism. NRSV accepts the Masoretic text. A key consideration here is lying. ▶**Lying**. It is an acceptable strategy in MENA societies for protecting and enhancing honor, yet everyone was aware of the difficulties it posed for daily living. Hence this proverb advises walking (that is, behaving) with integrity even if that means remaining bereft of inherited status, powerless ("poor"), rather than lying to improve one's lot. ▶**Rich and Poor**. Such is the behavior of a fool. He may think he has improved his lot, but it will end in disappointment.

**19:2** NRSV "desire" translates the Hebrew *nepeš* (throat, life, person, etc.) appropriately (see Prov. 20:3; 13:4, 25; 16:26). It relates to the heart–eyes symbolic body zone of the human person, the zone of emotion-fused thinking, understanding, knowing. The second line relates to the hands–feet symbolic body zone of the human person, the zone of purposeful action: here walking too swiftly, etc. One might also relate "desire" to the mouth–ears symbolic body zone, straddling two zones. ▶Three-Zone Personality. Thus the proverb cautions a person to act not only with complete knowledge but with caution, slowly and deliberately, so as not to miss the goal.

**19:4** In traditional peasant society, the wealthy constituted perhaps two but not more than ten percent of the population. The remainder were poor. ▶Rich and Poor: as others escape it. Poor is a revolving category. Some are falling into it as other escape it on a revolving basis (see Malina 2007: 15-36). As already noted frequently in this book, these are not primarily or principally economic markers. However, in this proverb it is important to remember that the wealthy, that is, those who had surplus, were expected to share it with others, to be patrons. ▶Patronage. They have many friends for two reasons: the poor seek patronage from the wealthy, and the wealthy increase their number of "friends" by being gracious to them. The literal Hebrew of the second line is poignant: the poor man's "friend [singular!] deserts him." Why would anyone want to be associated with a powerless person of no means?

**19:5** The language of this proverb clearly refers to the realm of the law court. NRSV "false witness" is literally "lying witness." The second line speaks of a "spouter of lies," a phrase common in Proverbs (Prov. 6:19; 14:5, 25; 19:9). ▶Lying. Lying was such an integral and acceptable element of MENA culture that it even affected judicial proceedings. One way of understanding the lie is that the liar says what the other person wants or expects to hear. As friend of the accused, the lying witness says what his friend wants to hear. Thus this proverb seeks to assure those who suffer injustice because of lying witnesses that the latter will not prevail. They will not escape or go free (Prov. 6:29; 11:21; 16:5; 17:5; 19:9; 28:20).

**19:6** The association of "generous" (person) with "giver of gifts" describes a wealthy person who fulfills his cultural obligation to be a patron. ▶**Patronage.** When the needy recognize such a person they do indeed seek his favor, which literally in Hebrew is to "stroke the face." The phrase belongs to the semantic field of honor, which means that those who hope to obtain largesse from this generous person sing his praises far and wide, thus broadcasting his honor to a wide audience. It ensures success for the petitioner and gains an increase of status for the benefactor. The proverb is not necessarily a critique of would-be beneficiaries.

**19:7** The text of the third line is corrupt and the Hebrew uncertain. The couplet that remains is an *a fortiori* statement: "if . . . how much more." The word "hate" does not describe an emotion. Rather, it connotes a preference for someone or something else (compare Matt. 10:37 and Luke 14:26; Prov. 11:15; 25:17). Those who prefer someone other than the poor man are literally "all the brothers." If poverty is a loss of status, a condition of powerlessness, the topic here is an adult family member whose situation shames the rest of the family. ▶**Rich and Poor.** Hence they separate themselves from him. Sadly, no brother acts as "redeemer" for him. (See comment on Prov. 17:17; 18:24.) All the more do friends keep their distance or even desert him. Such a person can only rely on God (Ps. 22:11). The proverb states reality and serves as a warning to avoid falling into poverty and thus losing one's inherited status.

**19:8** NRSV "wisdom" translates the Hebrew "heart," the symbolic body zone of emotion-fused thinking, understanding, hence wisdom. ▶**Three-Zone Personality.** The Hebrew word translated "oneself" is *nepeš* (throat; self, etc.). Thus the proverb clearly reflects the cultural understanding of body parts endowed with symbolic meaning. The vocabulary also reveals how intimately connected wisdom is with the total human person. Those who achieve understanding do themselves a real favor ("love themselves"). It is the key to happiness and success. "To keep understanding" is the technical language of formal instruction, education (see Prov. 5:2; 7:1-3). The one who pursues such instruction will indeed prosper (Prov. 16:20; 17:20: 18:22).

**19:9** See comment on 19:5. This proverb seeks to assure people falsely accused that false witnesses and liars will get their just deserts, if not in court then from God.

**19:11** See comment on Prov. 14:17, 29. In a culture whose core value is honor, or good reputation, always under threat from spontaneous outbursts of anger, this proverb reminds a person of the value of self-restraint. In particular, one can avoid serious consequences by choosing to ignore a challenge to one's honor (Prov. 10:12; 15:18; 17:9).

**19:13** Sirach 30:7-13 spells out the nature of the ruin a stupid son (NRSV "child") can inflict on his father. The positive description of an honorable son in Sir. 30:1-6, which obviously does not apply to a stupid son, fills out the picture of ruin. To this is added the picture of a "quarrelsome" wife. The JPS translation "nagging" intimates that she is quarreling with her husband. Given the gender-division of space in MENA culture and polygamy (one husband/many wives), it is perhaps preferable to assign the quarrels to rival wives rather than to husband and wife. Husband and wife (or wives) do not occupy the same space and rarely spend time together.

**19:14** The compiler of the book of Proverbs may have intentionally placed this aphorism here to contrast with v. 13. However, if we consider the advice on its own terms, the sense is that inheritance is assured because of the good management skills of the father (NRSV "parents"). However, the good character of a wife is a gift from God. In MENA cultures where marriages are arranged by the mother and father, each plays a distinctive role. Since boys and girls are raised together by the mother and all the women, it is they who determine the match. They are presumed to know the character of the prospective partners quite well. The father, the public face of the family, announces the match to the community. However, only God can read hearts (1 Sam. 16:7) and know the true character of a person. This same God, acting through the parents (who themselves were matched by their parents), can select well-suited partners or, from this proverb's perspective, choose a prudent or capable wife for the prospective husband. (See comment on Prov. 18:22.)

**19:15** NRSV "idle person" translates the Hebrew "idle *nepeš.*" Throughout the book of Proverbs the consequences of laziness are highlighted. Industriousness in agrarian societies is a matter of life and death, hence laziness is criticized and rejected. (See comment on Prov. 12:11.)

**19:16** "Commandment" in this proverb probably refers to the instructions of a teacher (see Prov. 4:4; 7:2). NRSV "will live" in Hebrew is "keeps his own *nepeš* [soul]." ▶ **Nepeš/soul.** Following this wisdom (or not) is a choice between life and death, typical advice in Proverbs.

**19:17** Recall that wealth and poverty are not primarily or principally economic designations in the Bible. They rather point to status, reputation, and honor-rating (Malina 1986a; 2001a; 2001b). ▶ **Rich and Poor.** However, the reference here may well be to those lacking means, since the language of the proverb is that of usury (lending, repayment). God identifies so closely with these poor and powerless as to repay their debts (see Prov. 14:31; 17:5).

**19:18** See comment on Prov. 13:24. The Hebrew literally says "discipline your son," reflecting the cultural practice of resorting to physical discipline in rearing him. The reason for this advice is that sons are raised by the women in the women's quarters with little to no influence from the father until puberty, when the son enters the man's world. They are privileged, pampered, and spoiled by the women. Hence fathers must now exact loyalty and obedience from the sons. Physical discipline teaches these effeminate boys how to be men. ▶ **Discipline.** Until puberty, boys live in the women's quarters. Don't know how to be a man, = gender ambiguity, no male role models, only women. The point is to administer discipline in order to bring about change in behavior, hence hope for the future. The second line advises moderation in discipline.

**19:19** The second line of this proverb is obscure and difficult to interpret. The first line once again describes the consequences of behaving violently, of not controlling one's temper. Whatever "penalty" may mean, there will be consequences for violent outbursts. This is an important reminder in an agonistic culture. ▶ **Agonism.**

**19:20** "Instruction" (Heb. *mûsār*) occurs more often in the book of Proverbs than elsewhere in the Bible. It means correction, discipline, rebuke, or even physical punishment by someone in command (God, father, human teacher, even "Wisdom"). ▶**Discipline.** The advice here is to listen, to be attentive and receptive in one's youth so that one might be a teacher later in life.

**19:21** See comment on Prov. 16:1, 9. In the final analysis the wise person will seek to do the will of God, that God's will may be established.

**19:22** As noted frequently in this book of MENA cultural analysis, lying was both an integral part of MENA societies and a source of great pain and frustration in day-to-day living. How could one know who was telling the truth, and when? The worst damage of lying was worked by perjury. A person calling God as witness would lie in a judicial proceeding (see Prov. 6:19; 14:5, 25; 19:9; 21:28). ▶**Lying.** Hence this proverb highlights loyalty (Hebrew: *ḥesed*) as the cultural value preferable to lying. Though one might lose the advantages gained from bribery by perjuring oneself, it is culturally preferable to be identified as loyal rather than as a liar.

**19:24** Humor in MENA societies is robust, indeed, ruthlessly teasing. This sense of humor is illustrated here and in related proverbs about laziness (Prov. 22:13; 26:13-16). It is intended to shame a person into being diligent and industrious rather than lazy. Youngsters quite likely heard this proverb and others similar to it many times as an incentive. The reference to the hands–feet and mouth–ears symbolic body zones demonstrates that laziness impacts the entire person, who does not seem to realize or care (heart–eyes symbolic body zone) that nourishment is essential to life. ▶**Three-Zone Personality.**

**19:25** While physical discipline is often a necessary goad to gaining wisdom in MENA culture, many learn from a simple word of exhortation. ▶**Discipline.** Scholars are not agreed on the precise meaning of "scoffer," but the simple person is inexperienced in life, prone to foolish behavior that risks disastrous consequences. However, unlike the scoffer, the simple person is amenable to persuasion by the experience of others and can gain wisdom (Prov. 21:11).

**19:26** This proverb deals with a wicked son. NRSV "children" implicitly imputes to daughters a power they do not have in MENA culture. The repetition of similar proverbs (Prov. 20:20; 28:24; 30:11) despite God's commandment (Exod. 20:12; Deut. 5:16) indicates that such brazen behavior was probably more common that one might imagine. What exactly did this wicked son do? The most likely explanation is that the parents are old and no longer able to manage the family property (the patrimony, the inheritance). In agrarian society, land, the patrimony, was at the heart of a family's survival. To jeopardize it or, worse yet, to lose it would be calamitous. The son, therefore, does a good thing in taking it over before his father's death. However, the proverb indicates that this son evicts his parents (or at least his mother), which is quite difficult to imagine. Where would they go? Who would care for them? Perhaps the best interpretation is to consider this proverb as describing the depth of shameful and disgraceful behavior by son toward his parents. The Latin dictum states: *qui potest plus, potest etiam et minus*: A person who can do the worst is also capable of lesser evils. Thus the wicked son who behaves shamefully would be one who robs his father of due honor and respect and causes his mother to separate herself from him. This is how Rashi (a twelfth-century French rabbi) translates the proverb : "A son who causes shame and disgrace robs his father, puts his mother to flight." **(See Jewish Study Bible, a.v.)**

**19:27** This is a very puzzling proverb, challenging to translate and interpret. NRSV follows the Jewish tradition based on Rashi: "My son, cease to stray from words of knowledge to hear discipline." The majority of scholars, however, offer a different translation: "My son, stop attending to correction; start straying from wise words." They interpret the proverb as biting irony. It is a sarcastic piece of advice not intended to be taken literally, at face value. Culturally, the ironic interpretation makes good sense. It is ruthless teasing (see comment on Prov. 19:24 above) that one might expect from father to son, or teacher to disciple.

**19:28** Once again the setting is judicial. NRSV "worthless" translates the literal Hebrew "Belial" (see comment on Prov. 16:27; compare NRSV 1 Kgs. 21:10, which translates this word as "scoundrels"). Perhaps a preferable rendition would be "malicious." Justice in Hebrew is *mišpat*. Israel recognized that the poor, indeed every person, has rights (*mišpatîm*; see Isa. 10:2; Job 36:6) that must be respected and honored, even by God (Job 34:5). To mock that is akin to blasphemy. Why does the malicious witness behave this way? He relishes iniquity as he enjoys food. The aphorism concentrates on the mouth–ears symbolic body zone. ▶**Three-Zone Personality**.

**19:29** The translation of the first line masks the passive voice, here the "theological" or "divine" passive. Just as fools merit flogging, so those who scoff at divine justice will receive divine punishment. God will not be mocked.

## Proverbs 20:1-30

1 Wine is a mocker, strong drink a brawler,
   and whoever is led astray by it is not wise.
2 The dread anger of a king is like the growling of a lion;
   anyone who provokes him to anger forfeits life itself.
3 It is honorable to refrain from strife,
   but every fool is quick to quarrel.
4 The lazy person does not plow in season;
   harvest comes, and there is nothing to be found.
5 The purposes in the human mind are like deep water,
   but the intelligent will draw them out.
6 Many proclaim themselves loyal,
   but who can find one worthy of trust?
7 The righteous walk in integrity—
   happy are the children who follow them!
8 A king who sits on the throne of judgment
   winnows all evil with his eyes.
9 Who can say, "I have made my heart clean;
   I am pure from my sin"?
10 Diverse weights and diverse measures
   are both alike an abomination to the Lord.

11 Even children make themselves known by their acts,
   by whether what they do is pure and right.
12 The hearing ear and the seeing eye—
   the Lord has made them both.
13 Do not love sleep, or else you will come to poverty;
   open your eyes, and you will have plenty of bread.
14 "Bad, bad," says the buyer,
   then goes away and boasts.
15 There is gold, and abundance of costly stones;
   but the lips informed by knowledge are a precious jewel.
16 Take the garment of one who has given surety for a stranger;
   seize the pledge given as surety for foreigners.
17 Bread gained by deceit is sweet,
   but afterward the mouth will be full of gravel.
18 Plans are established by taking advice;
   wage war by following wise guidance.
19 A gossip reveals secrets;
   therefore do not associate with a babbler.
20 If you curse father or mother,
   your lamp will go out in utter darkness.
21 An estate quickly acquired in the beginning
   will not be blessed in the end.
22 Do not say, "I will repay evil";
   wait for the Lord, and he will help you.
23 Differing weights are an abomination to the Lord,
   and false scales are not good.
24 All our steps are ordered by the Lord;
   how then can we understand our own ways?
25 It is a snare for one to say rashly, "It is holy,"
   and begin to reflect only after making a vow.
26 A wise king winnows the wicked,
   and drives the wheel over them.
27 The human spirit is the lamp of the Lord,
   searching every innermost part.
28 Loyalty and faithfulness preserve the king,
   and his throne is upheld by righteousness.
29 The glory of youths is their strength,
   but the beauty of aged is their gray hair.
30 Blows that wound cleanse away evil;
   beatings make clean the innermost parts.

*Textual Notes: 20:1-30*

**20:1** Some scholars translate NRSV "strong drink" as "beer" (Heb. *šēkār*).

While beer was produced in Egypt and Mesopotamia, it was not as common as wine in ancient Israel (Broshi 2001: 145, 165; Teachout 1986). The Hebrew word is best understood as a generic reference to all kinds of intoxicating drinks. This proverb attempts to discourage immoderate drinking by noting its consequences: disrespect for others ("scoffer"), carousing ("brawler"), and staggering ("led astray"—see Isa. 28:7). Similar warnings are repeated elsewhere in Proverbs (Prov. 23:19-21, 29-35; 31:4-5). Sad experience, however, would seem to be the best teacher in this regard. On the other hand, a later Judaic tradition concerning the celebration of Purim advises: "A man is obligated to drink on Purim until he no longer knows [the difference] between cursed [be] Haman and blessed [be] Mordecai" (b. Meg. 7b). ▶Normative Inconsistency. The point here, however, is how a wise man should behave.

**20:3** See comment on Prov. 15:18. ▶Agonism. An honorable person (literally "man") knows both how to avoid strife and how to curtail it if it has broken out. The fool prefers to be contentious (Prov. 15:18; 17:14; 18:6; 22:10). The word translated "quarrel" can also mean "lawsuit."

**20:4** See comment on Prov. 12:11. Here is yet another proverb criticizing laziness. That person will have nothing to reap (or eat!) at harvest time. Implicit in this proverb is the fact that the lazy person's entire family will suffer, since individualism is not a value in MENA cultures. ▶Collectivistic Society. The harvest time is August and September. Thus the time to plow ("in season") is after the early rains that fall in October–November (see Pilch 1999: 178–83).

**20:5** See comment on Prov. 18:4. The phrase "human mind" is literally in Hebrew "the heart of a man," referring to the heart–eyes symbolic body zone of the human body. ▶Three-Zone Personality. Since only God can read the human heart (1 Sam. 16:7), human beings are left with the challenge of drawing these purposes out and expressing them in words. The reference can be to the wise person or to another whom the wise person tries to understand.

**20:6** In MENA culture, a common exercise is "making oneself out to be (something)." Excess, exaggeration, and embellishment serve to establish and enhance the self-image one wants to project to others. This proverb is a reminder that in MENA society a person will "make himself out to be" loyal, trustworthy, faithful. The Hebrew word used in the first line, *ḥesed*, describes a characteristic of God: steadfast lovingkindness (see Deut. 7:9), which God's creatures ought to imitate. The question in the second line ("who can find . . . ?") expects a negative answer. In other words, such a person is either impossible to find in actuality, or at least rare. From another perspective, MENA cultures know full well the difference between the ideal (a truly faithful friend) and the real (many "who make themselves out" to be such). ▶ **Normative Inconsistency**.

**20:7** This proverb recounts what a "holy man" (NRSV "righteous," Heb. *ṣaddiq*) can expect as his patrimony: sons (NRSV "children") who follow in his footsteps. The Israelite tradition recognized two kinds of "holy men": the *ṣaddiq*, who kept the minimum requirements, and the *ḥasid*, who went beyond to make certain he kept the minimum. Each had an honorable status (Pilch 2011: 149). This proverb further expects that the sons of a holy man will be similarly honorable; they will, as it were, inherit his righteousness. Of course, this simplistic view was always troubling, since human experience did not always confirm the observation (see Jer. 31:29; Ezek. 18:1-20). NRSV "happy" translates the Hebrew *'ašrê*, which should more properly be rendered "honorable" or "truly honorable" (See Hanson 1994: 81–111; Prov. 3:18; 8:32, 34; 14:21; 16:20; 20:7; 28:14; 29:18; 31:28).

**20:8** Judgment and eyes refer to the heart–eyes symbolic body zone. ▶ **Three-Zone Personality**. Acting on behalf of God, the king separates the wicked from the just. His office entails the God-given ability to perform this duty properly (see 1 Kgs. 3:9-12, 16-28).

**20:9** A clear reference to the eyes–heart symbolic body zone as well as the hands–feet symbolic body zone ("sin" considered as deeds). ▶ **Three-Zone Personality**. The question anticipates a negative response. The proverb is a sobering corrective to the pervasive distinction in the book of Proverbs between the righteous and the wicked. Only God knows the true human condition (1 Sam. 16:7; Prov.

16:2; 21:2), something unattainable by the anti-introspective MENA personality.

**20:10** See comment on Prov. 11:1. Literally this proverb says: "a stone and a stone, an ephah and an ephah," echoing Deut. 25:13-16. Dishonest merchants used different measures in buying and selling. The critical point is that cheating others is "an abomination to the Lord" (see also Prov. 20:23). To appreciate this proverb one needs to remember that kinship is central in MENA societies. ▶**Kinship**. No one outside the family deserves truth, justice, fairness. The merchant thus behaves according to the cultural expectations. However, given the cultural conviction of limited goods, everyone tries to manage limited resources responsibly. ▶**Limited Good**. The buyer will benefit from fair prices and so will the seller. The buyer will be able to purchase more goods, and the seller will make more sales. Affirming that this dishonest practice is an abomination to the Lord is expected to motivate merchants to behave honestly.

**20:11** The Hebrew of the first line can be interpreted in two ways: "even a lad [Hebrew *nāʿar*] *reveals himself* in his deeds" (so the NRSV), or, "even a lad can *playact* in his deeds." The latter is linguistically and culturally preferable. The proverb is cast in *a fortiori* terms. "If a young man behaves this way, imagine how an adult will behave." MENA culture is fond of "making oneself out to be (something)" (see comment on Prov. 20:6). Individuals become very good at such pretense, which explains why no one believes it is possible to know another well at all. Human beings can only judge by externals; hence the popularity of playacting. Right deeds are the externals. There is no way to tell the true nature of a person. Only God can read hearts (1 Sam. 16:7).

**20:12** Two symbolic body zones are mentioned: mouth–ears (zone of self-expressive speech) and heart–eyes (emotion-fused thinking). The third zone (hands–feet, purposeful activity) is attributed to God, giving a clue to the meaning of this proverb. ▶**Three-Zone Personality**. While the human senses of hearing and seeing are key to attaining wisdom, they will succeed only if they attend to God, the creator of both. God is the source through which true wisdom can be gained.

**20:13** Explicitly, this proverb refers to the heart–eyes symbolic body zone, but implicitly it also includes the hands–feet, purposeful activity. ▶**Three-Zone Personality.** The one who loves sleep presumably does this in the daytime when he or she should be working. Instead, such a one will literally lose property or inheritance (NRSV: "come to poverty"). The imperative "open your eyes" urges a person to stay alert and keep busy, with the result that there will be plenty of food, thanks to due diligence.

**20:14** While a Western reader considers this a humorous observation about the market, a MENA teacher views it as important training for a young person, who must learn how to manage scarce resources. For the most part peasants strive for self-sufficiency and meet their basic needs by bartering (Oakman 1986: 65–67). ▶**Economy.** When bartering was not an option, the peasant had to commute a portion of his grain (or other materials) into money in order to pay rents and taxes and purchase goods. This might cost three-tenths of his production, leaving the remainder to sustain the family. Money, therefore, had to go a long way, and this proverb explains how to maximize its utility. In bargaining with a merchant one should try to negotiate a lower price, perhaps by decrying the value of the goods in question. If successful, the buyer will of course boast of his abilities, since it adds to his honorable reputation as a shrewd buyer and a caring provider for his family.

**20:16** Three people are involved in this proverb: (1) the stranger, whose trustworthiness is being guaranteed; (2) the guarantor, who gives his garment to the creditor to assure that the stranger will repay the debt (see Deut. 24:10-13); and (3) the creditor, the one making the loan. The proverb is addressed to the creditor: seize the garment! This caution against giving surety for a debtor is repeated a number of times in this book (Prov. 6:1-4; 11:15; 17:18; 22:26-27; 27:13; see comment on Prov. 11:15). The apparent conflict of this proverb with Deuteronomy is an example of MENA culture's distinction between the ideal

(Deuteronomy) and reality (Proverbs). (See comment on Prov. 12:17; 13:7-8; 18:19). ▶ **Normative Inconsistency.**

**20:17** The Hebrew phrase "bread of deceit" (NRSV "bread gained by deceit") can mean any material benefit (food, sustenance, livelihood) gained by dishonest means. However, much as in Prov. 4:17, this aphorism more likely refers to wicked deeds themselves, which give pleasure to the perpetrator (see Job 20:12-16). Thus what appears superficially to be a reference to the mouth–ears symbolic body zone actually refers to hands–feet (activity, deeds). ▶ **Three-Zone Personality.**

**20:18** This proverb is not at all about war, but rather about following advice and guidance in the struggle to succeed in day-to-day living (see Prov. 11:14; 15:22; 24:6). Thus it refers to the well-functioning heart–eyes symbolic body zone (advice and guidance) so that the hands–feet symbolic body zone (human activity) may be effective and salutary. ▶ **Three-Zone Personality.**

**20:19** See comment on Prov. 11:13. NRSV "gossip" is better rendered "one who slanders others" or something similar (Lev. 19:16). The prohibition "do not associate" is cast in the same Hebrew form as the commands of the Decalogue, indicating the seriousness of the warning. The aphorism makes clear reference to the mouth–ears symbolic body zone and the potentially damaging consequences of its slander. ▶ **Three-Zone Personality.**

**20:20-21** In the ancient world, cursing someone or something was not just wishing evil; rather, the words spoken irretrievably set in motion the evil intended (see Josh. 29:9-10; Ps. 62:4; Neh. 13:2; Job 24:18; Kitz 2014). Though it was long associated with word-magic, recent linguistic research identifies the curse as an "illocution," that is, an "institutionalized" performative utterance that depends on many subtle conditions to be effective (Thiselton 2006: 811). Whatever these conditions might have been, the deed itself merited the death penalty in the Torah (Exod. 21:17; Lev. 20:9; Deut. 27:16). Some scholars see a clue to the nature of the curse in the following proverb. A son scheming greedily or hastily to gain his inheritance (by requesting it before the proper time [Luke 15:12] or depriving parents of its benefits [Mark 7:11-12]) effectively curses his father and/or mother.

**20:22** More than once in our book we have noted that the court system in ancient Israel was not a guarantee that justice would be done (see comments on Prov. 12:17; 14:5; 17:15; 18:17; 19:5). One remedy was to work an out-of-court settlement if possible. This proverb, however, describes a situation in which a wronged person determines to seek justice on his own: "I will repay evil." The proverb echoes God's promise (Deut. 32:35-36) and urges patience to wait for God to redress the injustice. However, this proverb may be another instance of stating the ideal in full awareness that a different course will be taken in reality (Deut. 19:16-21). ▶**Normative Inconsistency.**

**20:23** See comment on v. 10 above.

**20:24** The first line is identical with (and perhaps a quotation from) the Hebrew of Ps. 37:23. The context of that psalm indicates that God leads a person along the right paths, and nothing is said about the person being unaware of the plan. The second line of this proverb begins with "how," which often suggests something is impossible (see Num. 23:8; 1 Sam. 10:27; Job 9:2; 25:4; 31:1). Thus the proverb seems to be a lament that it is impossible for a person to understand God's plan for life (see Jer. 10:23; Prov. 16:9). This is perfectly understandable—though stressful—in the peasant world. All theology is based on analogy. The peasant has no control over any part of his or her life; others do. If this is the experience with human beings, how much more is it true of experience with God?

**20:25** See comment on Prov. 20:21 above. Again the reference is to the mouth–ears symbolic body zone, the zone of self-expressive speech. ▶**Three-Zone Personality.** In the ancient world words were considered powerful and effective. They could not be retracted (see Isa. 55:10-11). Scripture reports the poignant story of Jephthah, whose vow cost him his only daughter (Judg. 11:19-40), a story quite likely known by those to whom this proverb would be addressed. Though the advice might seem commonsensical to a Western reader, in MENA societies people often speak before they think. These cultures prize spontaneity over planned and calculated activity, a preference that often results in disastrous consequences.

**20:27** This proverb alludes to Gen. 2:7, where God breathed into the first human's nostrils so that it became a living being. That breath/ spirit of God is a lamp that illuminates the human interior so that God is able to scrutinize every part. Given the non- and anti-introspective nature of this ancient MENA society, it is less plausible to identify the lamp as the human conscience that manifests a person's inner working to himself or herself. Only God can read the inner recesses of a human being (1 Sam. 16:7).

**20:29** On its face this proverb appears to be a simple observation. Youths have strength; the aged have reached old age (gray hair) thanks to living a righteous life (see Prov. 16:31). However, it can be interpreted as claiming superiority for age, since strength eventually diminishes, whereas long life is considered a reward for righteousness. A couple of cultural observations may be pertinent. One: Lifespan in the ancient world was typically not long; perhaps only three percent made it to their sixties. Few even lived into their thirties. ▶ **Age.**

Two: in contemporary Western medical research a person with fifty percent gray hair before the age of fifty is considered to have premature graying. However, this condition by itself has no bearing on morbidity or mortality (Glasser 1991). On the other hand, when coupled with other established coronary risk factors, graying of hair, male baldness, and facial wrinkling indicate an additional risk of myocardial infarction (Schnohr et al. 1995). None of this medical information, however, is applicable to the biblical record. As frequently repeated in this book, the heart was interpreted as a symbolic body zone in the Bible rather than as an important organ in the human body. ▶**Three-Zone Personality.** The early-third-century BCE Hellenistic thinker Erasistratus first understood the heart as a pump for blood in the human body, but none of his work survives except in Galen's critiques. Premature graying of the hair can of itself be caused by vitiligo, a non-life-threatening condition that afflicted the late pop singer Michael Jackson.

**20:30** The Hebrew text is obscure and scholars are not agreed on the interpretation of this proverb. In general it seems to claim that physical blows purify one's inmost being, but it does not explain how. Nevertheless, it tallies with the general cultural approval of physical discipline as an acceptable method of building the character of a young man. ▶Discipline.

## Proverbs 21:1-31

1 The king's heart is a stream of water in the hand of the Lord;
   he turns it wherever he will.
2 All deeds are right in the sight of the doer,
   but the Lord weighs the heart.
3 To do righteousness and justice
   is more acceptable to the Lord than sacrifice.
4 Haughty eyes and a proud heart—
   the lamp of the wicked—are sin.
5 The plans of the diligent lead surely to abundance,
   but everyone who is hasty comes only to want.
6 The getting of treasures by a lying tongue
   is a fleeting vapor and a snare of death.
7 The violence of the wicked will sweep them away,
   because they refuse to do what is just.
8 The way of the guilty is crooked,
   but the conduct of the pure is right.
9 It is better to live in a corner of the housetop
   than in a house shared with a contentious wife.
10 The souls of the wicked desire evil;
   their neighbors find no mercy in their eyes.
11 When a scoffer is punished, the simple become wiser;
   when the wise are instructed, they increase in knowledge.
12 The Righteous One observes the house of the wicked;
   he casts the wicked down to ruin.
13 If you close your ear to the cry of the poor,
   you will cry out and not be heard.
14 A gift in secret averts anger,
   and a concealed bribe in the bosom, strong wrath.
15 When justice is done, it is a joy to the righteous,
   but dismay to evildoers.
16 Whoever wanders from the way of understanding
   will rest in the assembly of the dead.
17 Whoever loves pleasure will suffer want;

whoever loves wine and oil will not be rich.
18 The wicked is a ransom for the righteous,
and the faithless for the upright.
19 It is better to live in a desert land
than with a contentious and fretful wife.
20 Precious treasure remains in the house of the wise,
but the fool devours it.
21 Whoever pursues righteousness and kindness
will find life and honor.
22 One wise person went up against a city of warriors
and brought down the stronghold in which they trusted.
23 To watch over mouth and tongue
is to keep out of trouble.
24 The proud, haughty person, named "Scoffer,"
acts with arrogant pride.
25 The craving of the lazy person is fatal,
for lazy hands refuse to labor.
26 All day long the wicked covet,
but the righteous give and do not hold back.
27 The sacrifice of the wicked is an abomination;
how much more when brought with evil intent.
28 A false witness will perish,
but a good listener will testify successfully.
20 The wicked put on a bold face,
but the upright give thought to their ways.
30 No wisdom, no understanding,
no counsel, can avail against the Lord.
31 The horse is made ready for the day of battle,
but the victory belongs to the Lord.

*Textual Notes: 21:1-31*

**21:1** God controls the *heart* of the king, the symbolic body-zone of emotion-fused thinking. ▶ **Three-Zone Personality**. As the stream of water fertilizes the arid land and is thus beneficial, God's control of waters and the king's heart is also beneficial (see Isa. 32:2).

**21:2** This proverb reflects the hands–feet (NRSV: "deeds," literal Hebrew "ways") and heart–eyes symbolic body-zones of a person ("sight," "heart"). ▶ **Three-Zone Personality**. However, as previously noted in this book, non-introspective MENA persons are easily deceived or mistaken. Only God can read hearts (1 Sam. 16:7; see comment on Prov. 16:2).

**21:3** The virtues of righteousness (ṣedāqā) and justice (mišpāṭ) are frequently linked in the Bible (see Prov. 2:9; 8:20). As this proverb notes, God cherishes them more than sacrifice (see Prov. 15:8; 21:27), as the prophet Samuel instructed Saul (1 Sam. 15:22). In a culture that accepts secrecy, deception, and lying as legitimate strategies in the service of honor, the qualities of righteousness and justice are eagerly desired because they are not common. ▶**Lying.** (On righteousness, see the introductory comment on Proverbs 10; on justice, see the comment on Prov. 13:23; 19:28.)

**21:4** Scholars recognize that the two lines of this proverb do not quite fit together. The first line is incomplete but describes the heart–eyes symbolic body zone of a wicked person ("haughty eyes"). ▶**Three-Zone Personality.** "Lamp of the wicked" in the second line is obscure. The Hebrew word translated "lamp" can be read as "tilled or cultivated land" (see Prov. 13:23). Whichever reading one accepts, the point is that either one will fail. The Hebrew word translated "sin" actually means to "miss the mark" (ḥaṭṭā't). This word of consolation assures that the wicked—either his household or his tilled land—will come to naught.

**21:5** People in MENA cultures tend to act spontaneously, without thought of the consequences. The hope is that some relative or friend will intervene if a person is hastily taking a course of action that can have damaging consequences. Thus this proverb is a caution against unreflective haste. Careful planning and calculated activity result in profit, haste results in loss.

**21:6** Once again, the Sage highlights the foolishness of lying. ▶**Lying.** The aphorism speaks of the misuse of the mouth–ears symbolic body-zone. ▶**Three-Zone Personality.** Anything of value obtained by lying is vanity (NRSV "fleeting vapor"; same Hebrew word as Eccl. 1:1) and potentially dangerous. The implication is that a party who suffers loss by this deceit will seek revenge. It is best not to run the risk.

**21:7** MENA cultures are agonistic, that is, prone to violence (Pilch 1997). ▶**Agonism**. The wicked who refuse to behave justly but rather engage in violence will eventually be caught up in it like fish in a net (see Hab. 1:15). The aphorism urges resisting the cultural tendency toward violence because it will inevitably harm the perpetrator.

**21:8** The Hebrew of this proverb is challenging to understand and translate. NRSV contrasts the behavior of the guilty (the Hebrew word is rare and obscure) with that of the pure (Hebrew *zak*, root of the name Zacchaeus ["Mr. Pure"], Luke 19:1-10). An alternative rendition of the aphorism seems preferable: "One's path may be winding and unfamiliar, but one's conduct is blameless and right" (NABRE).This is yet another reminder that people in non-introspective MENA cultures tend to judge others by externals (1 Sam. 16:7). This is at the root of the concept of the symbolic body zones that permeates the Bible. ▶**Three-Zone Personality**. But appearances are deceiving, and this strategy is unreliable. Given these limits on human perception and judgment, one should be very careful.

**21:9** This aphorism is repeated in Prov. 25:24, and the topic of a nagging wife is also treated in Prov. 21:19; 19:13; and 27:15. See comment on Prov. 19:13. While the reference in each case is to a wife (singular), the situation might plausibly be one of rival wives (e.g., Gen. 16:5-6; 1 Sam. 1:6). Given the gender-based division of space in ancient MENA dwellings, with women living in the women's quarters and spending precious little time with the husband, the quarrels and nagging plausibly occur between the women (Gregg 2005: 204; Eickleman 2002: 140–67). Clifford's proposal to replace "house shared" with "noisy house" on the basis of Akkadian enhances the import of this proverb (Clifford 1999: 190). Men spend most of their time outdoors anyway, hence the hyperbolic expressions in these proverbs (corner of a roof-top; wilderness).

**21:10** NRSV "souls" in this instance might preferably be translated "appetite" (compare the translations in Prov. 10:3; 13:2, 4). ▶ **Nepeš/ soul**. The reference once more is to the heart–eyes symbolic body zone. ▶**Three-Zone Personality**. This is a good link with "eyes" in the second line. The point of this observation is that wicked people are so obsessed with evil that they neglect their neighbor. In Hebrew there is an onomatopoetic connection between "evil" and "neighbor," a play on words much appreciated in this culture.

**21:13** It is important to remember that wealth and poverty are not primarily or principally economic designations in the Bible. They rather point to inherited status, reputation, honor-rating (Malina 1986a; 2001a; 2001b). ▶**Rich and Poor.** The poor person in this proverb is seeking help, quite likely from someone capable of and expected to give it (next of kin, patron, and the like). The cultural obligation incumbent on persons with surplus is to share it with the needy. For a person of means to ignore such a cry is damnable. Given that peasants in general have limited means and often live at the margin of subsistence themselves, they are notoriously selfish and reluctant to share. This proverb cautions that if a capable person ignores the plea, God in turn will not hear that one's request (the divine passive in the second line). For similar exhortations about the poor see Prov. 14:21, 31;17:5; 19:17; 22:9, 22-23; 28:27; Ps. 41:2.

**21:14** The topic of this proverb is allaying anger (literal Hebrew: nostril, face, nose) and wrath or strong rage. This is a common concern in an agonistic culture. ▶**Agonism.** Anger can lead to feuding, to violence, and perhaps eventually to bloodshed, which must be avoided at all costs. Hence the advice to resort to bribery.

**21:16** NRSV "assembly of the dead" translates the literal Hebrew "assembly of the Rephaim," that is, the inhabitants of Sheol (Ps. 88:11; Prov. 2:18; 9:18). It was not a place of punishment or pain and thus not equivalent to "hell" (Pilch 2012: 1-6). It was simply where the dead went. This proverb reprises a common theme from Proverbs 1–9, namely, choosing to walk along the correct path. To choose otherwise, as this proverb cautions, is to meet untimely and premature death.

**21:17** The key word in this proverb is "love." In MENA cultures this word does not carry emotional overtones. Rather, it means attachment or bonding, mainly to persons but also to other things including food (Gen. 27:4; Pilch and Malina 2009: 127–30). While wine and oil are staples in the Mediterranean diet, the association with "pleasure" (literally in Hebrew "joy") indicates a context of festivity (Eccl. 2:1, 2; 8:15; 9:7), especially banquets (Judg. 9:9, 13; Eccl. 9:7-8). Thus a man attached to or bonded with banquets will certainly not become wealthy but will lose what he has and suffer want.

**21:19** See comment on Prov. 21:9.

**21:20** Here is another contrast between the wise person and the fool. NRSV follows the Septuagint instead of the Hebrew, which reads "precious treasure and oil are in the wise man's dwelling." Precious treasure refers to fine wine (see 1 Chr. 27:27), thus again combining wine and oil as in v. 17. The point of the proverb is that a wise person knows how to manage and preserve precious resources, while the fool consumes them out of lack of understanding of a basic principle of peasant life: resources are finite in quantity and already distributed. There is no more where this came from. ▶ **Limited Good**.

**21:21** This proverb advises a person how to attain honor, the core cultural value of MENA societies, and life (see Prov. 8:18; 11:19; 12:28). ▶ **Honor and Shame**. The word "pursue" implies intense energy, dogged determination. To become a success in this cultural context by these standards requires due diligence.

**21:23** Here is yet another proverb dealing with the mouth–ears symbolic body-zone, the zone of self-expressive speech. ▶ **Three-Zone Personality**. This advice is repeated often in Proverbs. One must be careful about one's speech, for it will literally keep one's life (Hebrew *nepeš*) out of trouble; it will safeguard and preserve one's life.

**21:24** A plausible implicit context of this proverb might be Sir. 10:7: "Arrogance is hateful to the Lord and to mortals." The purpose of Proverbs is to form the culturally ideal person. Such a one would strive above all to please God and, of course, fellow mortals. Pride, arrogance, and haughtiness would be counterproductive. In other words, a "scoffer" ruins community.

**21:25** In pre-industrial agrarian society, peasants had to work very hard to support the family. All hands were necessary. Whoever was unwilling or refused to contribute to the family effort could suffer fatal consequences. The explicit reference is to the hands–feet symbolic body zone (hands, labor). ▶**Three-Zone Personality.** NRSV "craving" is literally appetite. The lazy man is not even willing to satisfy his hunger (see Prov. 13:4; 19:24).

**21:26** This proverb contrasts a greedy (NRSV: "wicked") person with a generous one. Since balanced reciprocity was a key strategy used daily by peasants to secure the necessities of life, a greedy or selfish person thwarts this strategy by refusing to enter into such dyadic relationships. ▶**Economy.** A righteous person, one who cares about the well-being of others and the entire community, enters freely into such exchanges since life itself depends on it.

**21:27** As noted in the comment on Prov. 15:8, this is the vocabulary of ritual, as in Deut. 7:25 (see also Prov. 11:1). Offerings made by people who displease God are abominations (see Isa. 1:10-17; 29:10). NRSV "how much more" is perhaps better translated "indeed," or "because." The second line would then explain why the liturgical sacrifices of incorrigibly wicked persons are abominations: because their intention (Hebrew *zimmâh,* calculation) is evil. Such a sacrifice is insincere, for the one offering it has no intention of reconciling with God. Perhaps it is just for show, for public consumption.

**21:28** See the comment on Prov. 19:5. Though many interpreters understand this proverb as contrasting a false witness with a truthful and reliable one, the reference to the "man who hears" (NRSV "good listener") in the second line may indicate a judicial setting (see Deut. 1:16, 17; 2 Sam. 14:17; 15:3; 1 Kgs. 3:11). It is the arbiter's decision that will endure (NRSV: "testify successfully").

**21:29** The contrast between the wicked and upright is presented in terms of the symbolic body-zones heart–eyes (face) and hands–feet (ways). ▶**Three-Zone Personality.** To put on a bold face is typical of MENA culture's practice of "making oneself out to be" (something), presenting a different "face" than one's authentic self (compare Prov. 7:13). This is obviously what a wicked person would do. Such a one feigns strength and determination and stubbornly pursues a course of action that has been insufficiently evaluated. The upright, in contrast, carefully consider their options and remain in control of their lives, their ways.

## Proverbs 22:1-16

1  A good name is to be chosen rather than great riches,
   and favor is better than silver or gold.
2  The rich and the poor have this in common:
   the Lord is the maker of them all.
3  The clever see danger and hide;
   but the simple go on, and suffer for it.
4  The reward for humility and fear of the Lord
   is riches and honor and life.
5  Thorns and snares are in the way of the perverse;
   the cautious will keep far from them.
6  Train children in the right way,
   and when old, they will not stray.
7  The rich rules over the poor,
   and the borrower is the slave of the lender.
8  Whoever sows injustice will reap calamity,
   and the rod of anger will fail.
9  Those who are generous are blessed,
   for they share their bread with the poor.
10 Drive out a scoffer, and strife goes out;
   quarreling and abuse will cease.
11 Those who love a pure heart and are gracious in speech
   will have the king as a friend.
12 The eyes of the Lord keep watch over knowledge,
   but he overthrows the words of the faithless.
13 The lazy person says, "There is a lion outside!
   I shall be killed in the streets!"
14 The mouth of a loose woman is a deep pit;
   he with whom the Lord is angry falls into it.
15 Folly is bound up in the heart of a boy,
   but the rod of discipline drives it far away.
16 Oppressing the poor in order to enrich oneself,
   and giving to the rich, will lead only to loss.

This segment of chapter 22 marks the end of the Solomonic collection. Proverbs 10:1–22:16 contains 375 proverbs (read in a single line instead of the format reported in NRSV and most translations). This is the numerical value of the Hebrew letters in the name "Solomon" reported in Prov. 10:1. **Since Arabic numerals are a contribution of the Arabs, other cultures used letters of the alphabet to stand for numbers.**

*Textual Notes: 22:1-16*

**22:1** As a collection of highly prized cultural values it is not surprising that the book of Proverbs ranks reputation and esteem (NRSV "favor") above wealth, silver, and gold. ▶**Honor and shame**. By definition, honor is a public claim to worth or value and a public acknowledgment of that claim. This is the essence of reputation ("good name") and favor ("esteem"—see Prov. 3:3-4; 13:15).

22:2 As frequently noted in this book, rich and poor are not primarily economic terms in ancient MENA societies. ▶**Rich and poor**. Basically, rich people have surplus and are obliged to share it—as patrons—with those in need. If a rich person does not share, the word *rich* should be translated and interpreted as "greedy." Poor people, on the other hand, are powerless or unable to fend for themselves. Thus the oppressed (politically unable), indigent (economically unable), sick and outcast (bodily and kinship unable), and unbelieving (religiously unable) need help from those with surplus (Malina 1986a: 154). This proverb emphasizes that both rich and poor are God's creatures deserving of respect (Prov. 14:31; 17:5; 29:13).

22:4 The syntax of this proverb is difficult. The word "and" is not in the Hebrew text. Thus some scholars translate: "the consequence or result of humbling is fear of the Lord, riches, honor, and life" (see Prov. 15:33; 18:12). ▶**Humility**. Humbling is a kind of self-deprecation, deliberately presenting oneself in a status lower than one deserves. This projects a message of neutrality, that is, not challenging the other person, who ought to respond by acknowledging the self-humbling person's rightful status. To behave this way relative to God is indeed "fear of the Lord," that is, revering God and acknowledging God's eminent status. God responds by endowing such a person with wealth, true honor, and indeed life. The proverb thus presents two cultural ideals: fear God, and always humble oneself. These gain the desired cultural rewards.

**22:5** NRSV "the cautious" translates the literal Hebrew "who guards his soul" (*nepeš*: the word can also mean "throat") ▶**Nepeš/soul.** thus relating to the mouth–ears symbolic body zone. ▶**Three-Zone Personality.** The import of the proverb, then, is quite serious. "Way" is common in Proverbs as a designation of one's life-journey. The perverse person's journey is filled with risk and threats, while the wise person is careful to preserve life.

**22:6** NRSV "children" is literally "boy, lad" in Hebrew. The proverb concerns the proper way for a father to train his son. While NRSV and other versions translate this proverb in a positive sense, the literal Hebrew gives pause: train the son "according to his way." Perhaps it is best to consider this an ironic piece of advice for a father, similar to Prov. 19:27. Leave the boy to his own designs and you will rue his adult behavior (see Sir. 30:7-11).

**22:7** Since the majority of the ancient world were indigent, they often had to seek assistance from those with surplus (the rich). **As noted, the poor was a revolving group. As some exited poverty, others fell into it.** As noted above (v. 2), the rich were expected to be patrons, that is, to treat clients as if they were kin, and thus to be generous with them. The client's obligation was to broadcast the generosity of the patron far and wide, thus expanding the patron's reputation (honor). But in some instances, if a patron could not be found, the needy person had to borrow with the obligation to repay. When this became impossible the borrower indeed became the literal slave of the lender. ▶**Rich and Poor.** In the contemporary world we would say "a word to the wise is sufficient."

**22:9** NRSV "generous" is literally in Hebrew "good of eye." It stands in contrast to the "evil eye," a belief common to MENA societies and forty-seven percent of the world's cultures today. ▶**Evil Eye.** Language about the evil eye is often translated "stingy," "miserly," "greedy," and the like. "Evil eye" rarely if ever appears in translations (Prov. 23:6; 28:22). It refers to the heart–eyes symbolic body zone. ▶**Three-Zone Personality.** The heart, which can generate good and evil intentions, projects its wishes through the eyes. "The eye is the lamp of the body" (Matt. 6:22-23), that is, it emanates what is in the heart (Gross 1999: 59–64). Thus this proverb praises the generosity of a person whom God blesses (divine passive) because she or he shares his or her limited resources with the poor.

**22:10** This proverb implies a community context disrupted by a scoffer (see Prov. 21:24). NRSV "quarreling" means bringing a lawsuit. Thus the scoffer dishonors (brings shame upon) others in the community either by threatening a lawsuit or by incessantly insulting them. ▶**Agonism.** Such a person must be ejected from the community.

**22:11** Commentators are not agreed on this verse because the Hebrew is so puzzling. However, from a cultural perspective the proverb relates to the heart–eyes and mouth–ears symbolic body zones. ▶**Three-Zone Personality.** A person in whom these zones are functioning well and appropriately will have easy access to people of power and authority.

**22:12** This proverb speaks of the Lord in terms of the symbolic body zones of heart–eyes ("eyes") and hands–feet ("overthrows") and of deceivers (NRSV "faithless") in terms of their heart–eyes ("knowledge") and mouth–ears ("words"). ▶**Three-Zone Personality.** Bernard de Géradon argues that the proper understanding of God creating human beings in the divine image and likeness ought not to be from the perspective of body and soul but rather from that of the three symbolic body zones (de Géradon 1974: 33–42). God, who alone can read hearts (1 Sam. 16:7), protects those who seek to live by wisdom and punishes their slanderers. In a culture where secrecy, deception, and lying are common acceptable strategies in human intercourse this proverb offers consoling information about God.

**22:13** Another humorous proverb about a lazy person (see Prov. 19:24; 26:13-15) who comes up with ridiculous excuses for not joining in the work of the family, so essential to the group's survival.

**22:14** The identity of this "loose woman" is not easy to determine: prostitute? wife of another? foreigner? However, the "loose woman" figures prominently in Proverbs 1–9, and in this verse the one with whom the Lord is angry will be seduced by her speech and be led to premature death.

**22:15** This is another of the proverbs recommending physical discipline in the raising of sons (Prov. 13:24; 22:26; 23:13; 29:15, 21).

**22:16** In this proverb "poor" and "rich" are very likely economic markers. Stealing from those who have little ("poor") in order to improve one's lot will only lead to personal loss, just as will offering bribes to the rich who may choose to ignore the petitioner and let him impoverish himself. ▶ **Rich and Poor.**

### III. Proverbs 22:17—24:22: The Words of the Wise

Scholars note that this segment of the book of Proverbs bears a striking relationship to an Egyptian work, *Instructions of Amenemope*, dating from around 1100 BCE. It existed before the Hebrew book of Proverbs and thus is not dependent on that work. Neither can the Hebrew work be considered dependent on the Egyptian work. Rather, both reflect a common tradition of educational literature known to Hebrew and Egyptian writers alike. Richard Clifford's commentary incorporates reflections on the *Instructions* into interpretations of Proverbs (Clifford 1999: 199–218). The clear relationship between the *Instructions* and Proverbs validates the anthropological decision to refer to this geographical region as MENA (Middle East and North Africa), a cultural continent sharing many elements in common. The culture of this region as reflected in these aphorisms continues to be the focus of our analysis.

The proverbs in this segment differ in form from those in the previous collection. The singular imperative dominates. This collection seems to have been a written (rather than oral) text for the student to study (Prov. 22:20). The students appear to be young men aspiring to public service, to becoming courtiers.

## Proverbs 22:17-29

17 The words of the wise: Incline your ear and hear my words,
and apply your mind to my teaching;
18 for it will be pleasant if you keep them within you,
if all of them are ready on your lips.
19 So that your trust may be in the Lord,
I have made them known to you today, yes, to you.
20 Have I not written for you thirty sayings
of admonition and knowledge,
21 to show you what is right and true,
so that you may give a true answer to those who sent you?
22 Do not rob the poor because they are poor,
or crush the afflicted at the gate;
23 for the Lord pleads their cause
and despoils of life those who despoil them.
24 Make no friends with those given to anger,
and do not associate with hotheads,
25 or you may learn their ways
and entangle yourself in a snare.
26 Do not be one of those who give pledges,
who become surety for debts.
27 If you have nothing with which to pay,
why should your bed be taken from under you?
28 Do not remove the ancient landmark
that your ancestors set up.
29 Do you see those who are skillful in their work?
they will serve kings;
they will not serve common people.

*Textual Notes: 22:17-29*

**22:17-21** Verses 17-18 of this prologue to the collection advise the student about the proper way to study: listen (ear, hear), memorize (apply your heart [NRSV mind]), reflect (keep them in your belly [NRSV within you]), and speak them as necessary. The three symbolic body zones are involved: mouth–ears, heart–eyes, and by implication hands–feet (speak, i.e., recall them for guidance in behavior). ▶ **Three-Zone Personality**. The student is to apply himself completely to this endeavor.

Verses 19-21 state the purpose of this teaching: to trust in the Lord.

The student must learn how to be a good messenger, reporting reliably what the sender and/or respondent want(s) to communicate. This describes the proper use of the mouth–ears symbolic body zone.

**22:22-23** Again it is important to recall that "poor" in the Bible is not primarily an economic indicator. (See comment on Prov. 17:5, but see also 22:16 above.) ►**Rich and Poor.** The poor are powerless and vulnerable, unable to defend themselves. "Poor" and "afflicted" are synonymous, though the latter term focuses more on helplessness. The "gate" in the Bible is the site for legal trials (Deut. 21:19; Amos 5:12; Prov. 24:7), hence the context of this advice is a judicial proceeding. "Cause" (Hebrew *rîb*) points to a legal case (Exod. 23:2, 3, 6; Deut. 21:5). The reason behind this advice is that God is the defense attorney for the poor and demands the death sentence for whoever robs them. Given the unreliability and unpredictability of law courts in antiquity, by leaving justice to God this proverb offers a powerful reason for behaving humanely and justly.

**22:24-25** The agonistic character of MENA cultures requires great restraint in keeping this cultural tendency in check. ►**Agonism.** In such a culture, normally conflict-prone, with the potential for violence and bloodshed, it takes great effort to overcome the tendency toward violence. Associating with unrestrained individuals and hotheads would only lead to trouble. (See comment on Prov. 15:18.)

**22:26-27** This advice appears often in Proverbs. (See comment on Prov. 11:15.) The cultural reason is belief in limited goods. ►**Limited Good.** The belief is that all goods are finite in quantity and already distributed. There simply is no more where this came from. Thus becoming a guarantor for the debt of another is risky. Most people slept on the floor, but archaeologists have found remnants of raised platforms (three or four feet wide and perhaps a foot off the floor) around a room. These served as divans during the day and beds at night. People did not undress to go to sleep in the ancient world. The prophet Amos railed against those who had extravagant beds (Amos 6:4).

**22:28** A more complete statement of this advice appears in Prov.

23:10-11. The cultural basis for this prohibition is the belief in limited good. ▶Limited Good. The land given by God is a finite quantity and already divided by the ancestors (literally "fathers"). The Law of Moses expressed this same prohibition (Deut. 19:14; 27:17; see comment on Prov. 15:25). Moving landmarks is theft.

### Proverbs 23:1-35

1 When you sit down to eat with a ruler,
   observe carefully what is before you,
2 and put a knife to your throat
   if you have a big appetite.
3 Do not desire the ruler's delicacies,
   for they are deceptive food.
4 Do not wear yourself out to get rich;
   be wise enough to desist.
5 When your eyes light upon it, it is gone;
   for suddenly it takes wings to itself,
   flying like an eagle toward heaven.
6 Do not eat the bread of the stingy;
   do not desire their delicacies;
7 for like a hair in the throat, so are they.
   "Eat and drink!" they say to you;
   but they do not mean it.
8 You will vomit up the little you have eaten,
   and you will waste your pleasant words.
9 Do not speak in the hearing of a fool,
   who will only despise the wisdom of your words.
10 Do not remove an ancient landmark
   or encroach on the fields of orphans,
11 for their redeemer is strong;
   he will plead their cause against you.
12 Apply your mind to instruction
   and your ear to words of knowledge.
13 Do not withhold discipline from your children;
   if you beat them with a rod, they will not die.
14 If you beat them with the rod,
   you will save their lives from Sheol.
15 My child, if your heart is wise,
   my heart too will be glad.
16 My soul will rejoice
   when your lips speak what is right.
17 Do not let your heart envy sinners,

but always continue in the fear of the Lord.
18 Surely there is a future,
   and your hope will not be cut off.
19 Hear, my child, and be wise,
   and direct your mind in the way.
20 Do not be among winebibbers,
   or among gluttonous eaters of meat;
21 for the drunkard and the glutton will come to poverty,
   and drowsiness will clothe them with rags.
22 Listen to your father who begot you,
   and do not despise your mother when she is old.
23 Buy truth, and do not sell it;
   buy wisdom, instruction, and understanding.
24 The father of the righteous will greatly rejoice;
   he who begets a wise son will be glad in him.
25 Let your father and mother be glad;
   let her who bore you rejoice.
26 My child, give me your heart,
   and let your eyes observe my ways.
27 For a prostitute is a deep pit;
   an adulteress is a narrow well.
28 She lies in wait like a robber
   and increases the number of the faithless.
29 Who has woe? Who has sorrow?
   Who has strife? Who has complaining?
   Who has wounds without cause?
   Who has redness of eyes?
30 Those who linger late over wine,
   those who keep trying mixed wines.
31 Do not look at wine when it is red,
   when it sparkles in the cup
   and goes down smoothly.
32 At the last it bites like a serpent,
   and stings like an adder.
33 Your eyes will see strange things,
   and your mind utter perverse things.
34 You will be like one who lies down in the midst of the sea,
   like one who lies on the top of a mast.
35 "They struck me," you will say, "but I was not hurt;
   they beat me, but I did not feel it.
   When shall I awake?
   I will seek another drink."

*Textual Notes: 23:1-35*

**23:1-3** Anthropologists identify meals in antiquity as "ceremonies." They were regular and predictable events in which roles and statuses in a community were affirmed or legitimated. ▶**Meals.** Thus this advice is less about etiquette than it is about appropriate behavior in a ceremony. A young, inexperienced courtier needs to learn the rules of the game. NRSV is misleading on two counts. First, the advice concerns not so much "what" is before you as "who," that is, the host. The courtier, after all, is interested in advancement and pleasing the host, the ruler. Second, the English phrase "put a knife to your throat" implies death. The advice is rather to restrain one's appetite. "Deceptive food" describes a meal that will not advance the guest's career and, of course, one that will not be satisfactory due to the need for restraint. The "ceremony" in this instance will not affirm or legitimate the young courtier's desired status. Sirach presents a more complete explanation of this advice (Sir. 31:12–32:13).

These verses also reflect all the symbolic body zones ("observe carefully," "desire": heart–eyes; "throat," "deceptive food": mouth–ears; implication of eating: hands–feet), thus indicating that the advice affects the whole person. ▶**Three-Zone Personality.**

**23:4-5** The advice given here that wealth is ephemeral contradicts the observation in other proverbs that wealth gained honestly does indeed last (Prov. 12:27; 14:23; 28:20). Such inconsistency is typical in MENA cultures. ▶**Normative Inconsistency.** The emphasis here may be on "wearing oneself out" in pursuit of wealth, that is, devoting one's total efforts to an ephemeral good.

**23:6-8** NRSV "stingy" translates the literal Hebrew "evil of eye" (Elliott 1991). ▶**Evil Eye.** Studies of the ethnographic data in HRAF (*Human Relations Area Files*) indicate that forty-seven percent of cultures in the worldwide sample, chiefly in the Circum-Mediterranean cultural continent, share this cultural belief. The evil intent in the heart is projected outward through the eyes (heart–eyes symbolic body zone). ▶**Three-Zone Personality.** Unless one knows how to protect oneself (e.g., by wearing apotropaic colors or insignia), one will indeed be damaged ("vomit up the little you have eaten"). The host may have felt culturally constrained to invite the guest, but "his heart is not with him." Hence he casts the evil eye on the situation, causing unpleasant consequences. Some scholars relying on *The Instructions of Amenenope*, chapter 11, believe the guest is uninvited and therefore like a thief, prompting the host to project the evil eye on him.

**23:10-11** See comment on Prov. 22:28. The basis for this prohibition is the cultural believe in limited goods. ▶**Limited Good.** All desirable and good things are finite in quantity and already distributed. In this case the issue is property. Moving the ancient landmarks is theft. The threat for such a violation is that God will be the redeemer, take the part of the "next of kin," and render justice to the orphan (and widow) who presumably have no other kin to help them (see Lev. 25:25). The Hebrew speaks of a *rîb*, a lawsuit, a serious matter.

**23:12** Here begins a new section no longer correlating, as the previous verses did, with the *Instructions of Amenenope*. It pertains to two symbolic body zones: heart–eyes ("mind") and mouth–ears ("ear," "words"). ▶**Three-Zone Personality.** What follows (Prov. 23:12-35) will address the third symbolic body zone (hands–feet, human activity).

**23:13-14** NRSV's inclusive language translation misrepresents the Hebrew text, which speaks of a young man and MENA culture. ▶**Discipline.** Boys and girls were raised together by the mother and other women in this rigidly gender-divided culture, with no influence from the father. At the age of puberty boys were pushed into the male world while girls stayed with the women. Boys then had to learn how to be men. The strategy was for fathers and the other men to apply corporal discipline to the young man (see Prov. 13:24; 22:15), hence this instruction to a father or teacher. "He will not die" does not refer to the potential result of physical discipline but rather to helping him avoid a premature and unfortunate end. Verse 14 has the sense of an imperative: "You must beat him . . ." in order to save him from that fate.

121

**23:15-16** These reflections assure a young man (NRSV inclusive rendition "child" misrepresents the culture) that acquiring wisdom will please a parent and/or teacher. Heart in v. 15 and "kidneys" (NRSV "soul"). ▶**Nepeš/soul.** and "lips" reflect the heart–eyes and mouth–ears symbolic body zones of a person. ▶**Three-Zone Personality.** Since "kidneys" are oriented toward action, these aphorisms describe a complete and well-rounded person.

**23:17-18** Scholars distinguish among envy, zeal, and jealousy (Hagedorn and Neyrey 1998: 17-20; see also Pilch and Malina 2009: 59-63, 209-12). Envy (Gk. *phthonos*) is a feeling of distress at another's success. Emulation (Gk. *zēlos*) is an incentive to match the success of another. Jealousy (Gk. *zēlos*) is defense of one's family, property, or reputation. The Septuagint translates the Hebrew of v. 17 with *zēlos*. Thus this proverb seeks to discourage a person from attempting to match the success of sinners who have violated the cultural belief in limited goods. ▶**Limited good.** Sinners have made gains at the expense of others. Envy carries the notion of seeking to destroy or deprive the other of good things. ▶**Evil Eye.** Emulation desires to match that success, undoubtedly by the same means. For similar advice regarding the wicked see Ps. 37:1; Prov. 3:31; 24:1, 19. A preferable alternative to NRSV's translation of the second line would be: "seek to emulate those who fear [or revere] the Lord at all times."

Verse 18 does not refer to a distant future (the next life) but rather to a happy and successful life here and now, ending with an honorable and not premature death.

**23:19-21** The parent/teacher advises "my son" (NRSV "my child") to behave according to his own instructed heart (NRSV "mind"), referring to two symbolic body zones: hands–feet ("walk" or "conduct oneself") and heart–eyes. ▶**Three-Zone Personality.** The idea is to resist peer pressure from evil companions.

Verses 20-21 echo Deut. 21:18-21, which describe a disobedient son. Considering how rare meat was in the ancient Israelite diet (MacDonald 2008: 61-76), one wonders whether these verses are hyperbole or refer to shameful behavior of foolish sons. The motive for the prohibition is that it will lead to poverty, that is, loss of status, and if not actual death (as in Deut. 21:20), then the equivalent of death: ejection from the family, one's key source of support. The reference to drowsiness may allude to laziness and failure to share in the communal family efforts at subsistence. These verses add another symbolic body zone to the preceding verse: mouth–ears, thus describing a son with misaligned purposes.

**23:22-25** Verses 22 and 25 form an inclusion signaling that the compiler intended this cluster of proverbs to be considered a unit, though the unity is difficult to perceive.

Verses 22, 24, and 25 echo the instructions of Proverbs 1–9. The closest emotional bond in MENA cultures is between mother and (eldest) son (Pilch 1993: 105). That bond is so close that Western culture would identify it as a relationship of codependent personalities. From this perspective it is easier to understand why an adult MENA son might "despise" his aged mother (v. 22). It is not much different with the father, whose cultural task is to instill obedience and loyalty in his son. These virtues do not come naturally to MENA sons, who are raised primarily by the women and are pampered and spoiled until the age of puberty. At that time, without a rite of transition, they experience the shock of being introduced into the male world where life is very different for them. The sissified males now will spend the rest of their lives trying to learn how to be men. Sirach 30:1-13 expands on the reflection in v. 24. Finally, v. 25 exhorts the son to bring joy and satisfaction to his parents by manifesting the good results of their parenting.

**23:26-28** The father demands that his son be obedient to him and follow his good example. Notice the symbolic body zones in v. 26: heart–eyes, the zone of emotion-fused thinking. ▶**Three-Zone Personality**. The verses that follow focus attention on proper sexual behavior (hands–feet symbolic body zone). They warn against the dangers of the prostitute and the "foreign woman" (NRSV "adulterer" is misleading in English). Traffic with a prostitute could result in pregnancy and put the inheritance at risk. "Do not give yourself to prostitutes, or you may lose your inheritance" (Sir. 9:6). Foreign women (outside the family; outside Israel) were viewed as immoral, but such dalliance would also incur the wrath of a slighted male (father, brother, or husband) responsible for the woman. Thus (v. 28) she is like a thief (stealing inheritance) and increases infidelity.

**23:29-35** This segment begins with a riddle in six questions (v. 29). The compiler of the book of Proverbs stated as his purpose at the outset to train the student in the skill of understanding riddles (Prov. 1:6). The answer is in v. 30: the person with all these problems is none other than a drunken brawler. The reference to mixed wines is to the practice of adding spices in order to increase the potency. In the Hellenistic period mixed wine referred to wine diluted with water (2 Macc. 15:39), but in earlier times mixing water with wine adulterated it (Isa. 1:22).

Verses 31-35 graphically describe a state of serious inebriation. The mere sight of wine in the cup entices the young man to drink it. Though the taste is pleasant, in the end it wreaks havoc like that of the bites of poisonous reptiles. Note the references to the heart (NRSV "mind")–eyes and mouth–ears in v. 33. ▶**Three-Zone Personality**. Hands–feet are involved in lifting the goblet but are unable to assist in self-defense (vv. 34-35). In the final analysis the alcohol-dependent youngster cannot wait to begin drinking again.

### Proverbs 24:1-22

1  Do not envy the wicked,
    nor desire to be with them;
2  for their minds devise violence,
    and their lips talk of mischief.
3  By wisdom a house is built,
    and by understanding it is established;
4  by knowledge the rooms are filled
    with all precious and pleasant riches.
5  Wise warriors are mightier than strong ones,
    and those who have knowledge than those who have strength;
6  for by wise guidance you can wage your war,
    and in abundance of counselors there is victory.
7  Wisdom is too high for fools;
    in the gate they do not open their mouths.

8 Whoever plans to do evil
  will be called a mischief maker.
9 The devising of folly is sin,
  and the scoffer is an abomination to all.
10 If you faint in the day of adversity,
  your strength being small;
11 if you hold back from rescuing those taken away to death,
  those who go staggering to the slaughter;
12 if you say, "Look, we did not know this"—
  does not he who weighs the heart perceive it?
  Does not he who keeps watch over your soul know it?
  And will he not repay all according to their deeds?
13 My child, eat honey, for it is good,
  and the drippings of the honeycomb are sweet to your taste.
14 Know that wisdom is such to your soul;
  if you find it, you will find a future,
  and your hope will not be cut off.
15 Do not lie in wait like an outlaw against the home of the righteous;
  do no violence to the place where the righteous live;
16 for though they fall seven times, they will rise again;
  but the wicked are overthrown by calamity.
17 Do not rejoice when your enemies fall,
  and do not let your heart be glad when they stumble,
18 or else the Lord will see it and be displeased,
  and turn away his anger from them.
19 Do not fret because of evildoers.
  Do not envy the wicked;
20 for the evil have no future;
  the lamp of the wicked will go out.
21 My child, fear the Lord and the king,
  and do not disobey either of them;
22 for disaster comes from them suddenly,
  and who knows the ruin that both can bring?

*Textual Notes: 24:1-22*

**24:1-2** This admonition repeats a theme expressed elsewhere in Proverbs (Prov. 3:31; 23:17; 24:19-20). It addresses the symbolic body zones of heart–eyes (envy, desire, hearts [NRSV minds]); mouth–ears (lips, talk); and hands–feet (be with them, that is, join their company and share in their violence; mischief). ▶**Evil Eye.** This describes a totally evil person. ▶ **Three-Zone Personality**. The young person is probably attracted to them by their apparent success.

**24:3-9** This cluster of proverbs is intended to demonstrate the value of wisdom to a young man attracted by the successes of wicked people. While the reflection about wisdom in vv. 3-4 may seem obvious to a Western reader, they mildly chide MENA personalities who in general never admit ignorance (Malina 1993: 117–19) and do not separate personal life from any role they might play. Inability to execute the expected role (build a house/household) would indicate that one is not a good father or spouse. This would cast self-worth and core sense of honor in doubt. Thus the statement encourages one to gain the requisite wisdom, understanding, and knowledge to meet this challenge.

Verses 5-6 present an illustration of the value of wisdom drawn waging war. Might alone does not suffice; one needs wisdom to plan an effective strategy. The advice is not so much about actual warfare as it is about the daily battles of living.

Verses 7-9 lampoon the fool, one who is not wise. In the agonistic MENA societies, insults are one means of attempting to control the behavior of others (Pilch 2014). ▶ **Agonism**. In this instance the attack is on the fool's lack of competence, an insult to his competence = face (Pilch 2014: 2). In v. 9, NRSV "sin" is more appropriately rendered "missing the mark," that is, the incompetent fool's plans miss the mark.

**24:10-12** Whybray (1994: 347) hypothesizes that these instructions refer to a person who has fallen prey to robbers who are about to murder him. Saving a life is a key value in the Israelite tradition (see Deut. 30:15-20 with God's challenge: "Choose life!"). Later rabbinic tradition commenting on Lev. 18:5 derived an obligation to save life from this verse: "Keep, then, my statues and decrees, for the person who carries them out will find life through them." The Hebrew phrase is *pikuaḥ nepeš* (to save a life). The Talmud notes: "To save life is tantamount to saving the whole world" (b. Sanh. 74a). With the exception of incest, idolatry, and bloodshed, it is permissible to disobey commandments in order to save a life. God accepts no excuse for failing to meet this obligation. This is one of the tasks of the next of kin, the redeemer (Sir. 30:6; Num. 35:12). In this instance the young man is being reminded of this obligation, which extends even to a fellow-Israelite (Lev. 19:17-18). Verse 12 highlights the fact that God repays each person justly. Humans should refrain from seeking revenge.

**24:13-14** Neither this nor any of the other three references to honey in Prov. 16:24; 25:16, 27 concerns physical delight in eating it. Rather, gaining wisdom is compared with this pleasure. Its reward is the assurance of a future and preservation from a premature death. In v. 13, NRSV "taste" represents *nepeš*, literally "soul" (or "throat," "desire," or "appetite"). ▶**Nepeš/soul.** As honey has a pleasant taste, so is wisdom for one's life if one has an appetite or desire for it. This is yet another challenge to cultural blindness to one's ignorance and a positive exhortation to pursue true wisdom.

**24:15-16** The emphasis here is on the righteous person. He is held up to the young man as a model to imitate. Though he seem to be overcome many times, in the long run he will be victorious. The wicked person who seeks to do violence to the property of the righteous one is an outlaw who will be tripped up and come to a tragic end. This is yet another exhortation against being swayed by the apparent success of wicked people.

**25:17-18** MENA societies distinguish carefully between in-groups and out-groups. ▶**In-group and Out-group.** The main in-group is one's household, extended family, and friends. Everyone else, in general, belongs to the out-group and is equivalent to an enemy. The cultural belief is that "they" are out to get "us." Hence rejoicing at the misfortune of an enemy, a member of an out-group, is normal (Ps. 58:4-12). This coexists with the divine exhortation to help a fallen enemy (Exod. 23:4-5). Thus a good and innocent person would empathize with the misfortune of others, even the wicked, who rejoice at others' misfortune (Ps. 35:11-16). This is yet another illustration of cultural normative inconsistency. ▶**Normative Inconsistency.**

The second verse is ambiguous. Yes, the Lord will be displeased, but the Lord's response is difficult to interpret in the text as it stands.

**24:21-22** The conclusion of this segment reminds the son (NRSV "child") to revere the Lord and the king, who have the power to punish transgressors.

## IV. Proverbs 24:23-34:
## Further Words of the Wise

23 These also are sayings of the wise:
  Partiality in judging is not good.
24 Whoever says to the wicked, "You are innocent,"
  will be cursed by peoples,
  abhorred by nations;
25 but those who rebuke the wicked will have delight,
  and a good blessing will come upon them.
26 One who gives an honest answer
  gives a kiss on the lips.
27 Prepare your work outside,
  get everything ready for you in the field;
  and after that build your house.
28 Do not be a witness against your neighbor without cause,
  and do not deceive with your lips.
29 Do not say,
  "I will do to others as they have done to me;
  I will pay them back for what they have done."
30 I passed by the field of one who was lazy,
  by the vineyard of a stupid person;
31 and see, it was all overgrown with thorns;
  the ground was covered with nettles,
  and its stone wall was broken down.
32 Then I saw and considered it;
  I looked and received instruction.
33 A little sleep, a little slumber,
  a little folding of the hands to rest,
34 and poverty will come upon you like a robber,
  and want, like an armed warrior.

An editor or the compiler of the book of Proverbs has arranged this text-segment into two groups, each having three components that correspond. This is the arrangement:

| The court of law | 1. Judges: vv. 24-25 | 4. Witnesses: v. 28 |
| Speaking and thinking | 2. Truthful speech: v. 26 | 5. Harmful speech: v. 29 |
| Work | 3. Positive view: v. 27 | 6. Negative view: vv. 30-34 |

*Textual Notes: 24:23-34*

**24:23-25** These verses (23-25) match Prov. 24:28, as indicated above. NRSV "[showing] partiality" is literally in Hebrew "recognizing the face" (Deut. 1:17; 16:19; Prov. 28:21). It is synonymous with "lifting the face" (see Prov. 18:5). Reference to "face" casts these observations into the realm of honor, the core cultural value of MENA cultures. ▶**Honor and Shame.** The one who judges dishonestly (proclaiming the guilty as innocent) behaves shamefully and earns universal dishonor. The honorable judge renders fair judgment and thereby augments his honorable status, gaining "the blessing of prosperity" (NRSV "a good blessing").

**24:26** This verse matches v. 29. The challenge for a Westerner in interpreting this proverb is to explain the meaning of a "kiss on the lips" in MENA society. In general, MENA cultures display emotions toward others more readily and spontaneously than is common in the West. The typical kiss—even by men greeting one another—is generally on both cheeks. Sometimes men rub noses, which appears to onlookers as a kiss on the lips.

Lovers kiss on the lips (Cant. 1:2; 7:9), but that is not relevant here. Perhaps the reference in the pseudepigraphical story of *Joseph and Aseneth* provides the appropriate insight. In this tale Jacob's son, Joseph, meets the Egyptian woman Aseneth and prays for her conversion. When she converts, and they meet again, they embrace each other "and kissed each other for a long time and both came to life in their spirit. And Joseph kissed and gave her the spirit of life, and he kissed her the second time and gave her the spirit of wisdom, and he kissed her the third time and gave her the spirit of truth" (*Joseph and Aseneth* 19.11). Just as God breathed (through anthropomorphic lips) the breath, spirit, and life into the first human creature (Gen.

129

2:7), so human beings can impart the same gifts to each other. Thus a truthful person in a culture that values secrecy, deception, and lying is a life-giving resource in an otherwise depressing and hopeless context. **24:27** This verse matches vv. 30-34. The appropriate context for understanding this proverb would seem to be the concept of ancestral land. Thus it is addressed not to a member of the elite but rather to a young man whose obligation to nurture his family is met by tilling the land surrounding the ancestral property. This is important because after meeting all external obligations the peasant might have had as little as twenty percent of annual produce remaining for meeting subsistence needs. It was therefore imperative to get as much from the land as conditions would allow. Then one could establish a family.

**24:28** This verse relates back to vv. 24-25 concerning the judge and legal trials. They caution against bearing false witness against one's neighbor (Exod. 20:16; Deut. 5:20). Here is yet another illustration of the prevailing cultural penchant toward deception and lying in defense of one's honor. ▶ **Lying.**

**24:29** This verse relates to v. 26 concerning truthful speech. Bearing false witness is harmful speech, and this verse illustrates the motivation for such behavior: seeking revenge. It usurps God's rights, as noted in v. 12d above. Though scholars think v. 29 was not originally associated with v. 28, the compiler has linked them, perhaps because they cover all three symbolic body zones: heart–eyes (witness), mouth–ears (deceive, lips), and hands–feet (do to others; pay back). ▶ **Three-Zone Personality.**

**24:30-34** This text-segment refers to v. 27 concerning work. It is an "example story." The father or teacher has passed by a field, makes an observation, and then draws a conclusion. The theme—common in Proverbs—is the sluggard or lazy person (Prov. 6:16-11; 26:13-16). Not only does his willful neglect rob him—and his family!—of sustenance; it also earns him a shameful reputation, since his failure is quite public. ▶ **Honor and shame.**

# V. Proverbs 25–29:
# Further Proverbs of Solomon Collected by the Servants of King Hezekiah

## Proverbs 25:1-28

1 These are other proverbs of Solomon that the officials of King Hezekiah of Judah copied.

2 It is the glory of God to conceal things,
 but the glory of kings is to search things out.
3 Like the heavens for height, like the earth for depth,
 so the mind of kings is unsearchable.
4 Take away the dross from the silver,
 and the smith has material for a vessel;
5 take away the wicked from the presence of the king,
 and his throne will be established in righteousness.
6 Do not put yourself forward in the king's presence
 or stand in the place of the great;
7 for it is better to be told, "Come up here,"
 than to be put lower in the presence of a noble.
 What your eyes have seen
8 do not hastily bring into court;
 for what will you do in the end,
 when your neighbor puts you to shame?
9 Argue your case with your neighbor directly,
 and do not disclose another's secret;
10 or else someone who hears you will bring shame upon you,
 and your ill repute will have no end.
11 A word fitly spoken
 is like apples of gold in a setting of silver.
12 Like a gold ring or an ornament of gold
 is a wise rebuke to a listening ear.
13 Like the cold of snow in the time of harvest
 are faithful messengers to those who send them;
 they refresh the spirit of their masters.
14 Like clouds and wind without rain
 is one who boasts of a gift never given.
15 With patience a ruler may be persuaded,
 and a soft tongue can break bones.
16 If you have found honey, eat only enough for you,
 or else, having too much, you will vomit it.
17 Let your foot be seldom in your neighbor's house,

otherwise the neighbor will become weary of you and hate you.

18 Like a war club, a sword, or a sharp arrow
　is one who bears false witness against a neighbor.

19 Like a bad tooth or a lame foot
　is trust in a faithless person in time of trouble.

20 Like vinegar on a wound
　is one who sings songs to a heavy heart.
　Like a moth in clothing or a worm in wood,
　sorrow gnaws at the human heart.

21 If your enemies are hungry, give them bread to eat;
　and if they are thirsty, give them water to drink;

22 for you will heap coals of fire on their heads,
　and the Lord will reward you.

23 The north wind produces rain,
　and a backbiting tongue, angry looks.

24 It is better to live in a corner of the housetop
　than in a house shared with a contentious wife.

25 Like cold water to a thirsty soul,
　so is good news from a far country.

26 Like a muddied spring or a polluted fountain
　are the righteous who give way before the wicked.

27 It is not good to eat much honey,
　or to seek honor on top of honor.

28 Like a city breached, without walls,
　is one who lacks self control.

The reference to Hezekiah, king of Judah (715–687 BCE), helps to date this collection. He undertook political and religious reforms after the fall of the Northern Kingdom (721 BCE). This reforming activity would have included preserving, copying, and editing sacred writings. Proverbs 25–28 were then added to the Solomonic collection (Proverbs 10–22). **Because of the description of Solomon's wisdom in 1 Kings 4:9-14, he is tranditionally considered the author of all wisdom. Clearly this segment, even if inspired by Solomon, is the work of Hezekiah.**

### Textual Notes: 25:1-28

**25:2-3** The focus here is honor, specifically the honor or reputation of God contrasted with that of the king, God's representative. ▶**Honor and Shame**. God's honorable status and reputation are inscrutable. No human can fully know or understand God. God remains mysterious. Kings, on the other hand, must be able to explain the mysteries of the world and solve the problems of life, so far as it is in their power. In Israel it was believed that "the wisdom of God was in [the king] to execute justice" (1 Kgs. 3:28). Even so, the heart (NRSV: "mind") of the king is no less difficult to understand. ▶Three-Zone Personality.

**25:4-5** This rather self-evident reflection points to a common concern of the peasant: righteousness. Under an honest and fair king the peasant can hope with confidence for just treatment. This is all the more possible if the royal circle is free from wicked advisors. (See the introductory comments on Proverbs 10.)

**25:6-7** While the context of this proverb is the royal court and proper behavior there, the advice is a reminder of the common MENA cultural value of humility. ▶Humility. In honor and shame cultures it is imperative not to impinge on the status of others or "make oneself out to be" more than one is. That is equivalent to grasping for an honor that might not be recognized. Thus a safe practice is to assume a position slightly lower than that to which one is properly entitled. Such behavior allows a host or person of status to publicly elevate the humbled individual to his rightful place. To be publicly sent to a lower place would be shameful (see Luke 14:7-11).

**25:7c-10** The cultural context for this advice is secrecy, deception, and lying. ▶Lying. As already noted, courts did not guarantee justice. It was always preferable for the disputing parties to work out their difficulties or to seek an arbitrator whose judgment would be definitive. Such a person would be at least five links removed in relationship from the disputing parties (see Luke 12:13-15). The neighbor can cause shame either by revealing something true and harmful or by simply lying. Moreover, a culturally plausible MENA interpretation of "what your eyes have seen" can include a fabrication presented as fact in support of a plaintiff who is also a friend. Once such an exchange is put in motion it is culturally obvious that the maligned party will retaliate. Verses 9-10, even if not connected with vv. 7c-8, highlight the principal concern: avoiding shame and ill repute, whether deserved or not. ▶**Honor and Shame**. (Compare Matt. 5:25-26).

**25:11-14** These four proverbs refer to speech, reflecting the mouth–ears symbolic body zone. ▶**Three-Zone Personality**. Three of them (vv. 11, 12, 14) are metaphors rendered by NRSV as similes. The images are simply juxtaposed with the object to which they are compared, with no connecting particle such as "like" or "as." The meanings are self-evident. In a culture where lying prevails, honest and helpful words are welcome (vv. 11, 12, 13). In contrast, empty promises are not only frustrating but can have harmful effect (v. 14). The Hebrew literally is "a gift of deception" (*šeqer*). If a patron does not extend the patronage promised, the client can suffer damage.

The reference in v. 11 to "apples" is curious, since this fruit was not introduced in ancient Israel during the Old Testament period. Similarly in v. 13, the reference to snow in harvest time refers to someone bringing it from the mountain tops rather than snow falling. NRSV "spirit" in v. 14 is literally "soul" (*nepeš*) in Hebrew, a word that can also mean throat or palate. ▶**Nepeš/soul**.

**25:15** The three symbolic body zones are reflected in this proverb. ▶**Three-Zone Personality**. Patience: heart–eyes; soft tongue: mouth–ears; and "break bones": hands–feet, even though this latter phrase is hyperbole meaning "is irresistible." Similar advice occurs elsewhere in this book. Proverbs 11:14 and 15:22 highlight the value of advising a person of higher status as appropriate. Proverbs 25:5 (see above) attests to the influence royal advisers might have on the king. Thus patience and gentle persuasion can prove very effective.

**25:16** The Hebrew word translated "honey" is more plausibly understood as a thick, sweet syrup distilled from cooking down fruit (MacDonald 2008: 39). Fruits native to the region include figs, pomegranates, grapes, apricots, dates, and apples (Borowski 2003: 70). The two references to honey in the Bible (Judg. 14:8; 1 Sam. 14:25-30) point to wild honey. The point of this advice is to caution against excess in enjoying pleasures. There is a narrow border between excessive pleasure and pain.

**25:17** This is curious advice in MENA cultures. The family is the center of one's world, and all outsiders—even neighbors unless they are related—are considered hostile, plotting to harm the family. Young children are trained and expected to wander freely in and out of other people's lives to snoop on them and report back to their family. ▶**Discipline**. This is culturally acceptable and expected (Matt. 19:14//Mark 10:13-16//Luke 18:15-17). Being too neighborly would cause the neighbor to become suspicious and to reject (a translation preferable to "hate") such visits.

**25:18** The context here is a judicial trial, the law court. Despite the commandment that prohibits bearing false witness (Exod. 20:16; Deut. 5:20), there are repeated references prohibiting perjury or describing its harmful effects (see Prov. 6:19; 12:17; 14:5; 19:5, 9), suggesting that it occurred frequently. This is understandable, if repulsive, in a culture that approves secrecy, deception, and lying either in the defense of one's honor or to take revenge on an enemy. ▶**Lying**. The comparison here is to weapons of war that cause death, precisely the result of false testimony against an innocent party.

**25:19** In MENA culture, trust is a very important value (Pilch and Malina 2009: 201–4). One would expect the family (especially the *redeemer*, the next-of-kin) to be reliable in time of trouble, but this is not always the case (Jer. 9:1-5). Trusted friends like the one mentioned in this proverb are no exception (see Ps. 41:10). Given the cultural assertion of inability to truly know other persons (1 Sam. 16:7), one can never be sure of whom to trust (Mic. 7:5). Thus to be betrayed in a time of need is similar to experiencing a bad tooth or lame foot, each unreliable for its task. Only God deserves such trust (Jer. 17:5; Prov. 3:5; 16:20).

**25:20** This verse is seriously corrupt in Hebrew (see Clifford 1999: 225; Murphy 1998: 198). The main point is the futility of trying to cheer up a sad or heavy heart by singing songs (compare Sir. 22:6a). Such thoughtlessness is compared to vinegar poured on soda (*natron*; NRSV translates the word as "wound"), which causes a hissing and fizzing, thus a negative result. From a positive point of view, in antiquity vinegar, diluted with water, was a refreshing drink. It resulted from light wine going sour; that is, the alcohol content was converted into acetic acid. Roman soldiers were fond of this drink (John 19:29) since it had cooling properties. It was also a sauce into which one dipped bread (Ruth 2:14).

**25:21-22** NRSV "enemies" is literally in Hebrew "one who hates you." The basic advice is to resist the temptation to exact revenge, but rather to come to the aid of such a person in distress, in the spirit of Exod. 23:4-5. This urges heroic behavior upon a person culturally schooled in taking revenge. The Wisdom tradition recommends leaving to God the punishment of one's enemies. Scholars are not agreed about the meaning of "heaping coals of fire on their heads." No proposed hypothesis has proven satisfactory. Whatever this means, the Lord will reward a person who practices such heroic self-restraint.

**25:23** The puzzle of this verse is that in Palestine it was the west wind (not the north wind) that brought rain. The west wind blows inland off the Mediterranean sea. Among the various proposed interpretations, the one based on a play on Hebrew words makes the best sense at the moment (Whybray 1994: 369). NRSV "backbiting tongue" is literally in Hebrew "a tongue of hiddenness." This prompted scholars to repoint the Hebrew word for north (ṣāpôn) to the Hebrew word for hidden or mysterious (ṣāpan). Thus as an unknown, mysterious wind brings dark clouds of rain (from the place in the sky where it has been stored), so does a hidden tongue darken the face of ("shames") the person affected by the slander, who understandably becomes angry.

**25:24** See comment on Prov. 21:9.

**25:27** The first line implies the sense of Prov. 25:16, but the second line is hopelessly corrupt in the Hebrew text. Compare various translations to see how it is interpreted. The sense would seem to be moderation with regard to pleasurable things such as honey and honor. ▶**Honor and Shame.** There is no way to increase ascribed honor, but it is indeed possible to increase acquired honor. **Ascribed honor derives mainly from birth. It can't be changed, augmented,**

**nor diminished. Honor is acquire by games of skill, prowess, ability to insult, etc.** Still, one must be careful because the consequences can be deadly. In the Gospel passion narrative, Pilate realizes "that it was out of jealousy [better: "envy"] that the chief priests had handed [Jesus] over" (Mark 15:10). The sense is that the chief priests envied the honor that the life and mighty deeds of Jesus gained for him, causing their honor to lessen. ▶**Evil Eye.** Honor is a limited good. ▶**Limited Good.** Therefore they had him put to death (Hagedorn and Neyrey 1998: 15–56).

**25:28** NRSV "lacks self control" translates the literal Hebrew "has no restraint over his *ruah*" (spirit)." "Spirit" refers to the heart–eyes symbolic body zone, while "has no restraint" refers to the hands–feet symbolic body zone. ▶**Three-Zone Personality.** Self-control is a major problem in MENA societies, which are inclined toward spontaneity, to acting without or before thinking. This is known as a preference for "being" rather than "doing" (Pilch and Malina 2009: xxv–xl). Relatives or friends are expected to intervene in spontaneous outbursts to prevent the person from harming self or others. In a parabolic reference Jesus noted that "the wind blows where it chooses, and you hear the sound of it, but you do not know where it comes from or where it goes" (John 3:8). In Hebrew and Greek the words *ruah* and *pneuma* respectively can mean wind, spirit, and breath. The cultural belief was that they are mysterious yet powerful (see Eccl. 11:5). Hence the proverb exhorts the student/disciple to learn and practice self-control; otherwise that person is vulnerable, like an unfortified city.

## Proverbs 26:1-28

1 Like snow in summer or rain in harvest,
   so honor is not fitting for a fool.
2 Like a sparrow in its flitting, like a swallow in its flying,
   an undeserved curse goes nowhere.
3 A whip for the horse, a bridle for the donkey,
   and a rod for the back of fools.
4 Do not answer fools according to their folly,
   or you will be a fool yourself.
5 Answer fools according to their folly,

or they will be wise in their own eyes.

6  It is like cutting off one's foot and drinking down violence,
    to send a message by a fool.

7  The legs of a disabled person hang limp;
    so does a proverb in the mouth of a fool.

8  It is like binding a stone in a sling
    to give honor to a fool.

9  Like a thornbush brandished by the hand of a drunkard
    is a proverb in the mouth of a fool.

10 Like an archer who wounds everybody
    is one who hires a passing fool or drunkard.

11 Like a dog that returns to its vomit
    is a fool who reverts to his folly.

12 Do you see persons wise in their own eyes?
    There is more hope for fools than for them.

13 The lazy person says, "There is a lion in the road!
    There is a lion in the streets!"

14 As a door turns on its hinges,
    so does a lazy person in bed.

15 The lazy person buries a hand in the dish,
    and is too tired to bring it back to the mouth.

16 The lazy person is wiser in self esteem
    than seven who can answer discreetly.

17 Like somebody who takes a passing dog by the ears
    is one who meddles in the quarrel of another.

18 Like a maniac who shoots
    deadly firebrands and arrows,

19 so is one who deceives a neighbor
    and says, "I am only joking!"

20 For lack of wood the fire goes out,
    and where there is no whisperer, quarreling ceases.

21 As charcoal is to hot embers and wood to fire,
    so is a quarrelsome person for kindling strife.

22 The words of a whisperer are like delicious morsels;
    they go down into the inner parts of the body.

23 Like the glaze covering an earthen vessel
    are smooth lips with an evil heart.

24 An enemy dissembles in speaking
    while harboring deceit within;

25 when an enemy speaks graciously, do not believe it,
    for there are seven abominations concealed within;

26 though hatred is covered with guile,
    the enemy's wickedness will be exposed in the assembly.

27 Whoever digs a pit will fall into it,
    and a stone will come back on the one who starts it rolling.

28 A lying tongue hates its victims,
    and a flattering mouth works ruin.

In this chapter, vv. 1-12 treat of the fool, vv. 13-16 of the sluggard (NRSV "lazy person"), and vv. 17-28 of persons who do damage to the community by their speech.

*Textual Notes: 26:1-28*

**26:1** One cannot attribute honor to oneself. By definition honor is publicly recognized and acknowledged by others. ▶**Honor and Shame.** The climate of Palestine knows two seasons: "dry" from April to September, when it never (or rarely) rains or snows, and "wet" from October to March. Harvests occur in the dry season: barley in April-May, wheat in June, and fruit (including olives and grapes) in late summer or early fall (Isa. 16:9). Just as snow in summer or rain during the dry harvest season is contrary to nature in this part of the world, so too is granting honor to a fool at any time.

**26:2** A curse is the expression of a prediction, wish, or prayer for harm or disaster upon a person or thing (Kitz 2014). While among primitive people curses for the most part were associated with magic, in Israel the curse was associated with God's power (Gen. 12:3, 8, 9; Exod. 9:14). When pronounced against an innocent person, as this proverb implies, the curse has no effect because God neutralizes it or turns it into a blessing (Deut. 23:6). Thus is it like a sparrow or swallow whose flight appears to the uninformed to be aimless.

**26:3** MENA societies readily resort to physical discipline to teach appropriate lessons (Pilch 1993: 101–13). Some commentators suggest the discipline here is heavier than that proposed for training youth (Prov. 23:13-14).

**26:4-12** These verses continue to reflect on the fool and his shameful weaknesses. In v. 11, comparison with a dog is intended as an insult (as in 1 Sam. 17:43 and 2 Kgs. 8:13). The first part of v. 11 is quoted in 2 Peter 2:22.

**26:13-16** These verses focus on the "sluggard" (ʿṣēl). NRSV "lazy" is culturally inaccurate. In MENA culture, taking initiative is not a virtue (Malina 1993: 135–36). It is preferable to maintain the status quo. One generally has to be asked or invited by another to do something; then if anything goes wrong it is that person's fault.

**26:13** This is a variant of Prov. 22:13, where the sluggard gives the full reason for refusing to take initiative. The truth or falsity of the claim matters not at all.

**26:14** The sluggard is like a door on its hinges that accomplishes nothing. The proverb could be intended to shame the sluggard into action, but it very likely will fail.

**26:15** This proverb is a variant of Prov. 19:24. The sluggard is not even willing to do what is necessary to sustain life. The statement is hyperbolic and ironic.

**26:16** According to MENA cultural values the sluggard considers himself to be wise. He follows the cultural cue that discourages taking initiative. From this perspective he considers himself to be wiser than others who might suggest an alternative course of action.

**26:17** The key word here is "meddles," that is, in view is one who on personal initiative gets involved in the quarrel of others. Such a foolish action is like grabbing the ears of a dog. In contrast, it is an honor to be asked by disputing parties to mediate their quarrel (Luke 12:13-15; see also Matt. 5:9). The ideal mediator is not kin but a highly esteemed person respected by all. This insures that the judgment will be fair and accepted by the parties (Patai 1983: 228–31).

**26:18-19** Understanding this proverb involves an appreciation for the MENA cultural values of secrecy, deception, and lying. ▶**Lying**. These are commonplace and expected in MENA culture. However, when a deceiver reveals that he was only joking it is important to recognize how humor is perceived in MENA cultures (Kuiper, et al. 2010: 149–73). Deceptive self-enhancing humorous comments ("I am only joking") are confusing and not acceptable to collectivistic personalities who are unable to distinguish between collective and individual self-construals. Thus this proverb's culturally appropriate observation that the use of deceptive humor renders the joker like a crazed archer who scatters deadly arrows without thought of the consequences.

**26:20-21** These verses highlight the harmful effects of careless use of language, specifically by people who provoke quarrels. Given the agonistic nature of MENA culture, quarreling and strife are commonplace. ▶**Agonism**. This is not a momentary lapse but rather a habitual practice. In these two proverbs the Sage compares such language to fuel for a fire. Without fuel, the fire dies out, but when supplied with fuel, a fire will rage. As one would strive to avoid the damage caused by fire, so one should be equally careful with language that might initiate and feed quarreling and strife.

**26:22** See the comment on Prov. 18:8, which is identical to Prov. 26:22.

**26:23** This proverb refers to two symbolic body zones: mouth–ears ("lips") and heart–eyes ("heart"). ▶**Three-Zone Personality**. The zones mentioned are improperly used; hence the proverb exhorts to a change of heart. The problem, however, is once again specific to MENA cultures, which give priority to appearances over reality (or the ideal over the real): a silver-looking glaze covering an earthen vessel. ▶**Normative Inconsistency**. NRSV and other translators interpreted the literal Hebrew "silver dross" as glaze. The reference is to lead monoxide, a residue of the process of purifying silver that looks like silver. NRSV and other translators also render the literal Hebrew "burning" (*dālaq*) lips with a proposed emendation: "smooth" lips. Whybray (1994: 378) relates "burning" to a kiss of warm friendship or love. More to the point, however, Prov. 16:27 describes the lips of a scoundrel as like a burning fire. In other words, appearances are deceptive, so beware!

**26:24-25** NRSV "an enemy" translates the literal Hebrew "one who hates." The point of these two proverbs relates to what was just noted above: dissembling is the standard mode of operation in MENA cultures. ▶**Lying**. It takes many forms. The Sage reminds one to be skeptical when an enemy speaks graciously. The suspicion—indeed the firm belief—is that the speaker intends to deceive. It is for this reason in MENA culture that if one wants to assure the listener that the truth is being spoken, the speaker will add an oath: "by the honor of my father," "so help me God," "Amen, Amen I say unto you," and the like. Without such an expression it is legitimate to suspect that the speaker is being deceptive.

**26:26** Life in such a cultural context was difficult indeed, even though it is the expected actual context. The hope is that somehow, somewhere, the truth will be made known. This proverb identifies a general gathering of the local community (Hebrew: *qāhāl*) as the place with the revelation would be made known, but it is difficult to know how this would occur. Ethnographic literature describes a variety of possible scenarios. In one instance the village master-liar uncovers the deceit of a visiting sheikh for the gathered community by trickery totally unsuspected by the visitor. In another case an entire village denies witnessing an event in a legal proceeding, but shares its knowledge in a community gathering called to resolve the issue at hand. Peasant communities have ingenious ways of discovering or revealing the truth when necessary. (See Matt. 10:26-27.)

**26:27** This proverb was popular in antiquity and reflects the ideal more than the real. It is echoed in Eccl. 10:8; Sir. 27:26; Pss. 7:16; 9:16. A threatened person would hope for this result, but it does not always happen.

**26:28** The Hebrew text is obscure and difficult to interpret. The general sense, however, is clear. Lying and deceit, so acceptable in MENA cultures, under certain circumstances works tragic results in everyone's life. ▶ **Lying**.

## Proverbs 27:1-27

1  Do not boast about tomorrow,
   for you do not know what a day may bring.
2  Let another praise you, and not your own mouth—
   a stranger, and not your own lips.
3  A stone is heavy, and sand is weighty,
   but a fool's provocation is heavier than both.
4  Wrath is cruel, anger is overwhelming,
   but who is able to stand before jealousy?

5 Better is open rebuke
   than hidden love.
6 Well meant are the wounds a friend inflicts,
   but profuse are the kisses of an enemy.
7 The sated appetite spurns honey,
   but to a ravenous appetite even the bitter is sweet.
8 Like a bird that strays from its nest
   is one who strays from home.
9 Perfume and incense make the heart glad,
   but the soul is torn by trouble.
10 Do not forsake your friend or the friend of your parent;
   do not go to the house of your kindred in the day of your calamity.
   Better is a neighbor who is nearby
   than kindred who are far away.
11 Be wise, my child, and make my heart glad,
   so that I may answer whoever reproaches me.
12 The clever see danger and hide;
   but the simple go on, and suffer for it.
13 Take the garment of one who has given surety for a stranger;
   seize the pledge given as surety for foreigners.
14 Whoever blesses a neighbor with a loud voice,
   rising early in the morning,
   will be counted as cursing.
15 A continual dripping on a rainy day
   and a contentious wife are alike;
16 to restrain her is to restrain the wind
   or to grasp oil in the right hand.
17 Iron sharpens iron,
   and one person sharpens the wits of another.
18 Anyone who tends a fig tree will eat its fruit,
   and anyone who takes care of a master will be honored.
19 Just as water reflects the face,
   so one human heart reflects another.
20 Sheol and Abaddon are never satisfied,
   and human eyes are never satisfied.
21 The crucible is for silver, and the furnace is for gold,
   so a person is tested by being praised.
22 Crush a fool in a mortar with a pestle
   along with crushed [like] grain,
   but the folly will not be driven out.
23 Know well the condition of your flocks,
   and give attention to your herds;
24 for riches do not last forever,
   nor a crown for all generations.
25 When the grass is gone, and new growth appears,

and the herbage of the mountains is gathered,
26 the lambs will provide your clothing,
    and the goats the price of a field;
27 there will be enough goats' milk for your food,
    for the food of your household and nourishment for your servant girls.

*Textual Notes: 27:1-27*

**27:1** Some scholars have noted the pedestrian quality of the proverbs in this chapter. Verse 1 actually reflects a key MENA cultural perspective, namely, a focus on the present (Pilch and Malina 2009: xxvii–viii). The Hebrew language has two tenses: perfect and imperfect. The perfect describes a completed action, the imperfect an action not yet completed. It is this second tense out of which a "future" evolves, but in MENA cultures the "future" is better expressed as "forthcoming." A process begun will eventually—in short order—be completed. Hence humans have no way of knowing what the morrow will bring. Their cultural focus is on today, the present.

**27:2** This verse is a reminder of the MENA cultural value of humility.
▶**Humility.** The idea behind humility is not self-effacement or putting oneself down. Rather, fully cognizant of one's rightful status, a person deliberately stays one step behind to allow others to publicly proclaim and elevate one to rightful status. The "other" and "stranger" are, of course, members of the same community.

**27:3** Compare Sir. 22:14-15.

**27:4** In contrast to the West, MENA cultures readily display emotions (see Malina and Pilch 2007: 138–54). Emotions are also understood and interpreted differently than in the West. For a contrast of American anger with Mediterranean anger see Malina and Pilch 2007: 151–52. *Anger* is generic and unspecified but is used almost synonymously with *wrath* in the Bible. Wrath is a determination to seek satisfaction or revenge for an outward, public, and widely acknowledged (by others) violation of personal honor. This indeed is perceived as cruel to the perpetrator. Jealousy is a defense of one's family, property, or reputation (Hagedorn and Neyrey 1998:15–56). It is not difficult to appreciate how an assault—perceived or imagined—on these concerns can elicit a cruel response. These three emotions are closely linked with the MENA cultural value of honor they are intended to protect, and the peasant understanding of limited good, "there is no more where this came from." ▶ **Limited Good.** Proverbs notes that wrath can be assuaged by a mild answer (Prov. 15:10) or a bribe (Prov. 21:14), but jealousy is not so easily deterred (Prov. 6:34-35) since it arouses wrath (6:34) and "rots the bones" (Prov. 14:30). Thus the proverb identifies jealousy as the most potentially damaging of the three.

**27:5-6** Both proverbs speak about friendship: v. 5 "love" (*'ahăbâh*); v. 6 "friend" (*'ôhēb*). In a "better than" proverb, v. 5 exalts honest and truthful rebuke over false love, which would remain silent. While insult is customary in MENA culture (sometimes only in jest), true friendship allows and requires honest if painful correction. Verse 6 repeats the same advice.

**27:8** NRSV "home" translates the Hebrew word that literally means "place." It refers to a person's place in God's universe (see Job 7:10; 8:18; 20:9). For the traditional peasant, mobility and traveling beyond one's "place" is deviant. There is no rational reason for it. Such travel removes one from kin and from one's life-sustaining network. The image of the bird that flees its nest is that of exile or banishment (Isa. 16:2-3), hence the context for the proverb is not a whimsical departure from home or an attempt to express one's independence. This would be shameful in MENA culture. Rather, it is being forced to abandon one's place in God's universe, a major tragedy (see Sir. 29:21-28).

**27:9** The second line of this proverb is so corrupt in Hebrew that it has been difficult to reconstruct. NRSV bases itself on the LXX. Others reconstruct the verse to something like "a friend's sweetness is better than one's own counsel." Anthropologists observe that MENA cultures are very fond of fragrance (Pilch 1999: 28–29). Perfume (literally in Hebrew "fat, oil") and incense (literally in Hebrew "smoke") were especially cherished by the Israelites, as this proverb indicates. For further information on this topic consult Duling 2014.

**27:10** The three lines of this proverb are completely independent of one another. They offer three different pieces of advice. NRSV "friend of your parent" translates the Hebrew "your father's friend." This first line is addressed to a young man, urging him to retain the family network of friends, something basic in MENA culture. In this agonistic culture it is "us" (family and its network of friends) against "them." We need all the help we can get, so it would be foolhardy to break bonds of friendship established by the patriarch to protect and assist the family.

The second line is puzzling (NRSV "kindred" translates the Hebrew "brother's house") since it contradicts the advice of Prov. 17:17 (see comment there). However, consistency is not a MENA value. ▶Normative Inconsistency. It is very likely that each of these contradictory pieces of advice relates to a specific situation, unknown to the modern reader.

Finally, the third line is somewhat puzzling since in ancient Israel the family lived in the compound of the patriarch. Either the needy person or the brother is away from the family compound. The first instance is more plausible: the needy person is away from the family but has made a good friend of the neighbor.

**27:11** This and the following verses (to v. 22) echo proverbs that were included earlier. In this case the son (NRSV "child") is urged to seek wisdom so that the father/teacher has a ready retort for anyone who reproaches him (compare Sir. 30:2-3). It relates to the honor rating of the father/teacher.

**27:12** This proverb is almost identical with Prov. 22:3.

**27:13** See comment on Prov. 20:16.

**27:14** While a straightforward, culturally-insensitive reading of this proverb prompts a humorous interpretation, MENA cultural considerations give pause. Cursing in these cultures is a serious thing with intended malicious consequences. The "blessing" is very likely a greeting (as in 1 Sam. 13:10; 2 Kgs. 4:29; 10:15). Delivered in a "loud voice," however, the greeting may be interpreted as insincere (Prov. 26:23-28). Finally, "early in the morning" could mean "insistently" (Jer. 7:13). Thus does the Sage urge critical judgment when evaluating apparently flattering behavior from others. One must be on guard against deception. ▶Lying.

**27:15-16** See the comments on Prov. 19:13 and 21:9. Given the strict gender separation in MENA cultures, our analysis interprets references to a contentious wife as one who is contending with rival wives in polygamous contexts. Such a wife is impossible to hide (literal Hebrew). The Hebrew of v. 16b is corrupt and translated variously: "to grasp oil in the right hand" (NRSV); "declare one's right hand to be oil" (JPS); "and his right hand meets oil" (Murphy 1998: 208); "the oil on her hand announces her presence" (Clifford 1999: 235); "and cannot tell north from south" (NABRE).

**27:17** This proverb strengthens the MENA cultural value of agonism. ▶**Agonism.** It is not simply an exhortation to dialogue and communication. Rather, the Sage encourages engaging in repartee, a mark of authentic manhood. Mastery of language together with the ability to endure physical pain without flinching are two ways of demonstrating one's manhood in MENA culture (Pilch 1993: 101–13).

**27:18** The meaning of this proverb is rather obvious. Taking care of one's master will give such a faithful servant a share in the master's prestige and honor. Sometimes parents are viewed as "masters" (Sir. 3:7—Greek *despotēs*, one of God's titles in the Septuagint: Sir. 23:1; 34:29). On the basis of Exod. 21:7 and Neh. 5:5, some rabbis concluded that children were like slaves to their father. Sirach does not intend that at all. He enjoins children rather to show love, honor, and care toward parents (Sir. 7:27-28).

**27:19** The Hebrew of this proverb has no verbs. Literally it reads: "like water, a face to a face, so the heart of man to man." While many translations (e.g., NRSV) interpret the water as a mirror reflecting the face, Clifford argues that the verse should be translated "face to face" as in Deut. 34:10 and Ezek. 20:35 (Clifford 1999: 240). The verse thus expresses a human being speaking directly and intimately to another, "as one face turns to another." He renders the next verse "one heart turns to the other." The meaning is that when two people speak "face to face" they speak "heart to heart." On the basis of 1 Sam. 16:3, which highlights the MENA cultural belief that human beings are non-introspective and that only God can read the heart, this proverb expresses the hope that speaking face to face gives people a glimpse of what might be in the heart of another, a hint of what the other person might be thinking.

**27:20** Abaddon ("place of destruction") is synonymous with Sheol, the abode of the dead. The traditional understanding is that these places have an insatiable appetite; they always want more. That the human eyes are similar points to a violation of the MENA cultural belief in limited goods. ▶**Limited Good.** All things of value are finite in quantity and already distributed. To cast lusty eyes on the property of others, a natural propensity according to this proverb, causes one to have an evil eye. ▶**Evil Eye.** Since it is culturally unacceptable to take the goods of others, one wishes destruction of those goods by casting an evil eye upon them. The proverb is thus a warning against this propensity.

**27:21** Praise is a key element of honor. ▶**Honor and Shame.** Honor by definition is a public claim to status or worth and a public recognition of that claim. Praise confirms one's claim to honor. However, the appropriate cultural response to praise is humility. ▶**Humility.** One denies the praise in hopes that it will be repeated even more emphatically (see Mark 10:17-18//Luke 18:18-19). Thus praise tests the person's cultural humility, which would verify his claim to honor.

**27:22** As has been evident throughout, the fool is a familiar foil to the wise person in Wisdom literature. The word describes more than stupidity or ignorance. It carries a moral connotation. The fool deliberately lives a life displeasing to God and is hopelessly incorrigible. That is precisely the meaning of this proverb. Glib reference to harsh physical discipline simply reflects the culture's comfort with this strategy.

**27:23-27** A peasant would not need to be reminded of the necessities for survival: food and clothing (Pilch 1999: 52–58; 135–40). The key, however, is probably in v. 24: "riches do not last forever." These verses are therefore an admonition to deal with the precious little one has rather than to lust after unproductive treasure that is subject to theft or seizure.

## Proverbs 28:1-28

1 The wicked flee when no one pursues,
   but the righteous are as bold as a lion.
2 When a land rebels it has many rulers;
   but with an intelligent ruler there is lasting order.
3 A ruler who oppresses the poor
   is a beating rain that leaves no food.
4 Those who forsake the law praise the wicked,
   but those who keep the law struggle against them.
5 The evil do not understand justice,
   but those who seek the Lord understand it completely.
6 Better to be poor and walk in integrity
   than to be crooked in one's ways even though rich.
7 Those who keep the law are wise children,
   but companions of gluttons shame their parents.
8 One who augments wealth by exorbitant interest
   gathers it for another who is kind to the poor.
9 When one will not listen to the law,
   even one's prayers are an abomination.
10 Those who mislead the upright into evil ways
   will fall into pits of their own making,
   but the blameless will have a goodly inheritance.
11 The rich is wise in self esteem,
   but an intelligent poor person sees through the pose.
12 When the righteous triumph, there is great glory,
   but when the wicked prevail, people go into hiding.
13 No one who conceals transgressions will prosper,
   but one who confesses and forsakes them will obtain mercy.
14 Happy is the one who is never without fear,
   but one who is hard-hearted will fall into calamity.
15 Like a roaring lion or a charging bear
   is a wicked ruler over a poor people.
16 A ruler who lacks understanding is a cruel oppressor;
   but one who hates unjust gain will enjoy a long life.
17 If someone is burdened with the blood of another,
   let that killer be a fugitive until death;
   let no one offer assistance.
18 One who walks in integrity will be safe,
   but whoever follows crooked ways will fall into the Pit.
19 Anyone who tills the land will have plenty of bread,

but one who follows worthless pursuits will have plenty of poverty.

20 The faithful will abound with blessings,
    but one who is in a hurry to be rich will not go unpunished.

21 To show partiality is not good—
    yet for a piece of bread a person may do wrong.

22 The miser is in a hurry to get rich
    and does not know that loss is sure to come.

23 Whoever rebukes a person will afterward find more favor
    than one who flatters with the tongue.

24 Anyone who robs father or mother
    and says, "That is no crime,"
    is partner to a thug.

25 The greedy person stirs up strife,
    but whoever trusts in the Lord will be enriched.

26 Those who trust in their own wits are fools;
    but those who walk in wisdom come through safely.

27 Whoever gives to the poor will lack nothing,
    but one who turns a blind eye will get many a curse.

28 When the wicked prevail, people go into hiding;
    but when they perish, the righteous increase.

*Textual Notes: 28:1-28*

**28:3** NRSV emends the Hebrew ("poor man") to "ruler" or "tyrant." The preferable translation is: "a poor man who extorts from another poor man" is like a rain that destroys rather than produces food. Some scholars think the context is tax farming, whereby a person bids for the right to collect taxes. But since he would have to pay the complete sum up front himself, it is difficult to imagine a poor person capable of such a bid. A more likely scenario is that depicted in Lev. 5:21-23; 19:13 (where the same Hebrew verb appears), namely, a simpler exploitation of a poor neighbor by an equally poor person. ▶ **Rich and Poor.** Given the scarcity of goods in the ancient world, it is easy to understand why peasants are notoriously selfish.

**28:5** The point here is justice (Heb. *mišpaṭ*; see Prov. 13:23; Isa. 10:2; Job 36:6), a right every person—even a poor one—possesses and that must be respected and honored, even by God (Job 34:5). The wicked have no understanding of this at all, while the righteous, that is, those who seek the Lord, understand it perfectly.

**28:7** "Law" in this proverb refers to instruction rather than the Torah. The Hebrew text concerns a son (singular) who obeys his father. NRSV offers the inclusive "children" and changes "father" to "parents." Such a son contrasts with a rebellious and disobedient son (see Deut. 21:18-21) who is described as a companion of gluttons. This family proverb reflects the MENA concern for its core cultural value: honor. ►Honor and Shame.

**28:8** The Torah forbade charging interest on loans to fellow Israelites (Exod. 22:24; Lev. 25:36; Deut. 23:20) but not to foreigners (Deut. 23:21). However, many directives in the Bible were ignored in practice. Apparently Israelites did charge interest to fellow ethnics. NRSV "exorbitant interest" is actually two words in Hebrew: interest and overcharge. Interest (*nešek*, related to "to bite") was deducted from the original loan yet had to be repaid in full. Overcharge (*tarbît*, related to "to increase") was an additional sum levied upon repayment. Clearly this was a burden for someone in financial distress. The proverb offers consolation to the beleaguered debtor by implying that divine Providence will have a generous person "pay back" to the poor what an unconscionable lender has extorted.

**28:9** Prayer is "a socially meaningful symbolic act of communication, bearing directly upon persons perceived as somehow supporting, maintaining and controlling the order of existence of the one praying, and performed with the purpose of getting results from or in the interaction of communication" (Malina 1980: 214; Pilch 1999: 123). This proverb says that the person who refuses to hear divine instruction will in turn not be heard by God when that person prays. The prayers of such a person are an abomination, unacceptable to God (Prov. 15:8, 29).

**28:11** Readers in Western culture might be tempted to conclude that this proverb attributes keen psychological insight to the poor person who can see through the façade of self-esteem put forth by a rich person. That would be a serious mistake (Pilch 1997b). According to the Bible, only God can read hearts (1 Sam. 16:7). It is a common practice for men in MENA cultures to "make themselves out to be" other than they know they are in point of fact. Thus a rich person by dint of his wealth considers himself "wise in his own eyes" (literal Hebrew). The shrewd poor person reads reality more clearly and truthfully. The judgment is based on external actions, as when Jonathan learns his father Saul's true attitude toward David through his external behavior (1 Sam. 20:11-34).

**28:13** This proverb can be considered a variant expression of "fear of the Lord." Fear of the Lord means acknowledging God, showing proper respect, and keeping the commandments. The Hebrew word translated "transgressions" refers to serious acts of rebellion, especially against God, whose reaction is to thwart that person's success in life. Conversely, confessing to God and turning from such offenses wins mercy and forgiveness from God (see Ps. 32:1-5). Moreover, God will bless that person's efforts with success ("prosperity").

**28:14** This is one of more than eighty makarisms (Greek *makarios*: how honorable!) in the Bible. "Happy" is not an appropriate translation (Hanson 1994: 81–111). The Hebrew word ʔašrê belongs to the semantic field of honor, thus is more properly translated "how honorable!" (see also Prov. 3:18; 8:32, 34; 14:21; 16:20; 20:7; 28:14; 29:18; 31:28). The proverb states that true honor involves caution and vigilance. Such a person will not slip up and incur shame. In contrast, a hard-hearted person, in the sense of someone bold and brash (see Exod. 3:7), will fall victim to what was not "feared" and will experience shame.

**28:16** The Hebrew of the first verse is quite corrupt, and so is variously emended and translated. The Jewish Study Bible is like the NRSV as reported here. NABRE offers a variation: "the less prudent the rulers, the more oppressive their deeds." Clifford (1999: 242) identifies the contrast in the verses as that between abundance and lack. "Who abounds in extortions is lacking in sense; those renouncing loot increase their days." The cultural context for this exhortation is belief in the finite quantity of desirable goods. ▶**Limited Good**. The sensible person, satisfied with what is possessed, will have abundant life. The greedy person eager to acquire more is simply stupid.

**28:17** The cultural context of this proverb is the role of the "avenger" (Hebrew: *gô'ēl*: next of kin; see Sir. 30:6; Lev. 25:25). Obliged to take revenge for a slight of honor against his family, the avenger might sometimes have unwittingly killed the wrong person. Hence cities of refuge were established where he could await a judgment on his culpability and avoid retaliation from his victim's relatives (Deut. 4:41-43; 19:1-13; Exod. 21:12-14; Joshua 20). This proverb (some scholars think it is not a proverb but rather a law mistakenly included in Proverbs) appears to highlight the different between the ideal (cities of refuge) and the real (the avenger will be a fugitive until he dies; no one will want to help him). ▶**Normative Inconsistency.**

**28:19** See comment on Prov. 12:11.

**28:20** The cultural context of this proverb is the peasant belief that all desirable good things are finite in quantity and already distributed. ▶**Limited Good.** The one hurrying to get rich would be considered greedy, which would be very shameful. ▶**Honor and Shame.** The suspicion is that haste in acquiring wealth suggests wrongdoing (Prov. 13:11; 20:21). God will punish such a person but bless a faithful person abundantly.

**28:21** "To show partiality" is literally in Hebrew "pay regard to faces." Though it is condemned in Deut. 1:17; 16:19, as with many condemned deeds in the Bible it seems to have been widely practiced. It was certainly a key element in patronage. ▶**Patronage.** Even God shows partiality (Mal. 1:2-3; Rom. 9:6-18). Here, however, the context would seem to be judicial, the law courts, and the issue is a paltry bribe ("piece of bread")—either for the judge or for witnesses—for the sake of which justice is thwarted.

**28:22** NRSV "miser" is literally in Hebrew "evil of eye." ▶**Evil Eye.** Ethnographic evidence indicates that forty-three percent of the world's cultures believe that certain people, especially those with ocular irregularities (amblyopia—lazy eye, joined eyebrows, etc.) are capable of causing damage and loss to things of value or beauty simply by their glance (Elliott). This is so because the eye projects the sentiments of the heart (heart–eyes symbolic body zone; Gross 1999: 58-64). ▶**Three-Zone Personality.** The person who has they evil eye hastens to acquire wealth (see v. 20 above) but may himself become the victim of another person's evil eye.

**28:23** Honor-based cultures strive to treat every person respectfully (unless circumstances dictate otherwise). ▶**Honor and Shame**. This means avoiding any word or deed that might shame another. Even a well-intentioned rebuke shames another person. Hence the basic cultural rule is to say what the other person expects to hear. Flattery is preferable to truth. ▶**Lying**. This proverb encourages honest and truthful rebuke (see Prov. 19:25; 25:12) that, while initially painful to the listener, will be appreciated later and bring favor to the critic.

**28:24** This is one of a cluster of proverbs concerned with proper respect for parents (Prov. 19:26; 20:20; 30:11, 17). The reference is probably to a son seeking to anticipate his inheritance before the death of his father (since inheritance is through the father, the word "mother" may have been inserted later). Sons, single and married, continued to live in the compound of the patriarch, while daughters moved and always lived with the husband's family. The Hebrew word rendered "robs" (*gāzal*) implies violence, while the word translated as "thug" (*mašḥît*) describes the worst kind of criminal, some would say a murderer. The son's misdeed is all the worse if he denies that it is a sin. He is no better than a base criminal.

**28:27** In this proverb, being poor refers to lacking something necessary for honorable living. It may be a coin, but it also can be some material item such as food or clothing. *Poor* need not have a monetary significance. ▶**Rich and Poor**. Sharing with the poor—however small the item might be—will be rewarded by God (Prov. 19:17). Refusing to share will bring curses—either from the suppliant or from God (Prov. 3:33).

## Proverbs 29:1-27

1 One who is often reproved, yet remains stubborn,
   will suddenly be broken beyond healing.
2 When the righteous are in authority, the people rejoice;
   but when the wicked rule, the people groan.
3 Who loves wisdom makes a parent glad,

but to keep company with prostitutes is to squander one's substance.

4 By justice a king gives stability to the land,
   but one who makes heavy exactions ruins it.

5 Whoever flatters a neighbor
   is spreading a net for the neighbor's feet.

6 In the transgression of the evil there is a snare,
   but the righteous sing and rejoice.

7 The righteous know the rights of the poor;
   the wicked have no such understanding.

8 Scoffers set a city aflame,
   but the wise turn away wrath.

9 If the wise go to law with fools,
   there is ranting and ridicule without relief.

10 The bloodthirsty hate the blameless,
   and they seek the life of the upright.

11 A fool gives full vent to anger,
   but the wise quietly holds it back.

12 If a ruler listens to falsehood,
   all his officials will be wicked.

13 The poor and the oppressor have this in common:
   the Lord gives light to the eyes of both.

14 If a king judges the poor with equity,
   his throne will be established forever.

15 The rod and reproof give wisdom,
   but a mother is disgraced by a neglected child.

16 When the wicked are in authority, transgression increases,
   but the righteous will look upon their downfall.

17 Discipline your children, and they will give you rest;
   they will give delight to your heart.

18 Where there is no prophecy, the people cast off restraint,
   but happy are those who keep the law.

19 By mere words servants are not disciplined,
   for though they understand, they will not give heed.

20 Do you see someone who is hasty in speech?
   There is more hope for a fool than for anyone like that.

21 A slave pampered from childhood
   will come to a bad end.

22 One given to anger stirs up strife,
   and the hothead causes much transgression.

23 A person's pride will bring humiliation,
   but one who is lowly in spirit will obtain honor.

24 To be a partner of a thief is to hate one's own life;
   one hears the victim's curse, but discloses nothing.

25 The fear of others lays a snare,
   but one who trusts in the Lord is secure.

26 Many seek the favor of a ruler,
　　but it is from the Lord that one gets justice.
27 The unjust are an abomination to the righteous,
　　but the upright are an abomination to the wicked.

*Textual Notes: 29:1-27*

**29:1** NRSV "Stubborn" translates the literal Hebrew "stiff-necked," a phrase describing people who refuse to accept reproof (Deut. 10:16; 31:27; Exod. 32:9; 2 Kgs. 17:14; Prov. 13:18; 15:10).

**29:3** Prostitution was condemned in ancient Israel, but it did exist, and males resorted to it. The cultural background is that young men want to be "experienced" and knowledgeable on their wedding night, but they also want to marry a woman who has not had sexual relations (see Gen. 24:16; also Pilch 2012a: 106–10). So the primary purpose of prostitution is to provide young men with the opportunity to gain the desired proficiency. In this proverb the Sage points out what was commonly known. Consorting with prostitutes causes one to run the risk of being disowned by one's father, not to mention wasting one's resources for fleeting pleasure. Worse yet is putting the inheritance at risk if the prostitute should conceive and bear a son. Obviously, a son (the word should be supplied in translations) who pursues wisdom gives more joy to a father (literal Hebrew) than a profligate son.

**29:4** NRSV "one who makes heavy exactions" is literally in Hebrew "man who exacts gifts." Though this could describe the acceptance of bribes it quite likely means "levies extortionate taxation." The fact that biblical Hebrew lacks specific words for taxation suggests that neither the vocabulary nor the practice was systematic or well developed in ancient Israel. Nevertheless, "taxes" included state taxes, tolls, rents, liens, various categories of tributes, religious dues, and labor levies (Oakman 2012: 63). The result was perpetual indebtedness among the peasantry. Hence the obvious meaning of this proverb is that a ruler who administers justice equitably (see Prov. 16:10; 29:26; 21:3, 15) builds up a stable nation. The one who imposes excessive "taxes" breaks it down.

**29:5** In MENA cultures whose core values are honor and shame, it is imperative never to shame another person. Thus in conversation one always says what the other wants to hear, whether or not it is true. Flattery is part of this strategy. One says complimentary things to a neighbor, even if they are not true. In this proverb the Sage warns that such speech sets the neighbor up for a tragic fall. From another perspective, to speak flattery (mouth–ears symbolic body zone) in contradiction to what one knows and thinks (heart–eyes symbolic body zone) damages the subject of the flattery (hands–feet symbolic body zone). ▶ **Three-Zone Personality**.

**29:7** The plausible context of this proverb is the legal system and its treatment of the poor. Keep in mind that "poor" is not always or primarily an economic designation. It often refers to powerlessness or to temporary loss of inherited status. ▶ **Rich and Poor**. Thus one difference between the righteous and the wicked is their empathy (or lack of it) toward those who have lost inherited status and perhaps seek to have it restored in the law courts.

**29:8** "City" in the ancient biblical world has practically nothing in common with modern cities. Thomas Carney observes that "the gulf between an ancient city and a modern one is immense" (Carney 1975: 86). Malina sketches the differences between ancient central places embedded in ruralized societies and modern cities situated in urban industrial and urbanized societies (Malina 2000: 27–31). Essentially, ancient cities are a bounded, centralized set of social relationships (Malina 2000: 40). This proverb contrasts scoffers with the wise. Scoffers "enflame" (literally "breathe out [upon]," which in its other occurrences in Proverbs has "lies" as its object: Prov. 6:19; 14:5, 25; 19:5, 9) a city. Thus the scoffer causes social unrest (perhaps with his lies) among the bounded social relationships ("city"), while a wise person knows how to reestablish calm.

**29:9** A number of proverbs discourage dealing with fools (Prov. 13:20; 14:7; 26:4). This one is not about going to law (as NRSV translates it) but rather disputing or arguing with another (see Jer. 2:25; Ezek. 17:20; 20:35, 36; etc.). Given the agonistic nature of MENA cultures, arguments and disputes are common events eagerly engaged in.

▶**Agonism.** The problem in disputing or arguing with a fool is that such a one refuses to follow the cultural rules but rather resorts to rant and ridicule. Thus whether the issue at hand is a problem to be resolved or just an agonistic exchange, the fool is not a worthy partner.

**29:11** MENA cultural value orientation is toward spontaneity, acting without thought of the consequences (Pilch and Malina 2009: xxx–xxxi). The cultural remedy for anticipated damaging behavior is for a kinsperson or friend to intervene and halt the action before any damage is done. Thus a wise person knows how to master self-control (Prov. 14:29; 16:32) or to have such safeguards in place, while the fool knows no self-restraint and does not seek help in controlling angry outbursts.

**29:13** This proverb is a variation on Prov. 22:2. Preferable to NRSV "have this in common" is "meet." The phrase "give light to the eyes" means "to allow to live" (see Ps. 13:4). Thus God has created both the poor person and the oppressor, and God will judge each accordingly.

**29:15** The NRSV translation is misleading. "Neglected" is literally "let loose" and often refers to animals (Job 39:5; Isa. 16:2). Animals are domesticated by the use of a staff (see Lev. 27:32; Ps. 23:4). A lad (masculine) undisciplined will bring shame to his mother. The mention of mother alone indicates that the context envisioned by the proverb is the early rearing of sons by all the women in the women's quarters (Pilch 1993). ▶**Discipline.** Sons are pampered and spoiled because they cement the mother's position in the family and will be her security in later years. When, at the age of puberty, they are ejected from the women's quarters without any rite of transition into the harsh world of the men, those men now have to teach them how to be men and how to act in proper male fashion (see Prov. 13:23; 19:18; 22;15; 23:13-14). This proverb advises the mothers/women to anticipate this and teach wisdom to young men by harsh physical discipline from the earliest age.

**29:17** This proverb adds to the theme found repeatedly in this book, namely, disciplining one's son (literal Hebrew; NRSV's inclusive language translation "children" distorts the cultural significance). (See the comment on v. 15 above; also Prov. 19:18; 23:13.) "Rest" quite probably refers to peace of mind derived from knowing one has raised a responsible son whose task in adulthood is to care for his parents. NRSV "give delight to your heart" is better interpreted as "providing food for your hunger" (see Hos. 9:4). "Heart" is literally "soul," (*nepeš*), a word that can also mean "throat" or "hunger." ►**Nepeš/soul.** The proverb urges disciplining young sons in order to produce responsible and loving adults.

**29:18** NRSV "prophecy" is literally in Hebrew "vision," the normal medium through which God communicates to human beings (1 Sam. 3:1). In the prophetic literature, vision refers to the vision of the prophet through which God gives instruction or directives for the people. Collectivistic personalities do not stand on their own two feet or march to their own melody. They rather heed authority (e.g., of God through the prophet) or follow the wisdom of the group. ►**Collectivistic Society.** This proverb considers the situation in which there is a lack of prophetic guidance from God (see Amos 8:11-12). People are discouraged; they cast off restraint. The second verse switches from the plural to the singular. "Truly honorable" (rather than "blessed" or "happy": see Hanson 1994: 81–111; Prov. 3:18; 8:32, 34; 14:21; 16:20; 20:7; 28:14; 29:18; 31:28) "is the one who heeds the instruction of the Sages, or possibly the priests" **(see Murphy 1998: 222).** Thus in the absence of divine guidance through prophecy a person can safely rely on wise instruction.

**29:19** This is yet another piece of advice about the value of strict physical discipline in MENA cultures. It is as necessary for slaves as for children (who sometimes are viewed as similar to slaves, Sir. 3:7). Words alone will not get a response, that is, obedience. The words will rather be met by silent resistance. Physical discipline is key to gaining the obedience of a slave.

**29:20** The key idea in this proverb concerns one who is "hasty in speech." MENA cultures value spontaneity, that is, action with no consideration of its effects or consequences. Spontaneity includes speaking too hastily without sufficient thought for the consequences.

Obviously such behavior has the potential to cause severe damage. Nevertheless, it is part and parcel of the culture's values and it is typical of a fool (Prov. 10:15; 12:16, 23; 14:30). Through hyperbole this proverb says it is even worse than the unguarded speech of a fool. The proverb seeks to encourage proper use of speech by a shaming comparison with the behavior of a fool.

**29:21** The saying promotes physical discipline for slaves.

**29:23** This proverb is still another reminder to practice cultural humility in order to gain honor. ▶**Humility**. (See the commentaries on Prov. 11:2; 16:18.)

**29:24** This proverb relates to Lev. 5:1-5, in which the victim of a thief pronounces a curse publicly to compel a witness (or accomplice) to testify to the injustice (see Kitz 2014 on the significance of curses in MENA cultures). Refusing to accept this obligation, the witness incurs divine judgment (severe penalty), which can only be avoided by subsequent confession and the offering of the appropriate propitiatory sacrifice. We have noted in this book that legal proceedings did not always ensure justice. Witnesses lied or refused to testify. This proverb is one more exhortation to speak the truth in the service of justice.

**29:25** Collectivistic personalities are always concerned about the opinions of others. They derive their honor status from others who can recognize and affirm or deny the claims. ▶**Collectivistic Societies**. Hence the Sage points out that trusting in the Lord is the key to security, rather than being gripped by trembling or terror at the prospect of what other human beings may think or say. Such fear becomes a trap that forces a person to follow a foolish or dishonest and thus shameful course of action. The book of Proverbs frequently reminds one of the importance of fearing, that is, respecting the Lord. The Sage knows only too well the power of the opinions of other people in collectivistic society.

## VI. Proverbs 30:1–31:9

### Proverbs 30:1-14: The Words of Agur

1 The words of Agur son of Jakeh. An oracle.

Thus says the man: I am weary, O God,
I am weary, O God. How can I prevail?
2 Surely I am too stupid to be human;
I do not have human understanding.
3 I have not learned wisdom,
nor have I knowledge of the holy ones.
4 Who has ascended to heaven and come down?
Who has gathered the wind in the hollow of the hand?
Who has wrapped up the waters in a garment?
Who has established all the ends of the earth?
What is the person's name?
And what is the name of the person's child?
Surely you know!
5 Every word of God proves true;
he is a shield to those who take refuge in him.
6 Do not add to his words,
or else he will rebuke you, and you will be found a liar.
7 Two things I ask of you;
do not deny them to me before I die:
8 Remove far from me falsehood and lying;
give me neither poverty nor riches;
feed me with the food that I need,
9 or I shall be full, and deny you,
and say, "Who is the Lord?"
or I shall be poor, and steal,
and profane the name of my God.
10 Do not slander a servant to a master,
or the servant will curse you, and you will be held guilty.
11 There are those who curse their fathers
and do not bless their mothers.
12 There are those who are pure in their own eyes
yet are not cleansed of their filthiness.
13 There are those—how lofty are their eyes,
how high their eyelids lift!
14 There are those whose teeth are swords,
whose teeth are knives,
to devour the poor from off the earth,
the needy from among mortals.

Some scholars consider Proverbs 30 and 31 a series of appendices to the book. Scholars are also not agreed on how much of Proverbs 30 belongs to the words of Agur. A good discussion of the opinions is presented by Richard Clifford (Clifford 1999: 256–58). We follow Clifford's outline.

*Textual Notes: 30:1-14*

**30:1-4** Agur is an unknown and presumably foreign, that is, non-Israelite sage. The identity of his father, Jakeh, is also unknown. It is possible that both names are fictitious, that is, that these were not historical persons. The point of the oracle (i.e., these verses) would seem to be a caution that the book of Proverbs' emphasis on wisdom as a supreme value should be balanced by piety, the recognition that true wisdom is a gift from God. What sounds at first like typical MENA cultural humility is in reality a true expression of a human being's relationship with God. ▶**Humility.**

Patrick Skehan offers a plausible interpretation of the significance of Agur (Skehan 1971: 42–43). Agur means "I am a sojourner," echoing the patriarch Jacob's description of himself ("the days of the *years of my sojourning* is a hundred and thirty years," Gen. 47:9). The denial of having knowledge of "the holy ones" (v. 3) reminds a reader of precisely such knowledge attributed to Jacob (Wis. 10:10). The allusion in v. 4 to ascending and descending a ladder reaching to the sky is yet another connection with Jacob (Gen. 28:12-13). Agur is thus a representation of Jacob/Israel, the Lord's son (Exod. 4:22). And who is his father, Jakeh? The Lord! The Hebrew for Jakeh (*yqh*) is an abbreviation of *Yhwh qādôš hû'* (The Lord, blessed is he—"an antecedent of the well-known *haqqādôš bārûk hû'*" (The Holy One, blessed is he; Skehan 1971: 43). The answer to the question in v. 4 is Agur (Jacob/Israel), the son of the Lord.

**30:5-6** Only God can give reliable knowledge, and that is contained in words from God. Hence no one should add to these words, pretending to have wisdom from a source other than God.

**30:7-10** Verses 7-9 present a model of prayer addressed to the Lord, composed by a pious and wise man and presented for imitation and reflection. Prayer is an act of communication addressed to a superior being in the hope of influencing that being to accede to the petitioner's request (Malina 1980: 214). It has an introduction (v. 7); requests or petitions (v. 8); and motives (v. 9). The request to be rescued from falsehood and lying is particularly significant in MENA culture which values or regards secrecy, deception and lying as legitimate tools in the defense of one's honor. ▶Lying. The request for "the bread of my portion," that is, only the food that I need, states a core value of MENA cultures: interpersonal contentment. This means a willingness "to acquiesce in human finitude and limitation and yet to strive to achieve a genuinely human existence, finite and free" (Malina 2010: 114). The typical Israelite expression of this core value is šālôm, "the presence of everything necessary for an adequately meaningful human existence realizing the core value" (Malina 2010: 132). For Israelites the replication of this core value took the form of studying and practicing Torah. The main idea is to avoid offending God.

**30:11-14** Each of these verses describes a kind of human behavior condemned in other parts of the book of Proverbs. The behaviors are unfilial (Prov. 19:26; 20:20; 28:24), or characterize the self-righteous (Prov. 16:2; 20:9), the arrogant (Prov. 6:17a; 21:4) and the rapacious (Prov. 1:10-19; 6:1, 7b; 12:6).

### Proverbs 30:15-33: Numerical Sayings

15 The leech has two daughters;
   "Give, give," they cry.
   Three things are never satisfied;
   four never say, "Enough":
16 Sheol, the barren womb,
   the earth ever thirsty for water,
   and the fire that never says, "Enough."
17 The eye that mocks a father
   and scorns to obey a mother
   will be pecked out by the ravens of the valley
   and eaten by the vultures.
18 Three things are too wonderful for me;
   four I do not understand:
19 the way of an eagle in the sky,

the way of a snake on a rock,
the way of a ship on the high seas,
and the way of a man with a girl.

20 This is the way of an adulteress:
she eats, and wipes her mouth,
and says, "I have done no wrong."

21 Under three things the earth trembles;
under four it cannot bear up:

22 a slave when he becomes king,
and a fool when glutted with food;

23 an unloved woman when she gets a husband,
and a maid when she succeeds her mistress.

24 Four things on earth are small,
yet they are exceedingly wise:

25 the ants are a people without strength,
yet they provide their food in the summer;

26 the badgers are a people without power,
yet they make their homes in the rocks;

27 the locusts have no king,
yet all of them march in rank;

28 the lizard can be grasped in the hand,
yet it is found in kings' palaces.

29 Three things are stately in their stride;
four are stately in their gait:

30 the lion, which is mightiest among wild animals
and does not turn back before any;

31 the strutting rooster, the he-goat,
and a king striding before his people.

32 If you have been foolish, exalting yourself,
or if you have been devising evil,
put your hand on your mouth.

33 For as pressing milk produces curds,
and pressing the nose produces blood,
so pressing anger produces strife.

This segment of Proverbs 30 features a poetic device (literary form) that is common in Semitic languages and literatures (Roth 1962: 307). This formula (x and x + 1) and variations occur thirty-eight times in the Hebrew Bible and Sirach (see Amos 1:3–2:6; Mic. 5:4; Eccl. 11:2; Prov. 6:16-19; etc.), and five times in this chapter: vv. 15b-16; 18-19; 21-23; [24-28]; 29-31).

*Textual Notes: 30:15-33*

**30:15-16** The two daughters of the leech are the suckers at the two ends of its body. The theme of these verses is the insatiable nature of the items listed: Sheol, barren womb, dry earth of Palestine, and fire.

**30:17** Resuming a theme that runs through Proverbs, these verses describe the fate that awaits an undutiful son. He will not be buried after dying, and vultures will consume his remains in the open field (1 Kgs. 14:11). The implication is that his own kin will dishonor him by refusing to bury him properly (Gen. 25:7-11; 35:29; 50:12, 24-26).

**30:18-19** The focus in this numerical proverb is on the "way," that is, road, course, or manner. The point is not *how* the first three things manage to be mobile, or that they leave *no trace*. Rather, their "way" or the "manner in which they act" is unrecoverable, truly something marvelous. The manner of the eagle, snake, and ship help focus on the mystery of mutual sexual attraction and how a man and woman establish a relationship. The Hebrew word for woman (*'almâh*) is the same one used in Isa. 7:14: a woman of marriageable and childbearing age.

**30:20** This apparently banal observation about an adulteress plays on a double meaning of the Hebrew (Clifford 1999: 266). "To eat" in the Talmud can also mean "to sleep with" (*b. Ketub.* 65.13-23). "Mouth" can also refer to the vulva (*b. Sanh.* 100a; *b. Menah.* 98a). The habit has become so ingrained that its guilt is completely denied.

**30:21-23** This third numerical proverb is intended to be humorous. The reversals here (except for the slave who would usurp the kingship) are hardly earthshaking. The focus is on the result of such unexpected reversals of social propriety, namely, intolerable conceit or arrogant behavior on the part of those who find their situations reversed. Once again it is well to remember that in MENA cultures marriages are arranged. The "unloved" (literally "hated") woman who finds a husband would be one whose parents finally manage to make a match for her, which, by the nature of marriage in MENA cultures, is the union of the honor of two families for the purpose of benefiting both

(Malina 2001a: 134–60). The maid who succeeds her mistress can achieve this by special favor from the husband (Gen. 16:1-6; 24:1-13) or the birth of a child (1 Sam. 1:1-8).

**30:24-28** This fourth numerical saying praises insignificant (the meaning of "small") beings that are capable of taking good care of themselves (the meaning of "wise"). The implication is that human beings who can acquire (presumably superior) wisdom are thereby able to overcome many natural disadvantages. The last example, "lizard" (more plausibly "gecko"), is a humorous comment. It is of no benefit to the gecko to be in a royal palace, but the fact that it gets there is a tribute to its insolent boldness.

**30:29-31** This last of the numerical sayings describes the leadership abilities of various animals and a king, manifest in their stately stride.

**30:32-33** As previously noted, MENA cultures accept spontaneous responses (especially from males) with no thought of the consequences. This proverb thus singles out two thoughtless behaviors: foolishly exalting oneself (thus neglecting the requisite cultural humility) ▶**Humility**, and intentionally devising evil, which always runs the risk of receiving a similar or worse evil in response. The advice is "hand to mouth," that is, do not do it! (See Judg. 18:19). Do not bring it to fruition. MENA cultures propose fantasy rather than effective action. Better to think about it, that is, take pleasure in imagining it than to actually execute it (Pilch 2007: 64–67).

Verse 33 presents the motive for the advice, emphasizing the word "churn" (NRSV "pressing": Clifford 1999: 268). Churning milk produces curds (Hebrew: ḥêm'âh, ghee, or ghi, a semifluid clarified butter, related to the Hebrew word for wrath, ḥēmâh). To churn the nose is to stir up anger, since the Hebrew word translated "nose" means anger, that is, the result will be a bloody nose for someone. And churning the anger of another person initiates feud, strife, even physical violence. The proverb proposes the ideal (self-restraint), while reality often requires the intervention of a third party (a "peacemaker") who stifles the violence before it get out of hand. Feud can lead to violence, which in turn can lead to bloodshed. There is no end to blood feud in MENA cultures. Hence it is best to nip it in the bud.

### Proverbs 31:1-9: The Words of Lemuel, King of Massa

1 The words of King Lemuel. An oracle that his mother taught him:

2 No, my son! No, son of my womb!
  No, son of my vows!
3 Do not give your strength to women,
  your ways to those who destroy kings.
4 It is not for kings, O Lemuel,
  it is not for kings to drink wine,
  or for rulers to desire strong drink;
5 or else they will drink and forget what has been decreed,
  and will pervert the rights of all the afflicted.
6 Give strong drink to one who is perishing,
  and wine to those in bitter distress;
7 let them drink and forget their poverty,
  and remember their misery no more.
8 Speak out for those who cannot speak,
  for the rights of all the destitute.
9 Speak out, judge righteously,
  defend the rights of the poor and needy.

*Textual Notes: 31:1-9*

**31:1-9** These verses are an example of "royal instruction" given by a Queen Mother to her son. While instruction was most often given by fathers, mothers—especially in the kingdom of Judah—had great power and familiarity with the intricacies of palace politics. This mother was well suited to provide shrewd advice to her son.

**31:1** Some scholars prefer to read v. 1 differently than does the NRSV. "The words of Lemuel, king of Massa . . . ." Massa is a North Arabian tribe, and mention of a king's name is usually followed by the name of his country. The several Aramaisms in these verses attest to the non-Israelite origin of the advice, though it would be pertinent in many kingdoms of the ancient Semitic world.

**31:2** The Hebrew of NRSV "no" is difficult to translate. Some scholars suggest something like "what troubles you?" or "what is it with you?" (See Gen. 21:17), implying a mild rebuke (Clifford 1999: 269).

**31:3-5** This exhortation cautions against excessive indulgence in sex and alcohol, which might cause the king to forget the poor. Again it is important to remember that "poor" in the Bible is not primarily an economic designation. ▶ **Rich and Poor**. The context seems to indicate that it is not the lack of resources that plagues these unfortunate folk; rather, it is their lack of status, power, and influence.

**31:6-9** Here the king is advised to advocate on behalf of the unfortunate. But rather shocking is also the advice to give strong drink to these people to help them forget their poverty and misery. Scholars are not agreed on what this advice might mean in reality. The bottom line, however, is that the king should use his authority to practice justice rather than wear it as a mark of superiority.

### VII. Proverbs 31:10-31:
### Hymn to the Capable Wife

10 A capable wife who can find?
　　She is far more precious than jewels.
11 The heart of her husband trusts in her,
　　and he will have no lack of gain.
12 She does him good, and not harm,
　　all the days of her life.
13 She seeks wool and flax,
　　and works with willing hands.
14 She is like the ships of the merchant,
　　she brings her food from far away.
15 She rises while it is still night
　　and provides food for her household
　　and tasks for her servant girls.
16 She considers a field and buys it;
　　with the fruit of her hands she plants a vineyard.
17 She girds herself with strength,
　　and makes her arms strong.
18 She perceives that her merchandise is profitable.
　　Her lamp does not go out at night.
19 She puts her hands to the distaff,
　　and her hands hold the spindle.
20 She opens her hand to the poor,

and reaches out her hands to the needy.
21 She is not afraid for her household when it snows,
   for all her household are clothed in crimson.
22 She makes herself coverings;
   her clothing is fine linen and purple.
23 Her husband is known in the city gates,
   taking his seat among the elders of the land.
24 She makes linen garments and sells them;
   she supplies the merchant with sashes.
25 Strength and dignity are her clothing,
   and she laughs at the time to come.
26 She opens her mouth with wisdom,
   and the teaching of kindness is on her tongue.
27 She looks well to the ways of her household,
   and does not eat the bread of idleness.
28 Her children rise up and call her happy;
   her husband too, and he praises her:
29 "Many women have done excellently,
   but you surpass them all."
30 Charm is deceitful, and beauty is vain,
   but a woman who fears the Lord is to be praised.
31 Give her a share in the fruit of her hands,
   and let her works praise her in the city gates.

This is an alphabetic acrostic hymn in praise of an ideal woman, similar to the alphabetic acrostic Psalm 112 in praise of the model man. In Hebrew each of the hymn's twenty-two lines begins with a successive letter of the alphabet. V. 10: **aleph (א)**: *ʾēšet* (from *ʾiššâ*, a wife, woman); v. 11 **beth (ב)**: *bāta* (entrusts), etc. It is carefully structured in chiastic form (vv. 10a-29a) with a chiasm in vv. 19-20 moving the action from within the home out to the public arena (Clifford 1999: 273).

"Capable" (v. 10a)
  "Her husband (v. 11a)
    "Her hand" (v. 19a)
      "Her fingers" (v. 19b)
      "Her palm" (v. 20a)
    "Her hand" (v. 20b)
  "Her husband" (v. 28b)
"Capable" (v. 29a)

It is hardly likely that such an ideal wife combining these sterling qualities existed in the ancient (or even the contemporary) world. Hence scholars argue persuasively that this hymn functions especially on the metaphorical level. It is primarily about Lady Wisdom, and what she offers to those who take up her invitation and join her in her household (McCreesh 1985: 25–46). The basis of the metaphor is the reality of a good wife, a veritable gift from God, who builds her house for the benefit of the entire family and even for those outside the family (e.g., the poor, her husband's mates, etc.). Thus, as Lady Wisdom has earlier in the book of Proverbs invited persons into her house (Prov. 9:1-5) to become her disciples, this concluding chapter spells out the happy results of accepting that invitation.

*Textual Notes: 31:10-31*

**31:10** The Hebrew word rendered here (and in Prov. 3:4; 3:13; 6:33; 18:22 as "find" should preferably be translated in these instances as "get, acquire" (*māṣāʾ*; Prov. 1:28; 3:4; 6:33; 8:35; 28:23). The question "who can find . . . ?" does indeed suggest something impossible. The fact is that in MENA cultures marriages are arranged (by the father, under the heavy influence of the mother, who knows the prospective partner-kin better than he does). (See comment on Prov. 18:22; compare Prov. 19:14.)

**31:18** The lamp that does not go out by night symbolizes prosperity (see Prov. 13:9; 20:20; 24:20).

**31:19-20** By repeating "hands" in each of these verses NRSV obscures the chiasm: v. 19: "hands," "fingers;" v. 20: "palms," "hands." "Open hands" describes generosity (Deut. 15:7-8). She extends her domestic industriousness outside the home, to the poor.

**31:21** Though snow is relatively rare in this climate, the ideal wife prepares her household for the eventuality by supplying a double portion of clothing. This is a preferable rendition of the Hebrew that is translated by NRSV as "crimson," which does not make sense in context.

**31:22** NRSV "coverings" more specifically refers to bedclothes. NRSV "purple" indicates that the clothing is luxurious, since purple was a very expensive dye (Pilch 1999: 19).

**31:23** While this verse may appear to contrast the wife's industriousness with the husband's leisurely activity at the gate (the place were business was conducted, disputes settled, and gossip spread), it actually reflects MENA values—of past and present—very accurately. Men's primary value orientation is toward spontaneity; women's is toward planned and calculated activity. Men represent the family to the outside world; women rule the interior of the household. It is precisely the activity of MENA women that makes MENA men's activities possible and intelligible.

**31:28-31.** NRSV "children" is literally "sons" in Hebrew. NRSV "happy" is better translated "honorable" (Hanson 1994: 81–111). Such a woman brings honor to the family and the entire household. ▶**Honor and Shame**. Since MENA women are embedded in relationships with men (father, brother, husband, sons), it is the men who benefit from their honorable behavior. They justifiably and proudly sing her praises (v. 29) as a woman who knows how to revere the Lord (v. 30).

**31:31** The hymn ends with a verse that can be viewed as a proclamation to the public assembly (Prov. 5:14; 26:26). Preferable to NRSV "give her a share" would be "extol or praise or celebrate her for her achievements" (Whybray 1994: 431; Murphy 1998: 245). Let her achievements be her claim to honor at the city gates.

# 2

---

# Reading Scenarios for the Book of Proverbs

These reading scenarios (see Preface) have been drawn from the *Social Science Commentaries on the New Testament* (Fortress Press), co-authored by Bruce J. Malina, John J. Pilch, and Richard L. Rohrbaugh.

## Adultery

Proverbs 5:1-23; 6:20-35; 7 address the topic of adultery, which is of concern throughout the Bible (e.g., Exod. 20:14; Deut. 5:18). In general, adultery means to "trespass on the honor of another male by having sexual intercourse with his wife, who is embedded in her husband" (Malina 2001: 238). By this definition a woman cannot commit adultery. On the part of the guilty male it is equivalent to theft (Prov. 6:30-35), that is, shaming another male by taking some good that is embedded in that male, the owner. But adultery—like marriage—is culture-specific and derives its meaning from its respective culture. Bruce J. Malina has sketched a useful history of marriage (including adultery) in Israel (Malina 2001: 134-60); eventually, adultery was viewed as an abomination to God (Lev. 18:20; Ezek. 22:11). The punishment was death (Lev. 20:10).The ancients' concern was the possibility of offspring. An adulterer put the family patrimony at risk, and this would be considered disastrous. Adultery was also given symbolic interpretation as infidelity to God and the covenant (Hos. 4:2, 13-14; Jer. 2:23-25).

Medical and social scientists, especially those who make use of the ethnographic data in the Human Relations Area Files (HRAF) at Yale University, prefer to speak of "extramarital sex" or an "extramarital relationship" instead of "adultery," which carries with it the notion of condemnation or sin in the Judaeo-Christian and Islamic world (Levinson 1995: 242–47). It has to be understood instead within the notion of marriage as "a culturally specific set of behaviors rather than as some abstract universal human institution" (Pilch 2012: 123). The meanings ascribed to marriage are culturally quite specific; hence the meaning of adultery is similarly culturally specific, as already noted.

## Age

For Westerners accustomed to long—and steadily increasing—life expectancies it is difficult to judge the significance of age markers in the Bible. In antiquity nearly a third of those surviving the initial months of infancy were dead before the age of six. By the mid-teens, sixty percent would have died. By the mid-twenties, seventy-five percent were dead, and by the mid-forties the figure reached ninety percent. Perhaps three percent of the population made it to their sixties. Few ordinary people lived out their thirties.

In 1990 archaeologists uncovered the burial chamber of Caiaphas, the high priest in Jerusalem, who is quoted in the Fourth Gospel as having said: "It is better for you to have one man die for the people than to have the whole nation destroyed" (John 11:50). The skeletal remains of more than sixty persons were found inside the large chamber. Their age distribution provides solid evidence that not even the elite escaped the high death rates noted above.

| Age of Individuals in Burial Chamber of Caiaphas (as determined by Skeletal Remains) | |
|---|---|
| 0-1 years | 10 |
| 2-5 years | 16 |
| 6-12 years | 14 |
| 13-18 years | 3 |
| 19-25 years | 1 |
| 26-39 years | 1 |
| 40+ years | 6 |
| Adult (age unknown) | 13 |

(Source: John Dominic Crossan and Jonathan L. Reed, *Excavating Jesus*
[HarperSanFrancisco, 2001], 243)

The ancient glorification of youth and veneration of the elderly (who in non-literate societies are the only repository of community memory and knowledge) are thus easily misunderstood. Many of the participants in or audience for biblical events would have been disease-ridden and looking at a decade or less of life expectancy.

## Agonism

The Greek word *agōn* refers to an athletic contest or any sort of contest between equals. Anthropologists describe ancient MENA society as "agonistic" because of its intensely competitive nature and the envy commonly directed toward successful persons. Men engage in constant struggle with other men for honor (the core MENA cultural value) and prestige, which is difficult to gain and easy to lose. Plato observed three parts of the human psyche always at war with one another: an appetitive part to satisfy hunger, thirst, and other bodily needs; a rational part that seeks the Good but often lacks the will to follow the pursuit; and a spirited part that loves honor and winning (Plato, *Republic*, 581b). Honor can also be destructive. "Doesn't his love of honor make him envious and his love of victory make him violent, so that he pursues the satisfaction of his anger and of his desires for honors and victories without calculation or understanding?" (Plato, *Republic*, 586d).

In the ancient world most forms of agonistic behavior can be viewed as challenges to reputation and honor that require a defensive—and victorious!—response. Why were the ancients so competitive and envious? There are four possible reasons. One, as Plato observed, love of honor (*philotimia*) pervaded the ancient world. Two, the common peasant perception was that everything of worth and value, including honor, existed in finite and limited supply. Three, envy naturally resulted from the success of others. Four, ancient MENA society was generally competitive for these highly desirable yet limited goods.

Thus, outside one's family or circle of friends every interaction was considered a challenge to honor, a mutual attempt to gain honor from one's social equal. It is important to remember that only equals can play the game of challenge and riposte. Gift-giving (bribes?), invitations to dinner, debates about law, buying and selling, arranging marriages, establishing cooperative ventures for farming, business, fishing, mutual help, etc.—all these interactions are governed by the rules of honor in the game known as challenge and riposte. The cues for agonism in MENA society are constant and steady.

## Collectivistic Society

In contemporary American culture we consider an individual's psychological makeup to be the key to understanding who a person might be. We see each individual as bounded and unique, a more or less integrated motivational and cognitive universe, a dynamic center of awareness and judgment that is set over against other such individuals and interacts with them. This sort of individualism has been and is extremely rare in the world's cultures and is almost certainly absent from the Bible.

In the ancient Mediterranean world such a view of the individual did not exist. There every person was understood to be embedded in others and had his or her identity only in relation to these others who formed this fundamental group. For most people this was the family, and it meant that individuals neither acted nor thought of themselves as persons independent of the family group. What one member of the family was, every member of the family was, psychologically as well as every other way. Mediterraneans are what anthropologists call "collectivistic" or group-oriented persons. They are "dyadic" or "other-oriented" people who depend on others to provide them with a sense of who they are.

Consider the following chart comparing dyadic, collectivist, or strong-group persons (MENA cultures) with individualist, weak-group persons (U.S.):

| Collectivist Person | Individualist |
| --- | --- |
| 1. Much concern about the effect of one's decision upon others (beyond friends and nuclear family). | 1. Much concern about the effect of one's decision on one's present standing and future chances. |
| 2. Persons are prepared to share material resources with group members. | 2. Those who are not part of the nuclear family are expected to provide their own material resources. |
| 3. Persons are ready to share less tangible resources with group members, for example, giving up some interesting activity for group ends. | 3. Generally a person is not expected to and will not share less tangible resources with others, often not even with nuclear family (for example, time to watch weekend football game). |
| 4. Persons are willing to adopt the opinions of others, especially those considered of high esteem in the wider group. | 4. Persons are expected to form their own opinions on a range of issues, especially politics, religion, and sex. Expert opinion accepted only in law and health, and this only for oneself and nuclear family. |
| 5. Persons are constantly concerned about self-presentation and loss of face, since these reflect on the group and one's position in the group. | 5. Unless others are involved in one's goals, there is little concern about one's impression on others. Embarrassment affects the individual (and at times the nuclear family), but not any group at large. |
| 6. Persons believe, feel, and experience an interconnectedness with the whole group, so that positive and negative behavior redounds to the group. | 6. Individualists act as though they are insulated from others; what they do is not perceived to affect others, and what others do does not affect them. |

| | |
|---|---|
| 7. Persons sense themselves to be intimately involved in the life of other group members, making a contribution to the lives of others in the group. | 7. The individualist's life is segmented. Persons feel involved in the lives of very few people, and when they are it is in a very specific way (for example, the teacher, the lawyer, etc.). |
| 8. In sum, strong-group people have "concern" for all group members. This is a sense of oneness with other people, a perception of complex ties and relationships and a tendency to keep other people in mind. The root of this concern is the need for group survival. | 8. In sum, weak-group people have "concern" largely for themselves (and nuclear family, at times). They are insulated from other people, feel themselves independent of and unconnected to others, and tend to think of themselves alone. |

Of course, persons enculturated in collectivistic societies are individuals, but there is a difference between the self in collectivistic societies and the self in individualistic societies (see Hofstede, Hofstede, and Minkov 2010: 89–134). Anthropologists commonly distinguish three distinctive selves: the privately-defined self, the publicly-defined self, and the collectively- or in-group-defined self.

(a) The *private self* is what I myself say about my own traits, states, behaviors. Who is it I think I really am in my heart of hearts?

(b) The *public self* consists of what the general group says about me. Who does that range of people with whom I regularly come in contact think I am? What do neighbors, merchants, teachers, and the like say about me? Do I live up to their expectations when I interact with them? And what do I think of all that these people think of me?

(c) The *collective* or *in-group self* is what the in-group says about me. Who do my parents say I am? What are their expectations for me? Did my family give me a nickname? What does it say about me? What are the expectations of my grandparents, aunts and uncles, cousins, and brothers and sisters in regard to who I am, how I should behave, what I will be? And what do I think of what these people think of me? What do my friends want me to do, over against what my parents want me to do?

To understand the self in terms of social psychology we need to know the way the defined self emerges in the contrasting collectivist and individualistic cultural types. Consider the following diagram in which the enclosed, boxed-in defined selves are expected to match in order to produce "truth."

| Collectivist Culture | Individualist Culture |
|---|---|
| **Privately defined self** | **Privately defined self** |
| **In-group defined self** | **Publicly defined self** |
| Publicly defined self | In-group defined self |

The types of self in bold form a unity in the respective cultures. What this chart makes clear is that in collectivist cultures there is a general conformity between private self and in-group self. Such people take in-group self-assessments far more seriously than do people in individualist cultures. Moreover, individuals are socialized not to express what they personally think, but to say what their conversation partner or audience needs or wants to hear from the in-group.

When it comes to dealing with in-group others, collectivist societies anticipate that individuals will often think one way and speak another. Individuals must keep their private opinions to themselves since such individual private opinions are insignificant and quite boring for the most part. Harmony, or getting along with in-group members, is valued above all sorts of other concerns. Saying the right thing to maintain harmony is thus far more important than telling what seems to be the truth to the private self. In fact, "truth" might be defined here as conformity between what the in-group thinks about some person, event, or thing and what the private self believes and knows. Collectivist persons are not expected to have personal opinions, much less to voice their own opinions. It is sufficient and required to hold only those opinions that derive from the social consensus of in-group members.

In individualist cultures, by contrast, the in-group self recedes. The public and private selves converge to form a single "objectively"- defined private self. Inconsistency between the public and private self is understood to be hypocrisy. One must think and say the same thing. Honesty, frankness, and sincerity are more abstract and less interpersonal for individualists. Everyone is expected to have an opinion on everything and others are supposed to act as though everyone's opinion counts for something.

The way in which the self is defined also determines behavior. The collectivist person represents the in-group and is presumed always to speak in its name. It is shameful to tell the truth if it dishonors one's in-group members or causes them discomfort. It is equally shameful to expect to be told the truth if one is not an in-group member. Out-group persons have no right to in-group truth.

In non-challenging situations out-group persons are almost always told what makes for harmony and what is to be expected. Making a friend feel good by what one says is a way of honoring the other, and that is far more important than "telling the truth." Thus in collectivist cultures the privately defined self and the in-group self tend to coincide. The person speaks in the name of the in-group in public.

By contrast, individualists as a rule fuse the privately and publicly defined selves. The privately defined self and the publicly defined self tend to coincide. The private self is in fact the acting public self. This is called "objectivity," and individualists value being objective in speech. To lie is to say one thing publicly while thinking another privately. Thus in individualistic cultures a person speaks in his/her own name in public.

In each type of culture a lie consists of splitting the selves included in the boxes above. Thus in an individualistic culture a lie is thinking one thing privately and saying another publicly. That involves splitting what one knows privately from what one says publicly. To a collectivist, however, a lie involves splitting private and in-group "truth." In a collectivist culture one's personal, private knowledge has nothing to do with truth.

The right to the truth and the right to withhold the truth belong to the "man of honor," and to contest these rights is to place a person's honor in jeopardy, to challenge that person. Lying and deception are or can be honorable and legitimate when directed to the out-group. To lie in order to deceive an outsider, one who has no right to the truth, is honorable. However, to be called a liar by anyone is a great public dishonor. The reason for this is that truth belongs only to one who has a right to it. To lie really means to deny the truth to one who has a right to it, and the right to the truth only exists where respect is due (in the family, to superiors, and not necessarily to inferiors or to equals with whom I compete). Thus to deceive by making something ambiguous or to lie to an out-group person is to deprive the other of respect, to refuse to show honor, to humiliate another.

A consequence of all this is that ancient collectivistic people did not know each other very well in the way we think most important: psychologically or emotionally. They neither knew nor cared about psychological development and were not introspective. Our comments about the feelings and emotional states of characters in the biblical stories are simply anachronistic projection of our sensibilities onto them. Their concern was with how others thought of them (honor), not how they thought of themselves (guilt). Conscience was the accusing voice of others, not an interior voice of accusation. Their question was not the modern one, "Who am I?" Rather, their questions were those asked by Jesus in Mark 8:27-30: "Who do people say that I am?" and "Who do you say that I am?" It was from significant others that such information came, not from oneself.

A recent anthropological-historical study (Fincher et al. 2008: 1279-85) concluded that, in contrast to individualism, collectivism serves as an antipathogen defense function. Thus the many advantages of individualism pale in comparison with its increased vulnerability to infectious diseases. Collectivism definitely proved to be a stronger defense against infectious disease; thus Fincher et al. conclude that collectivism emerged and existed in populations that historically have been characterized by a greater prevalence of pathogens.

## Discipline

The Hebrew word *mûsār* means "discipline" in the sense of punishment, chastisement—that is, to learn or teach a lesson by means of castigation. This is something like the Pavlovian approach. In Greek culture, however, *paideia* translates the Hebrew *mûsār* and is "the act of providing guidance for responsible living, upbringing, training, instruction." The verb *paideuein* means "to provide instruction for informed and responsible living," or "to assist in the development of a person's ability to make appropriate choices, practice discipline." It was the ideal of the Hellenistic world, namely, to form true humans.

The same could be said of ancient Israel, but the task of forming a "truly human person" took a different tack. In MENA culture women have inferior status relative to men. Even though the typical marriage partner in Israel for a man was his "father's brother's daughter" or patrilateral lateral cousin (absent that possibility, it would be a matrilateral parallel cousin), the bride was never fully accepted into the family until she bore a son. At this point the son became her "social security," for the emotional bond between mother and (usually firstborn) son is closer than that between husband and wife. Boys were reared exclusively by the women in the women's quarters in this rigidly gender-divided society until the age of puberty. They were pampered and spoiled. They were breast-fed twice as long as girls (2 Macc. 7:27); by the time they were weaned they could already speak. Demanding to be fed, they were immediately satisfied, which led boys to realize that—at least in the women's world—their word was law. It would not be difficult for such a boy, grown to adulthood, to compose a creation story in which God's word would work immediate results. "Let there be . . . and there was . . . ."

In the Israelite tradition the Bar Mitzvah has no conclusive evidence for the ritual as we know it today before the Talmudic period and did not exist in biblical times. There was no rite of passage for boys when they reached puberty and had to move into the men's world. It was a harsh and punishing experience, causing them to run back to the women's world, from which they were now repelled (Pilch 1993: 105; Malina and Rohrbaugh 2003: 386-7). They had to enter the men's world as harsh as it was and stood in stark contrast to the world of the women they had known until then. Never having had a male role model or male attention, the boy had to learn how to be a man.

Proverbs indicates that it was through severe physical discipline that boys learned how to suffer in silence and assert their manhood (Prov. 13:24; 19:18; 22:15; 23:13; 29:15, 17; compare Sir. 30:1-13). However, it was a lifelong struggle, for male adults suffered from gender ambiguity as a result of the circumstances of their early years. Jesus wanted to "mother-hen" Jerusalem before he died (Matt. 23:37-39), and Paul was in "labor pains" as he tried to "rebirth" his Galatian followers who had gone temporarily astray after false teachers (Gal. 4:19) (Pilch1993: 101–13). Jesus seems to have succeeded in this task of becoming a man according to Mark's account of his death, in which the centurion attested to his manliness (Mark 15:33–39).

In the context of a Middle Eastern boy's experience of growing up in the women's world, where he was pampered and spoiled, recall some adult experiences of men with women in the Bible. Though Abraham loved Hagar and Ishmael, Sarah forced him to turn them out (Gen. 21:10-11). Notwithstanding the fact that her sons were twins, Rebekah preferred her second-born (Jacob) to her firstborn (Esau) and helped Jacob to trick Isaac, her husband and their father, into giving Jacob the blessing (Genesis 27). Samson, who exhibited both brain (his riddle) and brawn (his murders), was brought to ruin by Delilah (Judges 13–16). A search of the Bible will turn up many more such instances in which women bested men. The presumably "negative" reflections about women by the Sages in Proverbs and Sirach, which are often judged by modern readers to be misogynistic and patriarchal, can be read from another perspective as expressing male fear of the power of Middle Eastern women. Female Middle Eastern anthropologists admit that women in that culture do indeed possess such power and use it effectively (Pilch 1993a: 104). This judgment is clearly confirmed by the advice of Lemuel's mother to her son, king of Massa, in the concluding chapter of Proverbs: "Do not give your strength to women, your ways to those who destroy kings" (Prov. 31:3). She knows how she has trained her daughters to manipulate men and so forewarns her son to be on his guard.

## Economy

There were two formal or free-standing social institutions in antiquity: kinship and politics. Economics and religion were substantive, that is, they were embedded in kinship and politics. There was kinship or household economics (Aristotle referred to this as *oikonomia*). This related to household management, that is, providing for the family, thus buying, selling, dowry, inheritance, and the like. And there was political or temple economics, which included taxes, tithes, redistribution, and the like. The same was true for religion, which was domestic (household gods, ancestor worship) and political (pilgrimages to Jerusalem, temple sacrifices, etc.). The notion of embedded economics is very difficult for Westerners to grasp and appreciate because the cultural context is dramatically different.

In antiquity, economics—whether domestic or political—was the social domain of all sorts of exchange: buying and selling, bartering and trading, borrowing and lending, tax, tribute, and tolls, mints and money, rents and leases, debts and redemption. Therefore the word *economics* in relation to antiquity primarily means provisioning for the household rather than, as in modern experience, referring to individual decisions about allocating scarce resources to a variety of ends (Hanson and Oakman 2008: 179–99).

The ancient economy was agrarian, that is, it was based on land ownership and farm production rather than hunting and gathering, fishing, or industrial activity. "Advanced" agrarian societies used iron tools, the plow rather than the hoe, and large animals (oxen, donkeys, horses) for plowing (1 Sam. 14:19-21; Jer. 52:16). This society was controlled by monarchs who gained and held power by brute force, namely, their military. Moreover, this economy produced surplus beyond what was necessary for subsistence, even though the surplus was siphoned off by the rulers. Furthermore, cities could exist and the population in general could increase. About ten percent lived in the urban areas, supported by the remainder who lived in the surrounding villages and tilled the soil (Fiensy 2010: 195–96).

This state of affairs produced two groups: the takers and the givers. The takers were the aristocrats (about one percent of the population), who lived in the city and did not work on the farm but lived off the surplus produced by the givers, the peasants (ninety percent). The other nine percent were retainers living in the city: landless merchants, craftsmen, day laborers, and the like. The peasants and the aristocrats held different views of reality. The peasant saw land and work as the way to feed his family rather than as a business for profit. The aristocrat saw the land and the peasants as personal "income." Thus aristocrats believed taxes and rents were justly owed to them, while peasants saw these as a burden on their work and their land.

The peasant managed to live by means of reciprocity. ▶**Generalized reciprocity** was giving something to someone with no hope of repayment. This would work only in the intimacy of the family. ▶**Balanced reciprocity** was the ongoing relationship between persons who could meet one another's needs by doing and owing favors to each other. This was the peasant's salvation. ▶**Negative reciprocity** describes how the aristocrats treated the peasants in general. They took with no promise of an exchange or a return.

### Evil Eye

Evil eye belief refers to the conviction that certain individuals, animals, demons, or gods have the power of causing some negative effect on any object, animate or inanimate, upon which they may look. Evil eye works voluntarily or involuntarily. The negative effects it can cause are injuries to the life or health of others, to their means of sustenance and livelihood, to their honor and personal fortune.

Basic to this belief was the notion that certain individuals, animals, demons, or gods had the power of injuring or casting a spell upon every object, animate or inanimate, on which their glance fell. Through the power of their eye, which could operate involuntarily as well as intentionally, such evil eye possessors were thought capable of damaging or destroying their unfortunate victims. In fact, though, such negative effects derived not simply from the power of their eye but from the condition of their heart, since eyes and heart worked in tandem. ▶**Three-Zone Personality.** A number of ancient Mediterranean informants have noted how the effects of the evil eye correlate with envy, a quality of the heart. The eye served to express the innermost dispositions, feelings, and desires of the heart. Numerous biblical passages illustrate this connection of eye and heart (Deut. 28:65; 1 Kgs. 9:3 LXX; Job 30:26-27; 31:1, 7, 9, 26-27; Prov. 15:30; 21:4; 44:18; Ps. 73(72):7; Isa. 6:10; Lam. 5:17; Sir. 22:19; 1 Cor. 2:9). Ephesians 1:18, for instance, speaks of "eyes of the heart" (cf. also 1 Clem. 36:2). Jeremiah 22:17 refers to eyes and heart intent on dishonest gain, shedding blood, and practicing oppression and violence. To understand the ancient Mediterranean perspective on the evil eye, consider how people of the time viewed the relationship between light and the eyes.

For the ancient Mediterranean, light was the presence of light, and darkness was the presence of darkness. That is, both light and darkness were positive entities, having no relationship to any source of light or darkness other than themselves. Thus the sun did not "cause" daylight nor did the moon or stars "cause" light at night. Day and night were simply the structured framework within which the sun and moon operated. Notice that in Genesis the sun, moon, and stars were created after the creation of light and darkness (Gen. 1:3-5, 14-19). While the sun and moon marked the changing of the seasons, they had no influence on the seasons any more than they influenced day or night. The relative darkness of winter was due to the cloudy sky, not to the low path of the sun. In fact, the sun was noted for its warmth rather than its light. Light was present due to the presence of light itself, not the presence of the sun. This meant that the onset of celestial light over the land was the dawn, and the coming of celestial darkness over the land was dusk (not sunrise and sunset).

In the story of creation, the creation of light set light itself apart from preexisting darkness, just as the creation of land (earth) set it apart from ever-present water (Genesis 1). Note that light (day) was created before the sun, and night before the moon. Dawn (morning) and dusk (evening) occur independently of the sun as well. The presence of light and land (earth) allowed for the coming of earthlings. Earthlings, human and otherwise, are created from earth, animated with the breath of life (Gen. 2:7), and endowed with the light of life (Ps. 56:14; Job 33:30), or "living light" as opposed to the light of the sky. Thanks to their living light, animate beings can see.

Sight consists of light emanating from the eyes of living beings (Gross 1999: 58–64). Just as the main humanly-controlled source of light is fire, so too it is because the eyes are made of fire that humans see. As Jesus says, "The eye is the lamp of the body" (Matt. 6:22). Aristotle observed: "Sight (is made) from fire and hearing from air" (*Problems* 31, 960a). "[V]ision is fire" (*Problems* 31, 959b). "Is it because in shame the eyes are chilled (for shame resides in the eyes), so that they cannot face one?" (*Problems* 31, 957b). The eye emits light that has an active effect on the objects upon which its glance falls. "Man both experiences and produces many effects through his eyes; he is possessed and governed by either pleasure or displeasure exactly in proportion to what he sees," one of Plutarch's dinner guests observes (Plutarch, *Quaestionum convivialium* 5.7, 681A).

Similarly, the Israelite tradition believed God's sky-servants (angels) were made of fire. Hence when they appear to humans they look like brilliant light. The fact that celestial bodies, such as stars or comets, emanate light means that they are alive. Stars, whether constellated or not, are living animate entities, as all ancients knew. That is why they move while the earth stands still at the center of creation. Since all living beings have light, light and life go hand in hand. In this perspective all light and life have their origin in the creative work of God alone; they can be handed on by human beings, but not created by them.

Envy thus proceeds from the heart through the eyes. The usual suspects thought to harbor evil eye abilities were family enemies, strangers, outsiders, and deviants as well as the physically deformed, the disabled, and the blind. Strangers and outsiders were presumed to be envious of the good things locals and insiders enjoyed; the socially deviant (criminals, traitors) were envious of those not caught and labeled as deviants, while the crippled and the blind were envious of those enjoying good health. Resident out-groups were stereotypically believed to be afflicted with the evil eye. Philo stereotypes the Egyptians as an envious and evil-eyed people in his writing against Flaccus: "But the Egyptian," he states, "is by nature an evil-eyed person, and the citizens burst with envy and considered that any good fortune to others was misfortune to themselves" (*Flaccus* 29).

This association of evil eye and envy is typical of ancient Mediterraneans. Israelite tradition, for example, is full of warnings against persons with the evil eye. "[The person with] a good eye will be blessed, for he shares his bread with the poor" (Prov. 22:9), but "evil is the man with an evil eye; he averts his face and disregards people" (Sir. 14:8). "An evil-eyed man is not satisfied with a portion, and mean injustice withers the soul" (Sir. 14:9). "An evil-eyed man begrudges bread, and it is lacking at his table" (Sir. 14:10; cf. also Sir. 18:18; Tob. 4:7, 17). "Remember that an evil eye is a bad thing. What has been created more evil than the eye? It sheds tears from every face" (Sir. 31:13). The glance and even the presence of such an individual were to be avoided because he or she was thought to have the power of injuring and destroying with his/her eye. "A fool," says Israelite wisdom, "is ungracious and abusive, and the begrudging gift of an evil-eyed person makes the eyes dim" (Sir. 18:18). "Do not consult with an evil-eyed man about gratitude or with a merciless man about kindness" (Sir. 37:11). "The evil eye of wickedness obscures what is good, and roving desire perverts the innocent mind" (Wis. 4:12).

In the Bible, envy manifests itself both on the tribal (Gen. 26:14; Isa. 11:13) and familial levels (Gen. 30:1; 37:11). As noted previously, it is associated with the worldview that prosperity occurs only at the expense of others, so that the few who prosper are wicked. Their prosperity must have been obtained by social oppression and will be punished by Yhwh in the end (Job 5:2; Pss. 37:1; 73:3; Prov. 3:31; 23:17; 24:1, 19; 27:4). The situations in which suspicion of an evil eye occurs in the Old Testament vary from famine and the begrudging of food to the starving (Deut. 28:53-57) and the sharing or non-sharing of food in general (Prov. 23:1-8; Sir. 31:12-31) to the lust after wealth (Prov. 28:22), the miserly unwillingness to share with those in need (Deut. 15:7-11; Sir. 14:3-10; 18:18; Tob. 4:1-21), consulting inappropriate counselors for advice (Sir. 37:7-15), evil eye fascination at the time of Enoch (Wis. 5:10-15), protection of fields with an anti-evil-eye device (Ep. Jer. 69), the control of the evil eye and other socially disruptive passions (Tob. 4:1-21). Further implicit traces of evil eye belief in the Old Testament can be found in passages that refer to the envy, hatred, greed, or covetousness of the eye or heart (e.g., Gen. 4:5; 30:1; 37:11; Exod. 20:17; 1 Sam. 2:32; 18:8-9; Ps. 73:3; Prov. 23:1; Jer. 22:17) or to protective amulets (e.g., Judg. 8:21, 26; Isa. 3:20) customarily used against the evil eye.

In the New Testament, references to the evil eye involved similar social and moral overtones. Jesus himself, according to the gospels, made mention of the evil eye more than once (Matt. 6:22-23; cf. Luke 11:34-36; Matt. 20:1-16; Mark 7:22). Among the explicit allusions to the evil eye is Paul's reference to the evil eye in his conflict with his opponents at Galatia: "O foolish Galatians, who has injured you with the evil eye?" (Gal. 3:1). This letter contains several indications that Paul had been accused by his detractors of having had an evil eye. Paul defends himself ("You did not shield your eyes from me and my portrayal of the Christ" [Gal. 3:1b]; "You did not spit in my presence" [Gal. 4:14]; "You would have plucked out your eyes and given them to me" [Gal. 4:15]) and counters this charge with an evil-eye accusation of his own: "It is not I, but rather my opponents who have the evil eye." "It is they," he implies to his Galatian readers, "and not I who have injured your children with their malignant envy and have caused divisions within your community" (see Gal. 4:17-18; 5:20, 26). In Galatians we have evidence of the way in which evil-eye accusations were employed by rivals to label and publicly discredit their opponents through appeal to the court of public opinion.

## Honor and Shame

All human societies use sanctions during early enculturation to gain compliance. These sanctions include guilt, shame, and anxiety. While all humans can experience all three of these sanctions, cultural groups emphasize one or the other. Unlike our Western, guilt-sanctioned society, Mediterranean societies of the first century (as in the traditional societies of that region today) had shame as pivotal sanction for non-compliance. The proof of the absence of shame was honor. The pivotal social value of honor kept the sanction of shame in abeyance. Concern for honor permeated every aspect of public life in the Mediterranean world. Honor was the fundamental value. It was the core, the heart, the soul. Philo speaks of "wealth, fame, official posts, honors, and everything of that sort with which the majority of mankind are busy" (*Det.* 122). He complains that "fame and honor are a most precarious possession, tossed about on the reckless tempers and flighty words of careless men" (*Abr.* 264). And note Rom. 12:10, where Paul admonishes Christians to outdo one another in showing honor, thereby acknowledging the value placed on honor among Christians as well.

Simply stated, honor is public reputation. It is having name or place. It is one's status or standing in the community *together with the public recognition of it*. Public recognition is all-important. To claim honor that is not publicly recognized is to play the fool. To grasp more honor than the public will allow is to be a greedy thief. To hang on to what honor one has is essential to life itself.

Honor is likewise a relative matter in which one claims to excel over others, to be superior. It thus implies a claim to *entitlements* on the basis of social precedence. As a result, honor and shame are forms of social evaluation in which both men and women are constantly compelled to assess their own conduct and that of their fellows in relation to each other. The vocabulary of praise and blame can therefore function as a social sanction on moral behavior. It is perpetuated by a network of evaluation, the gossip network, which creates an informal but effective mechanism of social control (Rohrbaugh 2007).

Honor is likewise a limited good, related to control of scarce resources including land, crops, livestock, political clout, and female sexuality. Because it is a limited good, honor gained is always honor taken from another. Legitimate honor that is publicly recognized opens doors to patrons; honor withheld cuts off access to the resources patrons can bestow. In a very pervasive way, then, honor determines dress, mannerisms, gestures, vocation, posture, who can eat with whom, who sits at what places at a meal, who can open a conversation, who has the right to speak, and who is accorded an audience. It serves as the prime indicator of social place (precedence) and provides the essential map for persons to interact with superiors, inferiors, and equals in socially prescribed or appropriate ways.

In ancient Greek and Latin literature, honor (*timē*) is at the center of a wide network of related values: power, wealth, magnanimity, personal loyalty, precedence, sense of shame, fame or reputation, courage, and excellence. It is no surprise, therefore, to find that the vocabulary of honor/shame is pervasive in the literature of antiquity. Josephus speaks of honors bestowed by Caesar, Vespasian, David, Saul, Jonathan, Augustus, Claudius, and the city of Athens (*BJ* 1.194; 1.199; 1.358; 1.396; 1.607; 3.408; *Life* 423; *AJ* 7.117; 6.168; 6.251; 13.102; 14.152; 19.292). He tells of the honor that belongs to consuls, governors, priests, village judges, and prophets (*B.J.* 4.149; 7.82; *A.J.* 4.215; 10.92; 11.309; 15.217). Philo speaks often of honor, glory, fame, high reputation, being adorned with honors and public offices, noble birth, the desire for glory, honor in the present, and a good name for the future (*Migr.* 172; *Leg.* 3.87; *Det.* 33; 157; *Post.* 112; *Abr.* 185; 263). In his *Roman Questions* 13, § 267A (*Moralia* IV, 25), Plutarch tells us that the Latin word "honor" is "glory, (*doxa*)" "respect," or "honor" (*timʹ*) in Greek. These are also the Greek words used to translate the Hebrew word for "glory" in the pre-Christian Greek translation of the Hebrew Bible, the Septuagint (LXX). English versions of the Bible often translate all these words with "glory." So the point is that "honor" and "glory" refer to the same reality, that is, the public acknowledgment of one's worth or social value.

Honor can be ascribed or acquired. Ascribed honor derives from birth: being born into an honorable family makes one honorable in the eyes of the entire community. By contrast, acquired honor comes from skill in the never-ending game of challenge and riposte. Not only must one win to gain it, one must do so in public because the whole community must acknowledge the gain. To claim honor the community does not recognize is to play the fool. Honor is a limited good, meaning that if one person wins honor, someone else loses. Envy is thus institutionalized and subjects anyone seeking to outdo one's neighbors to hostile gossip and the pressure to share. ▶ Evil Eye.

Challenges to one's honor could be positive or negative. Giving a gift is a positive challenge and requires reciprocation in kind. An insult is a negative challenge that likewise cannot be ignored. The game of challenge and riposte is deadly serious and can literally be a matter of life and death. It must be played in every area of life, and every person in a village watches to see how each family defends and maintains its position.

Since the honor of one's family determines potential marriage partners as well as with whom one can do business, what functions one can attend, where one can live, and even what religious role one can play, family honor must be defended at all costs. The smallest slight or injury must be avenged, or honor is permanently lost. Moreover, because the family is the basic unit in traditional societies rather than the individual, having a "flushed face" (*wajh* in Arabic, meaning a "face blushing due to being shamed"), as Middle Eastern villagers call it, can destroy the well-being of an entire kin group.

It also is important not to misunderstand the notion of "shame." One can "be shamed," and this refers to the state of publicly known loss of honor. This is negative shame. Being "thrown into outer darkness, where there will be weeping and gnashing of teeth" (Matt. 8:12; 13:42, 50; 22:12; 24:51; 25:30; Luke 13:28; see Acts 7:54) describes a reaction of persons who have been publicly shamed or dishonored.

By contrast, to "have shame" means to have proper concern about one's honor. This is positive shame. It can be understood as sensitivity about one's own reputation (honor) or the reputation of one's family.

It is sensitivity to the opinions of others and is therefore a highly desirable quality. To lack this positive shame is to be "shameless."

Women usually played this positive shame role in agrarian societies, meaning they were the ones expected to have this sensitivity in a special way and teach it to their children. People without shame, without this needed sensitivity to what is going on, make fools of themselves in public. Note the lament in Job 14:21 that a family's "children come to honor and they do not know it; they are brought low, and it goes unnoticed."

Perceiving status is as important as having it. Certain people, such as prostitutes, innkeepers, and actors, among others, were considered irreversibly shameless in antiquity because their occupations loudly announced that did not possess this sensitivity about their honor. They did not respect the boundaries or norms of the honor system and thus threatened social chaos.

Of special importance is the sexual honor of a woman. While male honor is flexible and can sometimes be regained, female honor is absolute, and once lost it is gone forever. It is the emotional-conceptual counterpart of virginity. Any sexual offense on a woman's part, however slight, would destroy not only her own honor but that of all males in her paternal kin group as well. Significantly, the order of those expected to defend (to the death) the honor of younger women, even married ones, runs: brother(s), husband, father. For older married women the son(s) is (or are) the primary defender of honor.

## Hospitality

Hospitality is the process of "receiving" outsiders and changing them from strangers to guests. This value clearly serves as a means for attaining and preserving honor, the MENA core cultural value. In the world of the Bible hospitality is never about entertaining family and friends. It is always about dealing with strangers. To show hospitality to strangers is to "receive" them. If strangers are not to be done away with, either physically or socially (see Matt. 10:14-23), their reception occurs in three stages:

(1) First, strangers have to be tested. Strangers pose a threat to any community since they are potentially anything one cares to imagine. Hence they must be evaluated both as to how they might fit in and whether they will subscribe to the community's norms. Officials (Josh. 2:2) or concerned citizenry (Gen. 19:5) might conduct such tests; the invasion of the outsider must be repelled (Mark 5:17: the Gerasenes ask the stranger Jesus to leave). An invitation to speak can be a test (Acts 13:14-15), while letters of recommendation can excuse one from a test, although sometimes not (e.g., 2 and 3 John; Rom. 16:3-16; 1 Thess. 5:12-13). The ritual of foot washing marks the movement from stranger to guest (see Gen. 18:4; 19:2; 24:32; lacking in Luke 7:36-50).

(2) Second, the stranger takes on the role of guest. Since transient strangers lacked customary or legal standing within the visited community it was imperative that they find a patron, a host. ▶Patronage. Hosts would be established community members. Through a personal bond with a patron (something inns cannot offer), the stranger was incorporated as guest or client. The traditional name for a protected client is "protegé." To offend the guest is to offend the host, who is protector and patron of the guest (poignantly underscored in the case of Lot, Gen. 19:1-10), yet such patronage can yield more trouble than honor (e.g., Prov. 6:1).

The rules of hospitality require the guest: (a) to refrain from insulting the host and from any show of hostility or rivalry; a guest must honor the host (Jesus eating with sinners neither accuses them of being sinners nor asks them to change: Matt. 9:10; Luke 5:29). (b) To refrain from usurping the role of the host, for example, making oneself at home when not yet invited to do so (in the home of another, Jesus heals when asked: Mark 1:30); taking precedence (see Luke 14:8); giving orders to the dependents of the host (Jesus refuses to command Mary: Luke 10:40); making claims or demands on the host or demanding or taking what is not offered (see Luke 7:36-50, where Jesus is the perfect guest, and the rules for traveling disciples: Mark 6:10 and parallels). (c) To refrain from refusing what is offered; to refuse is to infringe on the role of guest. The guest is above all bound to accept food (see Luke

10:18; the directives to disciples for their travels would force them to accept patronage: Mark 6:8 and parallels; see 1 Cor. 9:4).

On the other hand, the rules of hospitality require that a host: (a) refrain from insulting one's guests or from any show of hostility or rivalry and (b) protect one's guests and their honor, for guests individually are embedded in the host. Thus while fellow guests have no explicit relationship they are bound to forgo hostilities, since they offend their host in the act of offending one another. The host must defend each against the other since both are his guests (thus Paul's problem at the "Lord's" supper in 1 Cor. 11:17-34). (c) The host must also attend to the guests, granting them the precedence that is their due, showing concern for their needs and wishes or in general, to earn the good will guests should show. Note how in Luke 7:36-50 Simon the Pharisee fails on all counts with his guest, Jesus: no foot washing, no kiss, no anointing, not keeping away the sinful woman; the parable in Luke 7:40-41 represents Jesus' defense of his honor as guest. Finally, to fail to offer one's best is to denigrate the guest (John 2:10).

While element (a) is the same for both guest and host, elements (b) and (c) are complementaries. This assures that a stranger will rarely, if ever, reciprocate hospitality, hence its necessity and value (see Matt. 25:38, 43, among the traditional Judaic works of mercy). Yet while hospitality does not entail mutual reciprocity between individuals it can nevertheless be viewed as a reciprocal relationship between communities. Such hospitality to traveling Christians is both urged (see Rom. 12:13; 1 Pet. 4:9) and much practiced (e.g., Acts 17:7; 21:17; 28:7; Rom. 16:23).

(3) Third, the guest never leaves the host with the same status as upon arrival, for the stranger-guest will leave the host either as friend or enemy. If departing as friend, the guest will spread the praises of the host (e.g., 1 Thess. 1:9; Phil. 5:16), notably to those who sent the stranger to the host (e.g., Mark 9:37), but if as enemy, the one aggrieved will have to get satisfaction (e.g., 3 John).

In the context of the practice of hospitality John 1:10, "his own received him not" means that "Word made flesh" was given no welcome, shown no hospitality. In turn, Jesus gives this word of honor: "Truly, truly I say to you, he who receives any one whom I send receives me; and he who receives me receives him who sent me" (John 13:20; in the Synoptics, the saying is referred to a "child," that is, in the Gospel context, the least –Jesus-follower: Matt. 18:5; Mark 9:37; Luke 9:48). Of course, such sayings were significant in a world unused to travel and social services.

In the United States hospitality is reserved almost exclusively for friends. Strangers are directed to motels or hotels, and those in need are sent to social service agencies that regularly provide food and lodging to needy people who will remain anonymous throughout (Pilch and Malina 2009: 115–18).

## Humility

Humility is a MENA value that directs persons to stay within their inherited social status. The strategies for being humble include not presuming on others and avoiding even the appearance of lording it over another. Humble persons do not threaten or challenge another's rights, nor do they claim more for themselves than has been duly allotted them in life. They even stay a step below or behind their rightful status (e.g., the "unworthy" John, Mark 1:7). Thus humility is a socially acknowledged claim to neutrality in the competition of life.

Conversely, to attempt to better oneself at the expense of others, to acquire more than others, to strive for honors others now enjoy are all instances of proud and arrogant behavior. God humbles such proud people (Matt. 23:12; Luke 18:14; see Deut. 8:2, 16; Ps. 55:19), while exalting the humble (2 Sam. 22:28; Ps. 18:27; Luke 1:52; 14:7-11). Hence humility has precedence over honor (Prov. 15:33; 18:12). To humble or humiliate others is to shame them (e.g., Dinah in Gen. 34:2 is "humbled," since Hebrew has no word for rape; "women" are "humbled:" in Ezek. 22:10; Isa. 2:9, 11, 17). To humble or humiliate oneself is to declare oneself powerless to defend one's status (e.g., 2 Chr. 33:23; 36:12; Phil. 2:8), and then to act accordingly either factually (becoming powerless, like the low-born; see "humble in spirit" in Isa.

57:15; 66:2, or "the humble of the land" in Zeph. 3:12), or ritually (by a rite in which the use of power is set aside, symbolized by behavior typical of the low-born: fasting, rending garments, weeping, lamenting, confession—e.g., Lev. 26:41; 1 Kgs. 21:29; 2 Kgs. 22:8-20; Ps. 69:10). Such self-humiliation before God is praiseworthy and obtains God's favor (Prov. 3:34; Jas. 4:10; 1 Pet. 5:5-6; also 2 Cor. 12:21). Matthew's tradition insists that Jesus was no arrogant teacher, but "meek and humble of heart" (Matt. 11:29), and Matthew alone notes how Jesus' entry into Jerusalem is an unpretentious one: "Tell the daughter of Zion, 'Behold, your king is coming to you humble and mounted on an ass, and on a colt, the foal of an ass'" (Matt. 21:5, quoting Zech. 9:9); the horse was the traditional war animal of power and status; the ass was simple transportation.

Yet the gospel tradition notes that Jesus did not exhort to traditional self-humiliation. An indication of this is the tradition about Jesus and fasting. The traditional Hebrew name for fasting is (self-) humiliation (ta'anîth; see Isa. 58:5; Ezra 8:21). The tradition had it that Jesus did not fast (Mark 2:18-20; Matt. 9:14-17; Luke 5:33-39), nor did he expect his disciples to fast in public (Matt. 6:16-18). Rather, Jesus urged simply that one not challenge the honor of others (Matt. 23:12; Luke 14:11; 18:14), as though one were as powerless to do so as a child (Matt. 18:4). Such humility is a valued quality (Eph. 4:2; Col. 3:12). Humility is thus a means value, that is, a course of action or behavior that facilitates the realization of honor, the core value of Mediterranean culture.

In the Western world humility is not widely practiced. Because of this culture's emphasis on achievement it is imperative to record such achievements in resumés and record books and to publicize them in press-releases and newspaper reports (Pilch and Malina 2009: 118–20).

### Inclusive Language

Western culture in general and the English language in particular have paid special attention to matters of gender equality and related concerns in recent years. The traditional preference of the English language for masculine pronouns was especially called into question as offensive to women (and to some men). Hence English translations began to replace these references with inclusive ones: for example, humankind for man, child for son, and the like. Bruce Metzger, general editor of the New Revised Standard Version (NRSV 1990), explained the rationale for this change of translation practice thus:

> During the almost half a century since the publication of the RSV [Revised Standard Version], many in the churches have become sensitive to the danger of linguistic sexism arising from the inherent bias of the English language towards the masculine gender, a bias that in the case of the Bible has often restricted or obscured the meaning of the original text. The mandates from the Division [of Christian Education of the National Council of the Churches of Christ in the United States of America, sponsor of the RSV and NRSV] specified that, in references to men and women, masculine-oriented language should be eliminated as far as this can be done without altering passages that reflect the historical situation of ancient patriarchal culture. . . . In the vast majority of the cases . . . inclusiveness has been attained by simple rephrasing or by introducing plural forms when this does not distort the meaning of the passage. (From "To the Reader," by Bruce M. Metzger for the Committee on Translation.)

Other translations followed suit: The *New Century Version* (NCV, 1991), *Good News Bible: Today's English Version* 2nd edition (GNB, 1992), *New International Reader's Version New Testament* (NIRV, 1995), *The Contemporary English Version* (CEV, 1995), *New International Version Inclusive Language Edition* (NIVI, 1995), and the *New Living Translation* (NLT, 1996) among others.

Problems still remain in the translation of Proverbs. Here we find Proverbs that instruct fathers how to discipline their sons. Does the NRSV seem to misrepresent the meaning of the passages?

|  | RSV | NRSV |
|---|---|---|
| Prov. 13:24 (Hebrew) (son) (*ben*) | son | children |
| Prov. 22:15 (lad) (*na'ar*) | child | boy |
| Prov. 23:13-14 (lad) (*na'ar*) | child | children |
| Prov. 29:15 (lad) (*na'ar*) | child (left to himself) | (neglected) child |
| Prov. 29:17 (son) (*ben*) | son | children |
| Prov. 29:19 (servant) (*'ebed*) | servant | servants |

The ancient Hebrew language has words for "boy" and "girl," "son" and "daughter," but *no word* that really means "child" or "children." The culture was so rigidly gender-divided that its verb system was also gender-specific. This linguistic usage reflects the social system, that is, the deep gender-based divisions that existed in that culture. A considerate Bible reader or translator will seek to respect this aspect of biblical language and culture (Malina 1996: 54–64). To explore one example of the misrepresentation of biblical culture, compare the translation of Hebrews 12:3-11 in the RSV and the NRSV. Which is faulty?

| RSV | NRSV |
|---|---|
| 12:3 Consider him who endured from sinners such hostility against himself, so that you may not grow weary or fainthearted. | 12:3 Consider him who endured such hostility against himself from sinners, so that you may not grow weary or lose heart. |
| 12:4 In your struggle against sin you have not yet resisted to the point of shedding your blood. | 12:4 In your struggle against sin you have not yet resisted to the point of shedding your blood. |
| 12:5 And have you forgotten the exhortation which addresses you as **sons**?<br>  "My **son**, do not regard lightly the discipline of the Lord,<br>  nor lose courage when you are punished by him.<br>  12:6 For the Lord disciplines **him** whom he loves,<br>  and chastises every **son** whom he receives." [Prov 3:11-12] | 12:5 And you have forgotten the exhortation that addresses you as **children**—<br>  "My **child**, do not regard lightly the discipline of the Lord,<br>  or lose heart when you are punished by him;<br>  12:6 for the Lord disciplines **those** whom he loves,<br>  and chastises every **child** whom he accepts." [Prov 3:11-12] |
| 12:7 It is for discipline that you have to endure. God is treating you as **sons**; for what **son** is there whom his **father** does not discipline?<br>  12:8 If you are left without discipline, in which all have participated, then you are illegitimate children and not **sons**.<br>  12:9 Besides this, we have had earthly **fathers** to discipline us and we respected them. Shall we not much more be subject to the Father of spirits and live?<br>  12:10 For they disciplined us for a short time at their pleasure, but he disciplines us for our good, that we may share his holiness.<br>  12:11 For the moment all discipline seems painful rather than pleasant; later it yields the peaceful fruit of righteousness to those who have been trained by it. | 12:7 Endure trials for the sake of discipline. God is treating you as **children**; for what **child** is there whom **a parent** does not discipline?<br>  12:8 If you do not have that discipline in which all children share, then you are illegitimate and not **his children. (?)**<br>  12:9 Moreover, we had human **parents** to discipline us, and we respected them. Should we not be even more willing to be subject to the Father of spirits and live?<br>  12:10 For they disciplined us for a short time as seemed best to them, but he disciplines us for our good, in order that we may share his holiness.<br>  12:11 Now, discipline always seems painful rather than pleasant at the time, but later it yields the peaceful fruit of righteousness to those who have been trained by it. |

As St. Thomas Aquinas and the Scholastics taught: all theology is analogy. This means that everything human beings think, know, and say about God is based on human experience. And all human experience is culturally shaped and conditioned. Moreover, it is imperative to investigate what the sacred author wrote and intended. In the Letter to the Hebrews the Mediterranean author presents God in terms of a Mediterranean father (see the Proverbs listed above). He quotes Prov. 3:11-12, where the Hebrew very pointedly speaks of "sons" and the physical punishment Mediterranean fathers mete out to their sons but never to their daughters. Thus does the author draw a MENA cultural conclusion for the Mediterranean readers.

## In-group and Out-group

A person's in-group generally consisted of one's household, extended family, and friends. The boundaries of an in-group were fluid; in-groups could and did change, at times expanding, at others contracting. Persons from the same city quarter or village would look upon each other as an in-group when in a "foreign" location, while in the city quarter or village they might be out-group to each other. For Jesus to have a house in Capernaum is indicative of where his network of in-group relations was constituted. The first persons he calls to take part in his movement are from there, and that they so quickly respond is indicative of the in-group network there (See Mark 1:16-20).

In-group members are expected to be loyal to each other and to go to great lengths to help each other (Luke 11:5-9). They are shown the greatest consideration and courtesy; such behavior is rarely, if ever, extended to members of out-groups. Only face-to-face groups in which a person can express concern for others can become in-groups (Matt. 5:43-48). Persons interacting positively with each other in in-group ways, even when not actual kin, become "neighbors." The term refers to a social role with rights and obligations that derive simply from living socially close to others and interacting with them—the same village or neighborhood or party or faction. Neighbors of this sort are an extension of one's kin group (Prov. 3:39; 6:29; 11:9, 12; 16:29; 25:9, 17, 28; 26:18; 27:10, 14; 29:5). From one perspective the whole house of Israel were neighbors. The injunction in Leviticus to "love one's neighbor as oneself" (Lev. 19:18) dates to a time when the house of

Israel was confined to Judah (Judea). For the Levitical author, Israel marked a broad in-group, whether the injunction was carried out or not. In this light the parable of the "Good Samaritan" (Luke 10:29-37) seems to address the question of who belongs in Israel, especially since Israel extended far beyond Judea alone at the time.

The boundaries of the in-group were shifting ones. The geographical division of the house of Israel in the first century was Judea, Peraea, and Galilee. What all the residents with allegiance to the Jerusalem Temple had in common was "birth" into the same people, the house of Israel. But this group quickly broke into three in-groups: the Judeans, Peraeans, and Galileans. Jesus was not a Judean but a Galilean, as were his disciples. It was Judeans who sought to put Jesus the Galilean to death. All these geographically based groups had their countless subgroups, with various and changing loyalties. According to the Gospel story, Jesus shifted his geographical base from the tiny hamlet of Nazareth to the much larger village of Capernaum (see Mark 2:1, where Jesus of Nazareth is at home in Capernaum).

To outsiders, all these in-groups fused into one and were simply called "Judeans." Similarly, the house of Israel could look at the rest of the world as one large out-group, "the (other) nations" (Gentiles). Paul sees himself as a Judean living according to Judean customs, called Judaism, with allegiance to the God of Israel in Jerusalem in Judea, yet at work among Israelites resident around the Mediterranean, the "Dispersion."

Most such Judeans never expected to move back to Judea. They remained either resident aliens or citizens in the places of their birth, yet they continued to be categorized by the geographical location of their original ethnic roots. The reason for this was that the main way for categorizing living beings, animals, and humans in the ancient MENA world was by geographical origin. Being of similar geographical origin meant harboring in-group feelings even if one was long departed from that place of origin, a place that endowed group members with particular characteristics.

By asking another for a favor, one in effect extended to that person an implicit invitation to membership in one's in-group. Thus as Jesus set up his faction by recruiting core members with the invitation "Follow me," they of course expected something in return for complying (Matt. 19:27-29; Mark 10:28-30).

In-group members freely ask questions of one another that would seem too personal to North Americans. These questions reflect the fact that interpersonal relationships, even "casual" ones, tended to involve a far greater lowering of social and psychological boundaries in the ancient world than in present-day experience.

In dealing with out-group members almost "anything" goes. By current standards the dealings of ancient MENA types with out-group persons appear indifferent, even hostile. Strangers can never be in-group members. Should they take the initiative in the direction of "friendly" relations, only the social ritual of hospitality (being "received" or "welcomed") extended by an in-group member can transform them into "friends" of the group. ▶ **Hospitality**.

Because of in-group cohesion in the culture, the biggest obstacle to a person's joining a faction was the family, the primary in-group. Besides pointing up the trouble with Jesus' own family (Mark 3), the Synoptics report Jesus' words about the family as a hindrance to his task (Matt. 10:34-36; Luke 12:51-53).

Purity rules that distinguish between inside and outside (Leviticus) are replications of rules that distinguish in-group from out-group, thus keeping the boundaries between groups ever in the awareness of those observing the purity rules.

## Kinship

Kinship norms regulate human relationships within and among family groups. At each stage of life, from birth to death, these norms determine the roles we play and the ways we interact with each other. Moreover, what it meant to be a father, mother, husband, wife, sister, or brother was vastly different in ancient agrarian societies than what we know in the modern, industrial world.

Note, for example, the lists in Lev. 18:6-18 and 20:11-21. By New

Testament times these had become lists of prohibited marriage partners. They include a variety of in-laws for whom we do not prohibit marriage today (for example, see Mark 6:18). Moreover, for us marriage is generally neolocal (a new residence is established by the bride and groom) and exogamous (outside the kin group). In antiquity it was patrilocal (the bride moved in with her husband's family) and endogamous (marrying as close to the conjugal family as incest laws permitted). Cross-cousin marriages on the paternal side of the family were the ideal and genealogies always followed the paternal line of descent.

Since marriages were fundamentally the fusion of two extended families, the honor of each family played a key role. Marriage contracts negotiated the fine points and ensured balanced reciprocity. Defensive strategies were used to prevent loss of males (and females as well, whenever possible) to another family. Unlike U.S. families, which are essentially consuming units, the family was the producing unit of antiquity. Hence the loss of a member through marriage required compensation in the form of a bride-price. By far the strongest unit of loyalty was the descent group of brothers and sisters, and it was here that the strongest emotional ties existed, rather than between husband and wife.

Socially and psychologically, all family members were embedded in the family unit. Our individualism simply did not exist. The public role was played by the males on behalf of the whole unit, while females played the private, internal role that often included management of the family purse. Females not embedded in relation to a male (widows, divorcées) were women without honor and often viewed as more male than female by the society (note the attitude toward widows in 1 Tim. 5:3-16).

## Limited Good

George Foster, who specialized in peasant studies, formulated two key elements of peasant culture: dyadic contract and limited good. He discovered that peasants perceive all the world's cherished and valuable goods (e.g., wealth, land, happiness, honor, etc.) as finite in quantity, limited in supply, and already distributed. Life is a zero-sum game: There is no more where this came from. If someone suffered a loss of one of these goods, the suspicion was that someone else had acquired it.

> By "Image of Limited Good" I mean that broad areas of peasant behavior are patterned in such a fashion as to suggest that peasants view their social, economic, and natural universe—their total environment—as one in which all of the desired things in life such as land, wealth, health, friendship and love, respect and status, power and influence, security and safety *exist in finite quantity and are always in short supply*, as far as the peasant is concerned. Not only do these and all other "good things" exist in finite and limited quantities, but *in addition there is no way directly within peasant power to increase the available quantities.*
> (Foster 1965: 296; italics in original).

Two significant effects derive from such a perception. First, people are fearful of the realistically anticipated sanctions from others for attempting to improve their lot or station in life. Second, such ambitious people now become targets of envy by their neighbors. The neighbors perceive themselves as losing worth and value because of the gain of such good others achieve.

This contrasts with the Euro-American view that the economy is ever expanding because it is built on limitless resources. Everyone is capable of increasing her or his standard of living. Plutarch observes that those who hear an eloquent lecturer conclude that they are losing honor because of the speaker's success; hence they envy his accomplishments. "As though commendation were money, he feels that he is robbing himself of every bit that he bestows on another" (Plutarch, *On Listening to Lectures* 44b). In the Gospels, the disciples of John the Baptist complain to him about Jesus' success. John agrees, but insists that Jesus' increase is right and proper: "He must increase; I must decrease" (John 3:30; see Judg. 7:2).

## Lying

Since honor is the core cultural value in the Mediterranean world, and one's public claim to honor, value, worth, and reputation requires public acknowledgment, secrecy is one of a trio of strategies—the other two being deception and lying—that are employed in preserving honor. Actually, these are also cultural values. The more people know about a person, the fewer claims to honor that person can make. Hence the first step in maintaining one's reputation is secrecy, a formal, conscious, deliberate, and calculated concealment of information, activities, or relationships that outsiders can only gain by espionage. In other words, it is a selective sharing of information including refusal to share it, or leaking information as it is useful. One never gives "the truth, the whole truth, and nothing but the truth" to anyone. Given the nosey nature of this culture in which people always suspect they are not being told the truth, no one is satisfied with what is "leaked" or shared. They try to probe deeper to find the real truth. This then leads the secretive person to deception. Parables are a form of deception. "To you has been given the secret of the kingdom of God, but for those outside, everything comes in parables" (Mark 4:10). Notice that central to this process is a careful distinction between insiders and outsiders. Insiders are privy to the truth, but outsiders deserve nothing but secrecy, deception, and outright lies. ▶In-group and Out-group.

The third strategy for protecting honor is lying, that is, restricting the public dissemination of information over a period of time. Some anthropologists do not distinguish between deception and lying; they consider lying a form of deception. Whatever one decides, it is important not to impose upon lying in Mediterranean culture the moral evaluation it has in Western culture. Anthropologists have distinguished eight kinds of deception or lies used by contemporary Mediterranean people as a legitimate strategy in the service of maintaining or even gaining honor. These can also be found in the Bible. Each case reflects the public dimension of honor. (1) There is a lie to conceal the failure of an individual or group to live up to the highest level of requirements of the social code. A failure against honor can be concealed through lying so as to keep the appearance of maintaining honor. The son who tells his father he will go to work in the vineyard yet has no intention of so doing honors his father by responding respectfully, if not truthfully (Matt. 21:28-32). (2) Sometimes one fails without intending to do so. The failure would not escape notice in this society, so it must be covered with a lie. The expert in law who asks Jesus a question to which he knows the answer is shamed by Jesus. In an effort to regain his honor he lies again, asking another question to which his previous answer indicates he also knew the answer: who is my neighbor? (Luke 10:25-29). His lies fail him twice.

(3) Sometimes, to preserve one's honor one must besmirch another. It is fair to attack the honor of another by telling a lie of false imputation. In John 8:31-49, Jesus' opponents who have been losing each round of argument since v. 31 end by accusing him of being a Samaritan and having a demon (v. 48). This is a classic lie of false imputation.

(4) Other lies serve to avoid quarrels or trouble. The Middle East is not basically violent. It has a collection of strategies for defusing arguments because they can lead to violence that might result in bloodshed. Blood feuds last forever. Hence the mediator is key to squelching arguments. An even earlier step is to lie to avoid a quarrel or escape trouble, both of which can besmirch honor. Peter's threefold denial that he knows Jesus (Matt. 26:69-75) is clearly a series of lies to avoid getting involved. Jesus would understand this and accept it. However, it is also possible to interpret Peter's lies as an effort to cover an unintended failure. Having boasted with the others that he would die for Jesus rather than deny him (Matt. 26:35), he joined the others when all fled at Jesus' arrest (Matt. 26:56). Jesus would understand a lie attempting to avoid trouble, but it would be impossible to tolerate a lie to cover a breach of loyalty.

(5) Since honor is also measured by material possessions, one seeks to acquire them. However, such gain in the peasant world of limited good is shameful. Still, a (material) gain achieved by cheating on a

deal, or pretending to be cunning and shrewd, contributes to a person's achieved honor. Hence some lies are told for material gain (see 1 Kings 21). (6) At other times lies are told for sheer concealment, because the other has no right to know. Jesus conceals his travel plans regarding a visit to Jerusalem lest his opponents plot a surprise for him (John 7:1-12).

The expert in deception and lying in this culture is admired as a hero. (7) Thus some lies are told for pure mischief, just for the fun of it (2 Tim. 3:1-8) or to confuse authorities (Acts 5:1-11). (8) Finally, it is also and especially acceptable to lie on behalf of a friend, a guest, and certainly kin (Joshua 2). Thus some deceptions serve a defensive purpose while others are strategies of attack.

## Nepeš/soul

The Hebrew word "nepeš" (pronounced nefesh) is most often translated as "soul" but in actual usage it is polysemic. This means that the word has several other meanings, simultaneously. Recall that MENA cultures are non (perhaps even anti) introspective. Only God knows the interior of a person (1 Sam. 16:7). Humans can judge only by externals. Hence the many meanings attributed to this word which originally meant "throat" (Isa. 5:4; 29:8) From this meaning derived yet another, namely "breath" in the throat, as a sign of life (2 Sam. 1:9; 2 Kgs. 17:22) Thus the first creature whom God inflated with the divine breath became a nepeš hayy~h, a "living being," a phrase applied both to humans (Gen. 2:7)and animals (Gen. 1:21, 24). Finally,.the word can mean simply a person (Gen. 12:5; 46:46; Exod. 1:5; etc.) It is important to note that while "nepeš" in its early meaning designates "breath," and is similar to another Hebrew word ("ruah") which also means breath, and then spirit, each word has many idiomatic usages specific to itself.

"Nepeš"also describes interior states in a human being, viz., physiological, psychic, and psychological phenomena. "Nepeš" can be hungry (Prov. 10:3) and long for food and drink (Prov. 10:3; 25:25). It is the locus of emotions (Ps. 86:4; Jer. 6:16), of love and hatred (Gen. 34:3; 44:30). As noted above, it is similar to the word "rãah" (spirit) but invariably associated with b~Ñ~r (flesh, i. e., body). "Nepeš" can mean person, but "rãah" never does.

The OT does not reflect the idea that the"nepeš" exists apart from the body and survives death. It means "corpse" in Lev. 19:28; 21:1; nym 6:11). "Nepeš" was the whole person, the "living being" while b~Ñ~r was the whole person weak and perishing.

## Normative Inconsistency

When ambivalence and inconsistency provide positive outcomes, anthropologists call this "normative inconsistency." Nearly all societies have some form of normative inconsistencies, but the way in which a given society handles them differs. In the United States, for example, individualism is a core value and secret of America's greatness. However, no one should live for self alone. Children are considered a blessing, but no one should have more than she or he can afford to support and educate. (For a more complete list see Lynd 1939: 60–62; Williams 1970: 421–22.) In the Bible, Jesus cautions: "if you say [to your brother], 'You fool,' you will be liable to the hell of fire" (Matt. 5:22), yet he himself calls the scribes and Pharisees: "You blind fools!" (Matt. 23:17) in a chapter filled with insults. Or again, Jesus recommends "turning the other cheek" in reference to bearing insults (Matt. 5:39, the back hand, or left hand), yet throughout the Gospel, whenever approached by hostile, testing questioners, his first reaction is an insulting counter-question (Matt. 15:1-9). (For other examples see Malina 1986b: 45–47).

Inconsistency of norms and the experience of dissonance are normal in a social situation in which traditional values cannot be realized or actualized in daily living. This produces conflict both within the individual and between groups. One result is the spontaneous and prolific spawning of coalitions of various sorts: cliques, gangs, action sets, and factions. The individual is forced to deal with this sociological ambivalence and has two options: one, ignore the dissonance and seek totally consistent, inflexible behavior without options, which is extremism. This option leads ultimately to disaster, destruction of self (suicide) or the demise of the group or coalition. The second option is to accept the conflict and engage in a networking process in the social environment of one's birth. Once one learns the network, it can be "reconstructed" as necessary in order to produce a positive outcome, that is, a more or less satisfying life. Thus the person becomes a social, self-interested entrepreneur who learns how to manipulate norms and relationships for personal social and psychological benefit, while of course being manipulated by that network. This provides the person with contrary norms without loss of role or status, without loss of honor. Such a person simultaneously honors different commitments according to the circumstances. Thus Paul exemplifies such a person with multiple commitments: to the tribe of Benjamin, to Hebrews, to Pharisaism (Phil. 3:5), and to Christ as an Israelite and descendant of Abraham (2 Cor. 11:22-23). He is not a Gentile sinner but rather an apostle to Judeans living and enculturated among Gentiles, and even all things to all (1 Cor. 9:19-23).

Proverbs, a window into MENA culture reflected in the Bible, proposes a number of actions that confirm an acceptance of normative inconsistency. Bribes are generally criticized (Prov. 15:27) yet are acceptable as a means of avoiding imprisonment (Prov. 17:23; compare Matt. 5:25-26). The "ideal" in MENA cultures is for brothers to live in peace and concord (Ps. 133:1), but the "reality" is frequent dissension that is not susceptible of remedy (Prov. 18:19). Finally, the Torah encourages making loans to needy people and accepting a guarantee of repayment (Deut. 24:10-13; Prov. 20:16), while a number of proverbs caution against such a practice (Prov. 6:1-4; 11:15; 17:18; 22:26-27; 27:13; see the comment on Prov. 11:15). This is not only an example of the "ideal" contrasted with the "real" in MENA culture but also illustrates normative inconsistency, whereby, after making a careful analysis of the conflicting and contradictory circumstances of each case, one makes a response that should yield a positive outcome.

## Patronage

Patron-client systems are socially fixed relations of generalized reciprocity between social unequals in which a lower-status person in need (called a "client") has his or her needs met by having recourse for favors to a higher-status, well-situated person (called a "patron"). By being granted the favor, the client implicitly promises to pay back the favor whenever and however the patron determines. By granting the favor, the patron, in turn, implicitly promises to be open to further requests at unspecified future times. Such open-ended relations of generalized reciprocity are typical of the relation between the head of a family and his dependents: wife, children, and slaves. By entering a patron-client arrangement the client relates to his patron as to a superior and more powerful kinsman, while the patron sees to his clients as to his dependents.

Patron-client relations existed throughout the Mediterranean; we will examine the Roman version of the system as an example. From the earliest years of the Roman Republic the people who settled on the hills along the Tiber included in their families freeborn retainers called "clients." These clients tended flocks, produced a variety of needed goods, and helped farm the land. In return they were afforded the protection and largesse of their patrician patrons. Such clients had no political rights and were considered inferior to citizens, though they did share in the increase of herds or goods they helped to produce. The mutual obligations between patron and client were considered sacred and often became hereditary. Virgil tells of special punishments in the underworld for patrons who defrauded clients (*Aeneid* 6.60). Great houses boasted of the number of their clients and sought to increase them from generation to generation.

By the late years of the Republic the flood of conquered peoples had overwhelmed the formal institution of patronage among the Romans. A large population torn from previous patronage relations now sought similar ties with the great Roman patrician families. Consequently, patronage spread rapidly into the outer reaches of the Roman world, even if in a much less structured form. By the early years of the empire, especially in the provinces, we hear of the newly rich competing for the honor and status considered to derive from a long train of client dependents. The clients were mostly the urban poor or village peasants who sought favors from those who controlled the economic and political resources of the society.

In his *Epigrams*, Martial gives us many of the details of a Roman client's life. In the more formalized institution in Rome itself the first duty of a client was the *salutatio*, the early morning call at the patron's house. Proper dress was important. At this meeting clients could be called upon to serve the patron's needs, which might eat up much of the day. Menial duties were expected, though public praise of the patron was considered fundamental. In return, clients were due one meal a day and might receive a variety of other petty favors. Humiliation of clients was frequent, and little recourse was available. Patrons who provided more were considered gracious.

As the Roman style of patronage behavior spread to provinces such as Syria (Palestine), its formal and hereditary character changed. The newly rich, seeking to aggrandize family position, competed to add dependent clients. Formal, mutual obligations degenerated into petty favor-seeking and manipulation. Clients competed for patrons just as patrons competed for clients in an often desperate struggle to gain economic or political advantage.

A second institution that complemented the patronage system was the *hospitium*, the relation of host and guest. Such covenants were only between social equals and were often formalized in contractual agreements for mutual aid and protection that became hereditary. So long as a party remained in the city of the host, protection, legal assistance, lodging, medical services, and even an honorable burial were his due. Tokens of friendship and obligation were exchanged that sealed the contractual arrangement and could be used to identify parties to such covenants who had never met (for example, descendants). Such agreements were considered sacred in the highest degree.

Patrons, then, were powerful individuals who controlled resources and were expected to use their positions to hand out favors to inferiors based on "friendship," personal knowledge, and favoritism. Benefactor patrons were expected to generously support city, village, or client. The Roman emperor related to major public officials this way, and they in turn related to those beneath them in similar fashion. Cities related to towns and towns to villages in the same way. A pervasive social network of patron-client relations thus arose in which connections meant everything. Having few connections was shameful.

Brokers mediated between patrons above and clients below. First-order resources—land, jobs, goods, funds, and power—were all controlled by patrons. Second-order resources—strategic contact with or access to patrons—were controlled by brokers, who mediated the goods and services a patron had to offer. City officials served as brokers of imperial resources. Holy men or prophets also could act as brokers on occasion. In the Gospels, Jesus often acts as the broker for God, the one through whom clients obtain access to God's favor. An example is Matt. 8:13, in which Jesus acts as broker to bring the benefits of the patron (God) to the centurion's servant. In the authentic letters Paul presents Jesus as a broker, using the phrase "through Jesus Christ" (Rom. 1:8; 1 Cor. 8:6; 2 Cor. 3:4). The Deutero-Paulines use the same phrase to make that point (Eph. 1:5; Titus 3:6). Hebrews makes the same point by calling Jesus "priest" (5:6) and "high priest" (2:17).

Clients were dependent on the largesse of patrons or brokers to survive and do well in their society. They owed loyalty and public acknowledgment of honor in return. Patronage was voluntary but ideally lifelong. Having only one patron to whom one owed total loyalty had been the pattern in Rome from the earliest times, but in the more chaotic competition for clients and patrons in the outlying provinces, playing patrons off against each other became commonplace. Note that according to Matthew and Luke one cannot be a client of both God and the wealth-acquisition system (Matt. 6:24; Luke 16:13).

While clients boasted of being "friends" of their patrons (for example, Pilate as a "friend of Caesar"; John 19:12), friends were normally social equals, and having few friends was likewise shameful. Bound by reciprocal relations, friends were obligated to help each other on an ongoing basis, whereas patrons (or brokers) were not. Patrons, including the God of Israel, had to be cultivated. Divine worship, the service of God, entailed such patronage cultivation.

In the letters of Paul the language of grace is the language of patronage. The Greek word *charis*, translated in the NRSV as "grace," refers to the favor given by a patron. God is the ultimate patron, whose resources are graciously given. By proclaiming the gospel of God about the God of Israel raising Jesus from the dead with a view to an emerging kingdom of God, Paul in effect is announcing a forthcoming theocracy for Israel along with the ready presence of divine patronage. In Paul's proclamation Jesus is broker or mediator of God's patronage and proceeds to broker the favor of God through the Spirit of God.

## Politics

In the twenty-first century, Europeans and Americans generally believe there are four basic social institutions: kinship, economics, politics, and religion. These are conceived as separate social institutions, and people make arguments about keeping them separate. However, in the world of the Bible people attended to only two institutions as distinctive: kinship and politics. (After all, separation of "church" and state as well as the conceptualization of economics as a separate institution are eighteenth-century CE phenomena.) In the biblical period neither religion nor economics had a separate institutional existence and neither was conceived of as a system on its own with a special theory of practice and a distinctive mode of organization. Both were inextricably intertwined with the kinship and political systems.

Economics was rooted in the family, which was both the producing and consuming unit of antiquity (unlike the modern industrial society in which the family is normally a consuming unit but not a producing one). Hence there was a family economy. There was also a political economy in the sense that political organizations were used to control the flow and distribution of goods, especially luxury and temple goods and war materials. But nowhere do we meet the terminology of an economic "system" in the modern sense. There is no language implying abstract concepts of market, or monetary system or fiscal theory. Economics is "embedded," meaning that economic goals, production, roles, employment, organization, and systems of distribution are governed by political and kinship considerations, not "economic" ones.

Ancient Mediterranean religion likewise had no separate institutional existence in the modern sense. It was rather an overarching system of meaning that unified political and kinship systems (including their economic aspects) into an ideological whole. It served to legitimate and articulate (or de-legitimate and criticize) the patterns of both politics and family. Its language was drawn from both kinship relations (father, son, brother, sister, virgin, child, honor, praise, forgiveness, etc.) and politics (king, kingdom, princes of this world, powers, covenant, law, etc.) rather than a discrete realm called "religion." Religion was "embedded," meaning that religious goals, behavior, roles, employment, organization, and systems of worship were governed by political and kinship considerations, not "religious" ones. There could be domestic religion run by "family" personnel and/ or political religion run by "political" personnel, but no religion in a separate, abstract sense run by purely "religious" personnel. The temple was never a religious institution somehow separate from political institutions. In Hebrew one and the same word (*hêkāl*) means both "temple" and "palace." Nor was worship ever separate from what one did in the home. Religion was the meaning one gave to the way the two fundamental systems, politics and kinship, were put into practice.

Politics "is the study of the processes involved in determining and implementing public goals and in the differential achievement and use of power by the members of the group concerned with these goals" (Swarts, Turner, and Tuden 1966: 7). Politics involves an entire group, which could be village, region, or country, and its consciously held goals, such as protesting exploitative taxation, leadership in war, and the like. Power is the ability to make and enforce these decisions. Thus the concern is for uncovering the competition for power and the way those who have power seek to implement group goals.

Jesus' statement about rendering to Caesar and God their respective due (Mark 12:13-17; Matt. 22:15-22; Luke 20:20-26) has nothing to do with the separation of church and state (neither of which existed at that time) or with the notion of "two kingdoms" (Caesar's and God's). In trying to understand the meaning of Paul's statement about being subject to the governing authorities (Rom. 13:1-6) it would be similarly anachronistic to read back into the statement the modern idea of the separation of church and state. In such an anachronistic interpretation Paul would be exhorting Roman Jesus-group members to obedience to governing authorities. It is important to note that Paul does not refer to these Romans as citizens. This is another indication that they were Israelite resident aliens. Further, the governing authorities in question would be local officials that came into contact with residents of their city quarter. Paul notes that these city officials are "the servant of God to execute wrath on the wrongdoer" (Rom. 13:4). The mention of wrath points to a context of challenge-riposte, a context in which disobedience to authority is a dishonor for which those in authority must get satisfaction, that is, wrath.

What this means is that the relationship of subject to official is an interpersonal one in which disobedience personally dishonors the official. The reason for this is that ancient elites in Rome did not have an idea of juridical relations among various peoples. Instead, Roman statesmen dealt with other peoples in terms of good faith based on the analogy of clientelism. Rome presented itself as patron, it wanted persons to behave like clients. To behave otherwise was to be a rebel, an outlaw. Paul exhorted Roman Jesus-group members to be good clients and show honor to their patrons.

## Rich and Poor

The Hebrew and Greek terms for "poor" should be understood concretely, though not exclusively as economic in nature. The "poor" are persons unable to maintain their inherited honor-standing in society due to misfortune or the injustice of others. Because of this they are socially vulnerable, that is, religiously, economically, politically, and domestically. People who are maimed, lame, blind, and the like are "poor," regardless of how much land they might own. Similarly, a widow owning millions of denarii-worth of anything, yet having no son, was always "a poor widow." It was social misfortune rather than economic misfortune that made a person poor. Even if one were economically poor, as indeed the vast majority of humankind in antiquity was, cultural attention would remain riveted on the honor rating rather than goods. Thus being poor was a social reality that could in turn have had economic overtones or consequences, though the latter usually entered discussion only for the wealthy.

Central to understanding poverty is the notion of "limited good." ▶ **Limited Good.** In modern economies the assumption is that goods exist, in principle, in unlimited supply. If a shortage arises, more can be produced. If one person gets more of something, it does not automatically mean that someone else gets less. It may just mean that the factory worked overtime and more became available. In ancient Palestine, however, the perception was the opposite. All goods existed in finite, limited supply and were already distributed. These included not only material goods but also honor, friendship, love, power, security, and status as well—literally everything in life. Because the pie could not grow larger, a larger piece for anyone automatically meant a smaller piece for someone else.

An honorable man would thus be interested only in what was rightfully his and would have had no desire to gain anything more, that is, to take what was another's. Acquisition was, by its very nature, understood as stealing. The ancient MENA attitude was that every rich person was either unjust or the heir of an unjust person. St. Jerome asserted: "Every rich person is a thief or an heir of a thief" (*In Hieremiam*, 2.5.2, CCSL 74, 61). Profit-making and the acquisition of wealth were automatically assumed to be the result of extortion or fraud. The notion of an honest rich man in antiquity was an oxymoron.

To be labeled "rich" was therefore a social and moral statement as much as it might be an economic one. It meant the power or capacity to take from someone weaker what was rightfully not yours. Being rich was synonymous with being greedy (Prov. 15:27; 22:2). By the same token, being "poor" was being unable to defend what was yours. It meant falling below the status at which one was born. It was to be defenseless, without recourse.

In a society in which power brought wealth (in Western society it is the opposite: wealth "buys" power), being powerless meant being vulnerable to the greedy, who prey on the weak. The terms "rich" and "poor" therefore are better translated as "greedy" and "socially unfortunate." Fundamentally the words describe a social condition relative to one's neighbors. The poor are those who cannot be given a grant of honor; hence they are socially weak, while the rich are the greedy, the shamelessly strong.

Along with the palace, the other focal source of power (and so of wealth) in Israel was the Temple. Those priestly families in charge of the Temple were rich, a term that, as noted above, could be equally well translated "greedy" and "vicious." (T. Levi 18:2–14; Mark 12:38–44; Luke 20:45–21:2; tSot 15:3 "the crown of the sages is their wealth." The Babylonian Talmud observes that the Tannaim depicted as wealthy were all priests. Rubenstein 2003: 191–92). Given a limited-good view of the world, if the Jerusalem Temple personnel and their supporters were amassing wealth stored in the "den of thieves," then large numbers of persons were simultaneously becoming poor and unable to maintain their honor as "sons of Israel." See Malina 2007: 15–36.

## Three-Zone Personality

In the mid-twentieth century a Belgian Benedictine biblical scholar proposed a Semitic view of the human person he identified in the Bible and elsewhere (de Géradon 1954, 1958, 1974). Bernard de Géradon observed that, in contrast to the Greco-Roman world's view of the human person in terms of body and soul, people in the biblical world focused concretely on the body. They were not at all introspective; therefore philosophical and psychological interpretations are inappropriately ethnocentric and anachronistic (Pilch 1997b). Rather, human behavior in the Bible is evaluated on the basis of externally perceptible activity and in terms of the social functions of such activity. The human being is perceived as a socially embedded and interacting whole, a living being reacting to persons and things on the outside of the individual. The main framework of perimeters or boundaries of this interaction between the individual and the world outside the individual is described metaphorically, for the most part, using parts of the human organic whole as metaphors. Thus, most obviously, a human being is endowed with a heart for thinking, along with eyes that fill the heart with data; a mouth for speaking, along with ears that collect the speech of others; and hands and feet for acting. More abstractly, human beings consist of three mutually interpenetrating yet distinguishable zones of interaction with persons and things in the human environment: the zone of emotion-fused thought, the zone of self-expressive speech, and the zone of purposeful action.

In other words, the way human beings are perceived as fitting into their rightful place in their environments, physical and social, and acting in a way that is typically human, is by means of their inmost reactions (eyes–heart) as expressed in language (mouth–ears) and/ or outwardly realized in activity (hands–feet). These three zones comprise the non-introspective makeup of human beings and are used to describe human behavior throughout the ancient Near East, including the Bible, from Genesis to Revelation. De Géradon discovered and fully explicated this three-zone model. For a review of his insight see Follon (Follon 1976), and for its extensive application to the New Testament see Malina (Malina 2001a; 2012).

Recall that MENA descriptive approaches tend to be highly synthetic rather than analytic—more like floodlights than spotlights. A floodlight covers a whole area at one time, and movement of the light might intensify exposure in a given part of the area, yet the whole area always remains in view. Similarly, specific words covering one of the three zones would stand for the whole zone, while always keeping the total functioning human being in view, that is, the other two zones as well (de Géradon 1974: 18). Here is a representative list of such words and the zones they refer to:

**Zone of emotion-fused thought**: eyes, heart, eyelid, pupil, and the activities of these organs: to see, know, understand, think, remember, choose, feel, consider, and look at. The following representative nouns and adjectives pertain to this zone as well: thought, intelligence, mind, wisdom, folly, intention, plan, will, affection, love, hate, sight, regard, blindness, look; intelligent, loving, wise, foolish, hateful, joyous, sad, and the like.

In Western culture this zone would cover the areas referred to as intellect, will, judgment, conscience, core personality, affection, and so forth.

**Zone of self-expressive speech**: mouth, ears, tongue, lips, throat, teeth, jaws, and the activities of these organs: to speak, hear, say, call, cry, question, sing, recount, tell, instruct, praise, listen to, blame, curse, swear, disobey, turn a deaf ear to someone. The following nouns and adjectives pertain to this zone as well: speech, voice, call, cry, clamor, song, sound, hearing; eloquent, dumb, talkative, silent, attentive, distracted, and the like.

In Western culture this zone would cover the area referred to as self-revelation through speech, communication with others, the human person as listener who dialogues with others in a form of mutual self-unveiling, and so on.

**Zone of purposeful action**: hands, feet, arms, fingers, legs, and the activities of these organs: to do, act, accomplish, execute, intervene, touch, come, go, march, walk, stand, sit, along with specific activities such as stealing, kidnapping, committing adultery, building, and the like. The following representative nouns pertain to this zone: action, gesture, work, activity, behavior, step, walking, way, course, and any specific activity; and adjectives such as active, capable, quick, slow, and so forth.

In Western culture this zone would cover the area of outward human behavior, all external activity, human actions in and affecting the world of persons and things.

It is very unlikely that the persons using this derived etic model were explicitly aware of it. (Derived etic describes the model an outsider develops after testing many interpretation of indigenous data.) It seems more likely that the model served as an implicit pattern, an unarticulated set of significant areas that worked much as does the grammar of a native speaker who knows no explicit, articulated grammar. Yet whenever writers (or speakers in the document) describe human activity, they inevitably have recourse to the three zones, at times emphasizing only two of them or even one, with the others always in view in the background (de Géradon 1974: 18). This is the emic data from which de Géradon devised his etic model.

The idea is that all human activities, states, and behaviors can be and are in fact clumped in terms of these three zones. When all three zones are explicitly mentioned, the speaker or writer is alluding to a total and complete human experience. For example, the law of limited retribution in Exod. 21:24, restated in Deut. 19:21, and cited in part in Matt. 5:38 (the so-called law of Hammurabi) basically refers to limiting retribution within the whole range of human interactions covered by each zone: "*eye* for *eye, tooth* for *tooth, hand* for *hand, foot* for *foot.*" This "law" looks to righting restrictions placed upon individual social entitlements. If this legal formula derives from and expresses the three zones that make up a human being, it would obviously not be meant literally and concretely (except by persons who do not understand the culture or by persons in the culture who are at the concrete stage of cognitive development, that is, children and adults who are limited in understanding, by nature or by choice or experience).

A few more examples: "There are six things that the Lord hates, seven that are an abomination to him: haughty *eyes,* a lying *tongue,* and *hands* that shed innocent blood, a *heart* that devises wicked plans, *feet* that hurry to run to evil, a *lying witness* who testifies falsely, and one who *sows discord* in a family" (Prov. 6:16-19). In this seven-patterned proverb (shaped much like the seven days of creation in Genesis 1), we have two complete descriptions of the totally wicked person in terms of three zones, followed by the worst type of person in that culture, one who breaks up bonds of loyalty in a family of blood. Again, note how the prophet Elisha symbolizes his total living self as he lies upon the child he seeks to resuscitate: "Then he got up on the bed and lay upon the child, putting his *mouth* upon his *mouth*, his *eyes* upon his *eyes*, and his *hands* upon his *hands*; and while he lay bent over him, the flesh of the child became warm" (2 Kgs. 4:34). Or consider the description of the linen-clothed man in Daniel in what is obviously meant to be a total description: "His body was like beryl, his *face* like lightning, his *eyes* like flaming torches, his *arms* and *legs* like the gleam of burnished bronze, and the sound of his *words* like the roar of a multitude" (Dan. 10:6). The author of Revelation, perhaps taking his cue from Daniel, describes his celestial vision of the Son of man as follows: "His head and his hair were white as white wool, white as snow; his *eyes* were like a flame of fire, his *feet* were like burnished bronze, refined as in a furnace, and his voice was like the sound of many waters. In his right *hand* he held seven stars, and from his *mouth* came a sharp, two-edged sword, and his *face* was like the sun shining with full force" (Rev. 1:14-16). Again we have a description of function in terms of three zones, a portrayal of how this being relates to those with whom he comes in—a functional picture (de Géradon 1974: 35). It is the function of the organs rather than the organs themselves that is the focus of the ancient authors.

In addition to the dyads—heart–eyes, mouth–ears, hands–feet —it is possible to add yet another organ that seems peculiar to the Semites: the kidneys, often associated with the heart (Pss. 7:10; 26:2; Jer. 2:20; 20:12). Though the heart and kidneys together form the seat of intimate human impulses, the heart seems to orient them primarily in the direction of language while the kidneys point primarily toward external action. The primitive anatomical views of the ancient Israelites joined the kidneys with the hips and the articulation of their members, whence their immediate link with the movements of the legs, and accordingly with the arms. On the other hand, the heart, by its position, finds itself closer to the mouth, the breath of the word. "I the Lord test the mind and search the heart, [LXX adds: I examine the *kidneys*] to give to all according to their ways, according to the fruit of their doings" (Jer. 17:10). The Sage observes: "For Wisdom is a kindly spirit but will not free blasphemers from the guilt of their words; because God is witness to their inmost feelings [Greek *kidneys*] and a true observer of their hearts and a hearer of their tongues" (Wis. 1:6).

Ancient MENA cultures reveal a polyphasic system, i.e., a mixture consisting of various substances and solutions that are only partly miscible with one another. Such a system is characterized by or exhibits several successive peaks of activity. In animate beings the life source permeates the whole being yet is rooted in specific organs such as the blood, the fat around the kidneys, the heart, and the like. Animate human beings relate to beings in their environment in zones marked off by eyes–heart, mouth–ears, and hands–feet. These polyphasic features mark all animate behavior: of God and gods, spirits, people, and, of course, animals (de Géradon 1958; 1974: 33–42).

# List of Reading Scenarios

# Bibliography

Alonso Schökel, Luis, and José Vilchez. 1984. *Proverbios*. Nueva Biblia Española. Sapienciales 1. Madrid: Ediciones Christiandad.

Bargerhuff, Eric J. 2010. *Love that Rescues: God's Fatherly Love in the Practice of Church Discipline*. Eugene, OR: Wipf and Stock.

Barré, Michael L. 1981. "Fear of God and the World View of Wisdom." *Biblical Theology Bulletin* 11: 41–43.

Ben-Barak, Zafrira. 1980. "Inheritance by Daughters in the Ancient Near East." *Journal of Semitic Studies* 25: 22–33.

Borowski, Oded. 2003. *Daily Life in Biblical Times*. Atlanta: Society of Biblical Literature.

Broude, Gwen J. 1994. *Marriage and Family Relationships: A Cross Cultural Encyclopedia*. Santa Barbara, CA: ABC-CLIO.

Broshi, Magen. 2001. "Wine in Ancient Palestine: Introductory Notes." In *Bread, Wine, Walls, and Scrolls*, edited by Magen Broshi, 144–72. JSPSup 36. London: Sheffield Academic.

Carney, Thomas F. 1975. *The Shape of the Past: Models and Antiquity*. Lawrence, KS: Coronado Press.

Clifford, Richard J. 1999. *Proverbs: A Commentary*. Louisville: Westminster John Knox.

Crenshaw, James L. 1998. *Education in Ancient Israel: Across the Deadening Silence*. New York: Doubleday.

de Géradon, Bernard, O.S.B. 1954. "Le coeur, la bouche, les mains: Essai sur un scheme biblique." *Bible et Vie Chrétienne* 4 (1953–54): 7–24.

_____. 1958. "L'homme a l'image de Dieu." *Nouvelle Revue Théologique* 80: 683–95.

_____. 1974. *Le coeur, la langue, les mains: Une vision de l'homme.* Paris: Desclée de Brouwer.

Dobson, James. 1996. *New Dare to Discipline.* Wheaton, IL: Tyndale House.

Domeris, William R. 1995. "Shame and Honour in Proverbs: Wise Women and Foolish Men." *Old Testament Essays* 8: 86–102.

Duling, Dennis C. 2014. "Following Your Nose: Social-Historical and Social-Scientific Directions in New Testament Osmology." In *To Set At Liberty: Essays on Early Christianity and its Social World in Honor of John H. Elliott*, edited by Stephen K. Black, 145–69. Sheffield: Phoenix Press.

Eickelman, Dale F. 2002. *The Middle East and Central Asia: An Anthropological Approach.* Fourth Edition. Upper Saddle River, NJ: Prentice-Hall.

Elliott, John H. 1991. "The Evil Eye in the First Testament: The Ecology and Culture of a Pervasive Belief." In *The Bible and the Politics of Exegesis: Essays in Honor of Norman K. Gottwald on his Sixty-Fifth Birthday*, edited by David Jobling, 147–59. Cleveland, OH: Pilgrim Press.

Fensham, F. Charles. 1962. "Widow, Orphan, and the Poor in Ancient Near Eastern Legal and Wisdom Literature." *Journal of Near Eastern Studies* 21: 129–39.

Fincher, Corey L., Randy Thornhill, Damian R. Murray, and Mark Schaller. 2008. "Pathogen prevalence predicts human variability in individualism/collectivism." *Proceedings of the Royal Society B.* 275: 1279–85.

Follon, Jacques. 1976. Review of de Géradon 1974. In *Revue Philosophique de Louvain* 74: 159–61.

Foster, George. 1960. *Culture and Conquest.* Chicago: Quadrangle Books.

Glasser, M. 1991. "Is early onset of gray hair a risk factor?" *Medical Hypotheses* 39: 404–11.

Goodman, Felicitas D. 1990. *Where the Spirits Ride the Wind: Trance Journeys and other Ecstatic Experiences.* Bloomington: Indiana University Press.

Grant, Elihu. 1907. *The Peasantry of Palestine: The Life, Manners and Customs of the Village.* Boston and New York: Pilgrim Press.

Gregg, Gary S. 2005. *The Middle East: A Cultural Psychology.* Oxford: Oxford University Press.

Gross, Charles G. 1999. "The Fire that Comes from the Eye." *The Neuroscientist* 5: 58–64.

Hagedorn, Anselm C., and Jerome H. Neyrey. 1998. "'It was out of envy that they handed Jesus over' (Mark 15,10): The Anatomy of Envy and the Gospel of Mark." *Journal for the Study of the New Testament* 69: 15–56.

Hanson, K.C. 1994. "'How Honorable! How Shameful!' A Cultural Analysis of Matthew's Makarisms and Reproaches." In *Honor and Shame in the World of the Bible,* edited by Victor H. Matthews and Don C. Benjamin, 81–111. *Semeia* 68. Atlanta: Society of Biblical Literature.

Hoffner, Harry A. 1977. "ʾalmānâh, ʾalmānûth." *TDOT* 1: 287–91.

Hofstede, Gert, Gert Jan Hofstede, and Michael Minkov. 2010. *Cultures and Organizations: Software of the Mind. Intercultural Cooperation and Its Importance for Survival.* Revised and Expanded Third Edition. New York, NY: McGraw-Hill.

Howard, J. Keir. 2001. *Disease and Healing in the New Testament: An Analysis and Interpretation.* Lanham, MD: University Press of America.

Kitz, Anne Marie. 2014. *Cursed are You! The Phenomenology of Cursing in Cuneiform and Hebrew Texts.* Winona Lake, IN: Eisenbrauns.

Kotze, Zacharias. 2010. An Interpretation of the Idiom עין יקר in Psalm 35:19." *Journal for Semitics* 19: 140–48.

Kuiper, Nicholas A., Shahe S. Kazarian, Jessica Sine, and Margaret Bassil. 2010. "The Impact of Humor in North American Versus Middle East Cultures." *Europe's Journal of Psychology* 6: 149–73. www.ejop.org.

Levinson, David, ed. 1995. *Encyclopedia of Marriage and the Family. Vol. 1.* New York: Simon & Schuster Macmillan.

Lewis, Theodore J. 1992. "Belial." *Anchor Bible Dictionary* I: 684–86. New York: Doubleday.

Langston, Richard L. 1991. *Bribery and the Bible.* Singapore: Campus Crusade Asia Limited.

Lynd, Robert S. 1939. *Knowledge for What? The Place of Social Science in American Culture.* Princeton, NJ: Princeton University Press.

MacDonald, Nathan. 2008. *What Did the Ancient Israelites Eat? Diet in Biblical Times.* Grand Rapids: Eerdmans.

Malina, Bruce J. 1980. "What is Prayer?" *The Bible Today* 18: 214–20.

_____. 1986a. "Interpreting the Bible with Anthropology: The Case of the Poor and Rich." *Listening* 21: 148–59.

_____. 1986b. "Normative Dissonance and Christian Origins." In *Social-Science Criticism of the New Testament and its Social World*, edited by John H. Elliott, 35–59. *Semeia* 35. Decatur, GA: Scholars Press.

_____. 1993. *Windows on the World of Jesus: Time Travel to Ancient Judea*. Louisville: Westminster John Knox.

_____. 1996. "Mary and Jesus. Mediterranean Mother and Son." In Bruce J. Malina, *The Social World of Jesus and the Gospels*, 97–120. London and New York: Routledge.

_____. 1998. "Humility." In *Handbook of Biblical Social Values*, edited by John J. Pilch and Bruce J. Malina, 118–20. Peabody, MA: Hendrickson. Reprint Grand Rapids: Baker, 2009.

_____. 2000. *The New Jerusalem in the Revelation of John: The City as Symbol of Life with God*. Collegeville, MN: Liturgical Press.

_____. 2001a. *The New Testament World: Insights from Cultural Anthropology*. Third Edition, Revised and Expanded. Louisville: Westminster John Knox.

_____. 2001b. "The Kingdom and Political Economy." In Bruce J. Malina, *The Social Gospel of Jesus: The Kingdom of God in Mediterranean Perspective*, 97–111. Minneapolis: Fortress Press.

_____. 2007. "Every Rich Person is a Thief or an Heir of aThief: New Testament and Early Christian Perspectives on Wealth and Poverty." In *God and Mammon: Selected papers from the 2007 Annual Conference of the Theology Institute at Villanova University*, edited by Darlene Fozard Weaver, Ph.D., 15-36. Villanova, PA: Villanova University.

_____. 2010. *Christian Origins and Cultural Anthropology: Practical Models for Biblical Interpretation*. Eugene, OR: Wipf and Stock. Reprint of *Christian Origins and Cultural Anthropology: Practical Models for Biblical Interpretation*. Atlanta: John Knox, 1986.

_____. 2012. "The Idea of Man and Concepts of the 'Body' in the Ancient Near East." In *Menschenbilder und Körperkonzepte im Alten Israel, in Ägypten und im Alten Orient*, edited by Angelika Berlejung, Jan Dietrich, and Joachim Friedrich Quack, 43–60. Tübingen: Mohr Siebeck.

Malina, Bruce J., and John J. Pilch. 2000. *Social-Science Commentary on the Book of Revelation*. Minneapolis: Fortress Press.

_____. 2007. "The Wrath of God: The Meaning of ὀργὴ θεοῦ in the New

Testament World." In *In Other Words: Essays on Social Science Methods & the New Testament in Honor of Jerome H. Neyrey*, edited by Anselm C. Hagedorn, Zeba A. Crook, and Eric Stewart, 138–54. Sheffield: Sheffield Phoenix Press.

Malina, Bruce J. and Richard L.Rohrbaugh. 2003. *Social Science Commentary on the Synoptic Gospels*. Minneapolis: Fortress Press.

McCreesh, Thomas P. 1985. "Wisdom as Wife: Proverbs 31:10-31." *Revue Biblique* 92: 25–46.

Miller, Cynthia L. 2005. "Translating Biblical Proverbs in African Cultures: Between Form and Meaning." *The Bible Translator* 56: 129–44.

_____. 2006. "Translating Proverbs by Topics." *The Bible Translator* 57: 170–94.

Murphy, Roland E. 1998. *Proverbs*. Word Biblical Commentary 22. Nashville: Thomas Nelson.

Neyrey, Jerome H. 1998. *Honor and Shame in the Gospel of Matthew*. Louisville: Westminster John Knox.

Oakman, Douglas E. 1986. *Jesus and the Economic Questions of his Day*. Studies in the Bible and Early Christianity 8. Lewiston and Queenston, NY: Edwin Mellen Press.

_____. 2002. "Money in the Moral Universe of the New Testament." In *The Social Setting of Jesus and the Gospels*, edited by Wolfgang Stegemann, Bruce J. Malina, and Gerd Theissen, 225–48. Minneapolis: Fortress Press.

_____. 2012. *The Political Aims of Jesus*. Minneapolis: Fortress Press.

Oleson, John Peter. 1992. "Water Works." *Anchor Bible Dictionary* VI: 883–93. New York: Doubleday.

Patai, Rafael. 1983. *The Arab Mind*. Revised Edition. New York: Scribner's.

Pilch, John J. 1993. "'Beat His Ribs While He is Young' (Sir 30:12): A Window on the Mediterranean World." *Biblical Theology Bulletin* 23: 101–13.

_____. 1996. "Gestures." In *Eerdman's Dictionary of the Bible*, edited by David Noel Freedman, 172–76.

_____. 1997a. "Family Violence in Cross-Cultural Perspective: An Approach for Feminist Interpreters of the Bible." In *A Feminist Companion to Reading the Bible: Approaches, Methods and Strategies*, edited by Athalya Brenner and Carole Fontaine, 306–23. Sheffield: Sheffield Academic Press.

_____. 1997b. "Psychological and Psychoanalytical Approaches to Interpreting the Bible in Social-Scientific Context." *Biblical Theology Bulletin* 27: 112–16.

_____. 1999. *The Cultural Dictionary of the Bible*. Collegeville, MN: Liturgical Press.

_____. 2001. *Cultural Tools for Interpreting the Good News*. Collegeville, MN: Liturgical Press.

_____. 2007. *Introducing the Cultural Context of the Old Testament*. Eugene, OR: Wipf and Stock. Reprint with corrigenda of *Introducing the Cultural Context of the Old Testament*. New York and Mahwah, NJ: Paulist Press, 1991.

_____. 2011. *Flights of the Soul: Visions, Heavenly Journeys, and Peak Experiences in the Biblical World*. Grand Rapids: Eerdmans.

_____. 2012a. *A Cultural Handbook to the Bible*. Grand Rapids: Eerdmans.

_____. 2012b. "The Idea of Man and Concepts of the Body: Anthropological Studies on the Ancient Cultures of Israel, Egypt, and the Near East." In *Menschenbilder und Körperkonzepte im Alten Israel, in Ägypten und im Alten Orient*, edited by Angelika Berlejung, Jan Dietrich, and Joachim Friedrich Quack, 61–75. Tübingen: Mohr Siebeck.

_____. 2013. "Exploring Periods of Psychological Development in MENA (Middle East North Africa) Societies: A Tentative Model." *Biblical Theology Bulletin* 43: 88–102.

_____. 2014. "Insults and face work in the Bible." *Harvard Theological Studies* 70: 1–8.

_____. 2015. "Hospitality." *The Oxford Encyclopedia of the Bible and Theology* I: 498–501. Oxford: Oxford University Press.

Pilch, John J., and Bruce J. Malina, eds. 1998. *Handbook of Biblical Social Values*. Peabody, MA: Hendrickson. Reprint Grand Rapids: Baker, 2009.

Rohrbaugh, Richard L. 1996. "The Preindustrial City." In *The Social Sciences and New Testament Interpretation*, edited by Richard L. Rohrbaugh, 107–35. Peabody, MA: Hendrickson. Reprint Grand Rapids: Baker, 2003.

_____. 2007a. "The Preindustrial City in Luke-Acts: Urban Social Relations: A Study of Luke 14:15-24." In Richard L. Rohrbaugh, *The New Testament in Cross-Cultural Perspective*, 147–74. Eugene, OR: Wipf and Stock.

_____. 2007b. "Gossip in the new Testament." In Richard L. Rohrbaugh, *The New Testament in Cross-Cultural Perspective*, 125–46. Eugene, OR: Wipf and Stock.

Roth, Wolfgang M. W. 1962. "The Numerical Sequence x/x+1 in the Old Testament." *Vetus Testamentum* 12: 300–11.

Rubenstein Jefferey L. 2003. *The Culture of the Babylonian Talmud*. Baltimore and London: The Johns Hopkins University Press.

Schnohr, Peter, Peter Lange, Jorgen Nyboe, Merete Applevard, and Gorm Jensen. 1995. "Gray hair, baldness, and wrinkles in relation to myocardial infarction: The Copenhagen City Heart Study." *American Heart Journal* 130: 1003–10.

Skehan, Patrick W. 1971. *Studies in Israelite Poetry and Wisdom*. Catholic Biblical Quarterly Monograph Series 1. Washington, DC: The Catholic Biblical Association of America.

_____. 1979. "Structure in Poems on Wisdom: Proverbs 8 and Sirach 24." *Catholic Biblical Quarterly* 41: 368.

Smith, Mark S. 1998. "The Heart and Innards in Israelite Emotional Expressions: Notes from Anthropology and Psychobiology." *Journal of Biblical Literature* 117: 427–36.

Stansell, Gary. 1999. "The Gift in Ancient Israel." In *The Social World of the Hebrew Bible: Twenty-Five Years of the Social Sciences in the Academy*, edited by Ronald A. Simkins and Stephen L. Cook, 65–90. *Semeia* 87. Atlanta: Society of Biblical Literature.

Straus, Murray A., with Denise A. Donnelly. 1994. *Beating the Devil Out of Them: Corporal Punishment in American Families*. New York: Macmillan.

Swarts, Marc, Victor Turner, and Arthur Tuden, eds. 1966. *Political Anthropology*. Chicago: Aldine.

Teachout, Robert P. 1986. *Wine: The Biblical Imperative: Total Abstinence*. Columbia, SC: Richbarry.

Thiseltson, Anthony C. "Curse." *New Interpreters Dictionary of the Bible* 1: 810–12. Nashville: Abingdon.

Toverud, Guttorm, 1923. "The Influence of Diet on Teeth and Bones." *Journal of Biological Chemistry* 58: 583–600.

Vaux, Roland de, O.P. 1961. *Ancient Israel. Vol. 1: Social Institutions*. New York: McGraw Hill.

Westermarck, Edward. 1931. *Wit and Wisdom in Morocco: A Study of Native Proverbs*. New York: Horace Liveright.

Whybray, R. N. 1994. *Proverbs*. The New Century Bible Commentary. Grand Rapids: Eerdmans.

Williams, Robin M., Jr. 1970. *American Society: A Sociological Interpretation.* New York: Knopf.